THE
FINAL YEAR
OF WISDOM

ONE MAN'S JOURNEY
THROUGH CANCER

M. Duane Jordan
Compiled by Suzi Jordan Friend

Printed in the United States of America

First Printing, 2018

ISBN 978-1-7327557-4-1 (paperback), 978-1-7327557-0-3 (hardback)

Jordan Legacy Press
Phoenix, AZ 85087

ENDORSEMENTS

How do you respond to a friend who is facing terminal cancer? You search for kind words, encouraging words, anything that avoids the real issues your friend is facing. My friend, Duane Jordan faced the end of his own life from a terrible disease, yet what would conquer his body, never conquered his spirit! His journaling was not devoid of the harsh reality of his disease but was also filled with an unshakable faith in a God he knew and believed was in control. My last visit with him shortly before he passed away his humor came through when he asked for a burrito or taco, knowing he could not eat either. Read this book of his thoughts and musings as he walked through his own death's valley, and you will find the hope, and courage Duane found knowing that the end of this life is but the beginning of eternal life to those whose faith is in a Jesus Christ.

Dr. James R. Braddy
Superintendent Emeritus
Northern California/Nevada Assemblies of God

I worked beside this man of God, Duane Jordan; we prayed together often, and occasionally cried at the altar together. We remodeled, reshaped and enhanced a dress shop to be a more effective 'Storefront Church.' I could only aspire to be like him in my love and service to our Jesus. He was an example to me on how to be a follower of Jesus, even in his death.

The words written here are from Duane's heart. A heart that followed after Jesus with all he had to give. He died like he lived, trusting Jesus every hour. These words will encourage you, just as they did me. I am a cancer survivor, and Duane's written thoughts comfort me in my walk through cancer, and also in my walk toward eternity with my Jesus. I will read and reread these words, I am sure.

Bill Williamson
Author, www.books-4him-free.com

"Jesus said, "In this world, you **will** have trouble, but take heart! I have overcome the world." Nowhere is this promise more exemplified than in Duane Jordan's book, "*The Final Year of Wisdom.*" When faced with one of the greatest trials that can be thrown at a believer in Christ, Duane's light shined the greatest with grace and wisdom. Duane's words recorded during the darkest moments he endured will inspire, encourage, and give hope to the physically healthy or the physically challenged. Duane truly overcame this world with power and victory in Christ! Don't miss how Duane leaned on God to accomplish this hope!

I highly recommend this book for a revelation into the most intimate thoughts expressed during what we will all face one day, seeing Jesus face to face.

Pastor Gary Morefield
Lead Pastor of Green Valley Christian Center
Henderson, Nevada

Impacting Three Generations:

One of God's greatest gifts to my family was a couple named Duane and Fran Jordan who loved my children and grandchildren, and faithfully walked them through many years of testing, trials, and tribulation that always ended in spiritual victories. Duane and Fran's motto was: OPEN HEART; OPEN HOME! They shepherded the family of God with humility, grace, and true servanthood. Like the ancient prophet, Enoch, who was eulogized in Scripture as a man "who walked with God," so Duane walked with God, and his walk inspired, encouraged, and challenged all he met to do the same. His spiritual pilgrimage will call you to rise above all circumstances and stand firm in God's unchangeable love and grace.

Rev. Doris Johnson
President, Bernard Johnson Ministries

Thank you, Pastor Duane, for obeying God's call to shepherd the flock of God. You offered friendship, a listening ear, strong and encouraging leadership to our children, an open door to our home, and loving support in our time of need. The Apostle Paul's inspired words about ministry are echoed in our remembrance of you, as spoken in II Corinthians 6:3-4, and 12. v.3 Giving no offense in any thing, that the ministry be not blamed, v.4 But in all things commending ourselves as the ministers of God, in much patience, in afflictions, in necessities, in distresses, v. 12 On our part there is no constraint (Scofield) I have told you all my feelings; I love you with all my heart. (The Living Bible)

Beth Mapes (Daughter of Doris Johnson)
Teacher at Crook County Christian School, Prineville, Oregon

I remember Pastor Duane being a man of such strong conviction. He loved his family and church so dearly, but he was also firm and unwavering when it came to right and wrong – something I didn't quite understand or appreciate enough at the time. The love he and his family showered on us during their time in Prineville will be something I always treasure. Duane and Fran were just such good and caring friends. Through them, I came to realize that ministry isn't a normal job that quits at 5:00; it is a full time, all-in commitment to loving people.

Alexia Koetitz (Granddaughter of Doris Johnson)
U.S. Military Wife/Friend

Very few people have been as influential in my life as my pastor, Duane Jordan. It is difficult to put into a few words the magnitude of that influence during some of the most pivotal and influential years of my life. The Bible tells us that one man scatters seed, another waters, but it is God who gives the growth. As my pastor for nearly 25 years, Duane played both roles of planting seeds, and also faithfully watering the seeds planted by himself and others. When I left for college he gave me a book, and inside the cover, he wrote, "I dare you to read this, and then try to stay out of the ministry."

While he felt the story of that pastor's calling would speak directly to me, it was actually his own example to follow that was far more influential. He had an incredible ability to not only see the gifts and callings in others but to challenge them to walk in obedience to them. Thank you, Duane, for your unwavering belief in me, and others, and for your commitment and obedience to faithfully disciple me as a shepherd. I am where I am today, serving in ministry, largely because of your faithful commitment to disciple and your unwavering love for His Church. Thank you for loving me well and for your faithful example. Well done, good and faithful servant.

> Aaron Mapes (Grandson of Doris Johnson)
> Pastor on Staff/Elder
> Calvary Chapel, Prineville, Oregon

Friends!!

Have you ever been blessed with a relationship that is so significant that it literally becomes a "game-changer" in your life? This was the gift the Lord allowed us when my wife Nola and I met Pastor Duane Jordan. As a fresh "bull-in-the-china-closet" Bible school graduate, I became the associate to a man who took my raw, unrefined energy and unwaveringly shepherded me. Pastor Duane had such a deep reservoir of joy that he lavishly embraced me with, as well as all those around him. This Holy-Spirit-generated enthusiasm fueled his decisions, his, behavior, his goals, and the way he invested in people. When you met him, he embraced you thereafter as a friend; and I always felt like I was part of his family. And once you were, you somehow knew he was praying for you (sometimes through the night hours), would not hesitate to challenge you or correct in the spirit of love, and would loyally go to bat for you in any way that he could.

Pastor Duane taught Nola and me that ministry is not in getting a three-point sermon perfectly tailored, or to have a five-step plan, or to pray with a certain tone of voice. Rather, he demonstrated passion for his Lord as I saw him kneel during countless night services, seeking God. As I watched him spend hours with the broken-hearted going through traumas, as I saw him give from his pocket when he didn't have much in there to begin with, and as I saw him laugh with others as they chuckled over one of his corny, and I mean *corny*, jokes!

When Nola and I moved from our first three years of ministry in Prineville, Oregon, I can recall him saying to me, "You know, Steve, you should call me 'Duane!'" It was his way of saying to me that I was sort of "growing up," and that he no longer considered himself my boss, but my partner in kingdom building. All these years later, my respect for him has only grown by leaps and bounds as he continually demonstrated the example of leaping out in faith and giving all those around him the gift of acceptance and the chance to take the leap with him!

Duane was like my Elijah, and I was his understudy. He may not have gone to heaven in a fiery chariot, but somehow, I imagine his home going was pretty spectacular—that's how much I esteem his influence in my life. Of course, he would be the first to tell you that he wasn't perfect. But, he sure celebrated the Name of the One who is the Author and Perfector of our Faith! Pastor Duane pointed to Jesus and the Cross and showed us with his daily routine that God can take an ordinary and obedient man and do extraordinary things!

I know that as you read this book, you will feel God fan into flame His Spirit within you. We know that right along with the Lord we can say, "Well done, Pastor Duane!" Although sometimes I still feel like that "Bull-in-the-China-Closet," I truly feel challenged to bear the torch that Pastor Duane ran passionately with. Thank you, Pastor Duane, for gifting us with the vigor of a life well lived and as 1 Cor. 10:31 expresses, … "whatever you do, do it all for the glory of God!"

Grateful to have Pastor Duane, Fran and his family in my life!

Rev. Steve and Nola Slater
Lead Pastors of Living Waters Church, Fallbrook, CA

A SPECIAL NOTE
FROM THE COMPILER

The following pages have been reviewed countless times for editing, yet, I am sure you will find some grammatical and spelling errors. It was my intent to do as little editing as possible to provide an "unedited" version of my dad's journey, yet at the same time, doing it with excellence, to the best of my ability. One of the challenging issues with compiling this book was Dad posted/wrote on three different platforms. I had to line the dates up and merge them into one. Sometimes you'll see things that seem to be duplicated, but I left them in to show a little more detail. I promised Dad before he passed that I would make sure his writings would be published. It has taken me years and many tears to finish it. This was an intensive labor of love that also walked me through the grieving process. My dad's words have inspired, encouraged, and comforted me through it and continue to do so. I am grateful we are able to put it all in book form, so he can continue to help others.

This book is dedicated in memory of my dad and in the name of his legacy….

—Suzi

A NOTE FROM FRAN

I have had such a good, blessed life! Even walking through hard times, I cannot complain. I have fallen in love twice in my life! Once with my first husband, Stan Tatro, who was killed in 1986 in an auto accident, and then with my second husband, Duane Jordan. This book is about my second husband's journey through cancer and finally his entrance into Heaven!

As you read about the daily struggles he (we) went through, may you always keep in mind how very much our loving Heavenly Father cares for us! We may not get to choose everything that happens to us in our lives, but I am so glad our Father sees ahead and knows how to comfort and strengthen us just when it is needed.

If I were to leave this earth today, I would leave with no regrets! My only prayer is that those I leave behind will not forget the way to meet up with me in Heaven! Life is not about houses, land or money but it is about relationships between people.

As with living and dying, it is an individual path. No one's journey is exactly like another's. Also, in being the one left behind, each of our grieving processes are different. So, I have learned to not panic. Just relax and take your time walking through life and death, as there is deep meaning in each process.

Please enjoy this book as you get a glimpse into our wonderful family. My children, their spouses, and my grandchildren have each walked through their own grieving process. My children have actually walked through it twice. If you have a friend or loved one fighting a battle between life and death, I pray this book will give you strength and be an encouragement to you.

—Fran

Duane, Mary, Suzi, and Rob Jordan, 1985

Stan, Fran, Jenny and Jon Tatro, 1985

"The Jordan Bunch"

A NOTE FROM ROB

I've often been asked in various leadership settings who inspires me or who my role model was growing up. As I listened to the other responses around me, many were inspired by wealthy entrepreneurs, famous athletes, or other prominent figures in our society. Nothing wrong with that at all, in fact, many of those people have inspired me too. The person that really came to mind however when asked those questions was my father, Duane Jordan. I was privileged to have grown up in a pastor's home and saw the enormous impact that my dad had on the people and communities that he served in. I watched him serve day in and day out, selflessly always putting others needs before his. His leadership style and his love for people has shaped me into the person I am today. I am so thankful for the godly influence he had on my life. I miss so much the ability to just pick up the phone or send a text when I need some advice or maybe work through a tough situation. I can remember times when I would be frustrated with someone, especially in a work environment, I would call my dad to sort of vent. It would usually end with him praying for me, but more importantly praying for the person I was complaining about. He showed me in a nice way that the problem wasn't always the other person or maybe that person was going through a difficult time themselves. One of my dad's favorite scriptures was Romans 8:28(NKJV) – "And we know that God causes everything to work together for the good of those who love God and are called according to his purpose for them." Time after time that was true in my family's life through difficult situations.

Perhaps my dad's greatest strength was being an encourager. As you read through the pages of this book, I think you'll have a sense of why that's true for me. I'm not really sure at what point in my life that my dad stopped being just a dad, but I can tell you that he was much more than just a dad to me – he was my best friend. I couldn't wait to spend time with him, and I miss him more than you can imagine today. The last year of his life as he walked through his battle with cancer, I made at least 30 trips to Boulder City, Nevada to spend time with him and Mom(Fran). These were tough times, especially towards the end when he spent so much time in the hospital. I saw my strong dad start to lose his strength and losing weight to where he was literally skin and bones. Amazingly, however, those were some of our best times together. I'm so thankful we were able to share those quiet times.

We had some incredible one on one time that I would not trade for anything. He may have lost his physical strength, but I was able to witness in him the true strength and measure of a man. Through his weakest and darkest moments, he was still positive, upbeat and encouraging to those around him. I saw him interacting with the nurses during his stay, even praying with them over struggles they were having – once again putting others before his own needs.

The healing that we were hoping and praying for didn't turn out the way we had planned and life sort of fell apart as we knew it, but I find comfort in knowing that he is rejoicing in heaven today and someday we will be reunited. My dad didn't leave enormous wealth, but he left a legacy, and a true example of how to live life and I will take that over money and wealth any day. Thank you, Dad, for being an amazing example to me and my wife Jenny and to your granddaughters Erika and Amy – they all adored you. We miss you and love you so much.

—Rob

A NOTE FROM JEN

I miss my dad. It took me until I was in my 30's and marrying my second husband to call him that. After all, I couldn't betray my daddy by calling another man dad. At first, he was just the guy my mom married. Then he was the guy who butted into my family and made things more upside down and screwed around than they already were because he didn't do things like my daddy.

He was nothing like my daddy, except that they were both ministers. I understood my mom's need to remarry just not as it applied to me. My daddy was dead. It was up to me to take care of myself, my mom, and my little brother because I was 11 years old and of course capable of doing such a thing.

But Duane was a champ. He was patient. He was kind. And he loved my mom. He loved her so much that he put up with all my crap. My anger, my bitterness, my hurt, my rebelliousness. He CHOSE to love me through all of it. He was there for me, just there, when I needed him. He was a buffer between my mom and me when needed. Which as I got older got to be more and more.

Let's just describe it as Mom as June Cleaver to my Peg Bundy.

When I got married the first time, which turned out horrible, he was there to help pick me up and dust me off. He was there to move me across the country with my two little girls, Kalani and Kaia. He was there to encourage me as I went back to school and got my nursing degree. He was the best grandpa my two little girls could possibly have during that time of their lives.

When I met my current husband, he did what all good dads do… (stern face) "What are your intentions with my daughter?" My Michael and I got married with my parent's permission and blessing (this time), and my dad did our wedding ceremony. He had officiated my brothers' and sister's weddings, and it was important to me that he did ours as well.

He was a friend and confidante to my husband who also misses him greatly. "There's no one left that I can talk to like I was able to talk to Pop. He was the one person who didn't judge me for being anything other than me."

When life would go south as it is prone to do, frequently. I could talk to my dad. His words of wisdom resound even now. One of the scriptures he would often say to me is Jeremiah 29:11 (ESV/NLT): "I know the plans I have for you, says the Lord. Plans for good and not evil. Plans to give you a future and a hope." I often tend to pair this with my daddy's favorite verse Hebrews 11:1 (KJV): "Now faith is the substance of things hoped for, the evidence of things not seen."

I miss my daddy and my dad. I know now that part of respecting my father's memory is to love my dad, Duane, who God put into my life because I needed him. I am so fortunate to have been able to have two strong, godly men in my life. I respect Dad so much for hanging in there! Loving my mom so much to put up with me! Holding on to God when I'm sure he wanted to strangle me (just a little lol). And most of all for loving me in spite of myself.

I miss you Dad. I love you.

—Jen

FOREWORD

I had two older brothers, Laurance and Duane. Both were my heroes. Laurance was much older than Duane and me. Both were men who loved God.

From my earliest remembrance, Duane was my best friend. I followed him like a shadow. He was the leader, and I followed. I learned a lot by observing him. If he didn't get hurt, I would follow. If he did; I wouldn't. As he got older, he wanted his space, but I wanted to be around him. During high school, he said his song was "No Never Alone." He made friends easily. And he had a lot of them.

In high school, I remember a time when I was sitting in the back seat of one of the cars Duane had. I think it was the 1953 Ford. We had parked next to a curb on the main street in Homedale, Idaho. Suddenly a young man ran up to the car, to the open window where Duane was sitting. Without warning, he hit Duane in the face. A little terrifying to say the least. The young man said, "You going to fight me?" Duane responded, "No." To which the guy asked: "Why not?" Duane responded, "Because the Bible says to turn the other cheek." Duane turned his head to which the guy punched him again. The man left.

I was stunned because it happened so quickly. I knew I could not be of any help to Duane. But I was proud of my brother.

We attended a small Assembly of God Church in Homedale, Idaho during our grade school through high school years. It was during that time that a revival happened in that little church. Eight weeks of meetings almost every night. Those weeks of revival impacted our lives in powerful ways.

Duane went off to college after high school. He was the first for our family. College only lasted for one quarter for Duane because of finances, and then he came back to Idaho to work.

When it came my time to graduate high school, I enlisted in the Air Force and headed off to boot camp. Duane was married that summer. It wasn't long before the draft board selected his name, and Duane followed me by enlisting in the Air Force. The military and work prevented us from living close to each other for close to 10 years, but we stayed in touch.

Duane returned to Northwest College (now Northwest University) in Kirkland, Washington to follow God's call to become a pastor. During his senior year at Northwest, my family and I moved to Kirkland so that I could complete my college education. That was a great time for us to reconnect. Following graduating from Northwest, Duane took a position in Riggins, Idaho as Pastor of the Assembly of God church. It was a small town, with a small church. The congregation took a chance on an inexperienced young man. He was a pastor there from 1977 to 1983, he loved the people of that community, and they loved him and his family.

In 1981 my family and I moved to New Meadows, Idaho to pastor the Assembly of God church. Only 35 five miles apart; we would travel often to his town to see him and his family.

One of the years that he was in Riggins, following the high school graduation, a tragedy occurred. Some of the graduates were celebrating, and the car they were in went off the road and into the Salmon River. Duane and many of the townspeople were searching for the passengers along the river banks. It happened that our mother was visiting Duane and family that weekend. She related to me this story:

She was praying for those searching, and while praying, she said she had a vision of Jesus. He was standing on the hills overlooking Riggins. She said to me: "It was strange because he was wearing the same shirt Duane had on."

Wherever Duane went to minister, he loved his community. It was as if Jesus was in him wearing Duane's clothes, loving people through Duane. I believe that was what the Lord revealed to my mother.

This book is from Duane to us. He wanted to finish it before he died, but the energy to do it just was not there.

On March 15, 2012, my brother went into surgery to investigate a problem he was experiencing. As a result of the surgery, a prognosis was given that he would only live months; not years. The pages of this book are from his postings on a care page and Facebook to whoever would read them.

Duane's first post following the surgery, March 27, 2012, contained the following paragraph:

> "Bottom line is I will probably not live to be 80 years old and maybe much less without a miracle. As you pray, I ask that you pray that my time will be best used for the Kingdom of God and that Fran and I become fearless as we face the future. Love you all."

I can barely write because of my emotions. I miss him so much. He asked those of us who read his posts to "pray that my time will be best used for the Kingdom of God," and we did.

I want to share three responses that Duane received to his posts. I will not edit them.

Ps. 71:17
Carol Dash June 12, 2012

I am so thankful for all your posts, Duane. They are such an encouragement for Richard and me. I was reading in Psalm 71 today while Richard was in treatment. vs.17 says, 'Since my youth, O God, you have taught me, and to this day I declare your marvelous deeds. Even when I am old and gray, do not forsake me, O God, till I declare your power to the next generation, your might to all who are to come.' NIV. I remember the years when we were 'youths' here in Homedale and attending Homedale A/G. God has had his hand on us four younger 'kids,' even when we lived in not the greatest of places. He is still keeping us, no matter what choices we have made, and He's allowing us to pass down our faith in Him to our next generation. I won't say we're old, but I am gray, but the Lord willing, we will be old someday--hanging on to that hope! For some reason, I feel weepy today--Richard is so worn out from the treatments, and hearing how you've been hurting, makes me cry with you. Love you so much--so thankful that Fran's family has been there to help you this week!

Grace and Peace!
Doris Johnson June 14, 2012

Grace and Peace! I arrived from Brazil after 37 very busy, exciting days, and haven't yet gotten unpacked! So much to do, so little time. I have two of my oldest and dearest friends in critical situations, one in Scotts Valley and the other here in San Jose so I have tried to spend time with them. I have managed to read your updates and remind our Sunrise Prayer Group to pray for you. Also, Beth shared with me a long letter you have sent her. As I read, I remembered several years ago when in Brazil when one of our great missionary heroes, Don Stamps, the author of the Pentecostal Study Bible also known as the Fire Bible, was stricken with cancer and suffered one year of horrible treatments at the Cancer Center in Houston, Texas. During that time he was completing his work on the Study Bible. After his promotion to Glory, I was quite angry with God for allowing such a humble servant to suffer so much. One day the Spirit said to me... HE WAS AN OVERCOMER AND HE MODELED MY GRACE. That kind of stopped me dead in my tracks. That was probably ten years ago or more. Today all three of his children are in ministry, two of them on the Foreign Field. I had to admit that if God's grace was sufficient for him, then it was also sufficient for his dear wife, Linda, and his three children. From that tragedy??? his wife became another person, an activist for the Study Bible, traveling to many countries, after a lifetime of quiet passiveness that was absolutely mind-boggling. There are some things I guess I will never understand, like why the Lord took Bernhard home at age 63 when he was winning 100,000 souls a year for the Kingdom. But the old hymn still rings true... "Bye and bye, when the Morning comes, all the saints of God are gathered home, we shall tell the story HOW WE'VE OVERCOME and we'll understand it better bye and bye!" We love you and pray daily for you. Doris Johnson and Family

Inheritance
Patricia Kanno October 16, 2012

Nothing is certain in this life. For those of us who have retirement funds and such, it's fortunate, but even these are not certain--they can be taken away in a moment. What's certain is Christ. I thought it would be great to have an inheritance from our parents, but as they grew older, all I cared about was that they would be well taken care of in their last years. I think the best inheritance is what you've already given your family--the love of Jesus and YOUR love...period! I continue to pray for God's will for you...for healing. We love you so much and want you with us for as long as possible. But if and when the time comes that your fight against cancer gets too much for you, it's okay to let go -- we know whether you live or die, you're with Christ.

Reply: Inheritance
Martin Duane Jordan October 17, 2012

How can my little sister be so wise and smart? I appreciate your words very much. Thank you for loving your bigger brother. Our experiences with Mom and her three husbands were a wealth in itself. Just seeing how God provided for Mom for 99 years is a comfort in itself.

I haven't meant to write a book as a forward, but I suppose I have. As you read these pages that follow, you will hear the words of a man who was loved by family, friends, the people of the churches he pastored, and by God. His request that I quoted earlier: ***"I ask that you pray that my time will be best used for the Kingdom of God and that Fran and I become fearless as we face the future. Love you all";*** was answered.

His pages were viewed over 100,000 times as he wrote them.

If you are facing a challenge in your life or the life of someone you love, you can find help and hope in Duane's words to us.

As I am writing this I was reminded of the words of Jesus in Matthew 22:32 ***"…'I AM THE GOD OF ABRAHAM, AND THE GOD OF ISAAC, AND THE GOD OF JACOB'? He is not the God of the dead but of the living."*** My brother's body is in a grave in Boulder City, Nevada. But Duane is not there. He is in the presence of Jesus, the One he lived his life for. If you have fear about the future, make a decision to put your faith in Jesus in the present. He will be with you always, and you will always be with Him.

—Lyle Jordan, brother, and friend

ACKNOWLEDGEMENTS
FROM THE COMPILER

Special thanks to the following which without your help, this book of legacy would not have been completed:

Fran Jordan for being a sounding board and supportive of this project; for your input and contributions.

Ed, my husband, for listening, encouraging, dreaming, and supporting this project in countless ways.

My children Matt, Mary, & Abbey for your positive encouragement to persevere.

Rob & Jenny, Jen & Mike, Jon & Rebekah and your amazing children for your encouragement and support.

My dad's siblings: Lewanna, Clara, Lyle, Patricia, and Carol for the editing help, information, & encouragement you gave.

Jill Leebrick for your hours of editing and encouragement.

Linda Crosby for your **endless** amounts of helpful advice.

Missy Shaw for your input, editing, and encouragement.

Judi Braddy for your advice and direction.

Michelle Dana for your resources at the inception of this project.

Daren Lindley for your publishing advice.

To so many other family and friends: thank you for the support you've given along the way.

It's been such a long journey, if I've missed anyone, please forgive me. We hope you are encouraged by the words that you read here.

—Suzi

PREFACE

The following excerpt is taken from the beginning of my dad's CaringBridge account he had just started... I thought it was an appropriate way to begin.

—Suzi

I am grateful for CaringBridge as a new way to communicate what is going on in my life as I battle cancer.

Being on Hospice causes me to reflect my feelings about dying and causes me to fight to grab hold of life. This is my theme:

Psalm 118:17 NKJV
I shall not die, but live, and declare the works of the Lord.

John 10:10 NKJV

The thief does not come except to steal, and to kill, and to destroy. I (Jesus) have come that they may have life, and that they may have it more abundantly.

I hope you are blessed by the words I write daily expressing my journey of life with cancer...

PRÉCIS

On February 21, 2012, I was told that I had stage IV stomach cancer. The doctors believed the best way to fight this cancer was to remove the stomach. The night before surgery my wife Fran and I prayed that something would happen that I would not have to lose my stomach. That prayer was answered in a way that we were not expecting. The surgeon found the cancer had moved outside the stomach and was reaching into other areas of my organs and for him to try to remove the stomach would only spread the cancer, so he put a feeding tube in me and closed me back up. After healing from surgery, I began a very violent chemo program which included a trial drug from UCLA and after eight rounds my body had come to the place I could no longer tolerate the treatment. The plan was to continue the UCLA medicine as it did not cause a lot of side effects. However, a growth was detected in my kidney, and it was biopsied and was diagnosed as kidney cancer. Since the UCLA program was a trial, I could not continue as I now had two active cancers. Shortly after that, during some very painful days, we found that there was fluid buildup in my abdomen. I was scheduled for a drainage procedure, and they drained 5. 1 liters of fluid from my abdomen. It was tested and found to be cancerous, and the oncologist said he had done as much as he could do and wrote an order for me to be admitted to hospice. So here I am, in December, alive three months longer than the surgeon thought I would be, battling for my life. The following pages are written for my own good; to journal my battle and my faith in the God I have always trusted.

February 25, 2012

Romans 8:28 NKJV

And we know that all things work together for good to those who love God, to those who are the called according to His purpose.

We have had a lot of life changes, and you may or may not have heard that we retired from our church as of January 1, 2012. I have been so busy from that time till now that I don't know how I pastored in the past. Lol. I was recently offered a contract by the State of Nevada to be the Chaplain at the Nevada State Veterans Home here in Boulder City. The day I started I was called by a doctor, who was treating a bacterial type of ulcer in my stomach, to come in for an emergency consultation. He told us that biopsies revealed that I have stomach cancer. With further tests, it was found the cancer was localized in the stomach, and they want to remove the stomach very soon and start chemo. The veteran's home director has assured me they want me to stay on as Chaplain so I will be working toward that goal. We are trusting that God is directing our decisions and our steps and we will do what conventional medical wisdom says to do unless the Holy Spirit directs otherwise. We believe and hold on to the truth of Romans 8:28 and Psalms 118:17. Thank you for your prayers and concern.

Thanks for all the positive replies and the prayers and good wishes. Hope heaven doesn't get tired of hearing about me from so many who promised to pray... lol. I understand that if they have to take all or part of the stomach, I can survive like those who have had gastric bypass surgery. Should be an adventure... will find out more next week. For now:

2 Timothy 1:12 MSG/NKJV

... Nevertheless, I have no regrets... for I know whom I have believed and am persuaded that He is able to keep what I have committed to Him until that Day.

February 26, 2012

Proverbs 2:4-9 NKJV

If you seek her (wisdom) as silver, and search for her as for hidden treasures; Then you will understand the fear of the Lord, and find the knowledge of God. For the Lord gives wisdom; From His mouth come knowledge and understanding; He stores up sound wisdom for the upright; He is a shield to those who walk uprightly; He guards the paths of justice, and preserves the way of His saints. Then you will understand righteousness and justice, Equity and every good path.

[We] Have Chapel Service at Nevada State Veterans Home this morning. What a great place getting to help people who served our nation. We have a beautiful chapel... Fran is playing the baby grand today. Then we have a service at Boulder City's newest retirement center. Only the second Sunday service since it opened. The chapel has an atrium with a great view. Busy day...

———

... What a great piano player Fran is. She played in a way that got the people in the Veterans Home and Lakeview Terrace singing with lots of energy. I think we sang a total of 14 songs in the two places... we saw such good responses to the music and to the word of God in these amazingly sharp and alert seniors. We had a total of 27 people, all over 75 years old, praising God and enjoying having their names all remembered. I hope some of my friends will think about donating some time to bless the lives of people who have given so much so we can have what we have.

February 28, 2012

Proverbs 16:1 NASB

*The plans of the heart belong to man,
but the answer of the tongue is from the Lord.*

Today was one of those days that I had to depend upon the Lord to help make my paths straight and to give an answer out of wisdom that is from the Lord.

In the week since I was told I have stomach cancer, I have had many people tell me about all the amazing herbs, diets and treatments that they know about which are all outside of conventional medical knowledge. I agree, there are lots of helpful and sometimes curative treatments that the FDA has not approved, but I have been through that maze before when my first wife was dying of breast cancer years ago, and trying all those things thrust at us became almost more overwhelming than the cancer. Not much has changed in the type and scope of those treatments and what has been offered sounds just as it did years ago, and none of them did her any long-term good. The bottom line is every person has to find someone and something to put their faith in along with their faith in God. The peace of trusting is priceless.

———

Romans 15:13 NLV

Our hope comes from God. May He fill you with joy and peace because of your trust in Him. May your hope grow stronger by the power of the Holy Spirit.

Today we tried the "trusting in His leading" in my new challenge in life and have found peace. We met with a surgeon, and he laid out all the scenarios of what stomach cancer is doing, can do and how to treat or not treat this disease. He gave to us what we feel were very honest and straightforward answers to every question we asked him. I had done a lot of online research, and his answers were in line with what I had read. He told me I have a very nasty disease that will not give up, and although treatable, there will always be a threat of recurrence. Fran and I are praying about our options and will meet again with him on Thursday to move towards a treatment, either with him or another direction. We know that our God is our healer and we are at peace with that.

March 4, 2012

Joshua 1:9 NLV

"Have I not told you? Be strong and have strength of heart! Do not be afraid or lose faith. For the Lord your God is with you anywhere you go."

We had other blessings as Boulder City Assembly, the church I retired from has asked us to join them for church this Sunday so they can pray for us because of the health challenges I am facing. Calvary Chapel of BC gave Fran and me both handmade quilts that have dozens of scriptures on them so we can wrap ourselves in the Word of God as we rest in His promises. My Chaplain position at Nevada State Veterans Home helps me keep a perspective that each day is a gift.

What a treat Fran and I have had this last week. On Sunday, friends, Rich and Judy, who were in the first church I pastored, came to town and we had a great time enjoying each other's company. What precious people. Then on Wednesday Fran and I were blessed when a friend I graduated from high school with called and we met for dinner. Terry, Karen, and I have kept in contact for over 50 years. The awesome thing is that both couples after all these years still love Jesus Christ and we have so much in common. Thank you, Lord, for good friends. Then my oldest son and family came to spend the weekend, and we are enjoying them so much. I am rich in family and friends.

Talking about blessings, two of my kids, Jen and her family and Jon and his family live here in BC... So awesome to be able to see them so often... New grandson Caiden is so much fun... as are two granddaughters who live here.

I have decided to go forward with surgery. Will know in a couple of days when that will happen. Lots of different scenarios that can happen as they deal with the cancer... trusting that God has led me to this decision.

No matter:

> *"My (faith) is built on nothing less than*
> *Jesus' (Christ) and righteousness;*
> *I dare not trust the sweetest frame,*
> *But wholly lean on Jesus' name."[1]*

March 5, 2012

Good words to live by today...

> *Proverbs 3:5-8 NKJV*
>
> *Trust in the Lord with all your heart, and lean not on your own understanding; In all your ways acknowledge Him, and He shall direct your paths. Do not be wise in your own eyes; Fear the Lord and depart from evil. It will be health to your flesh, and strength to your bones.*

What a good day for Fran and me. We were able to attend BC Assembly with a lot of our family... The church was full, and there was an excitement there, not because we came back, but because of the belief God is moving the church forward. Pastor Marvin preached a great message, and the church then prayed for me... it was such a blessing. Saw some other miracles there today too. The new Mr. and Mrs. Alex Lingle had a beautiful wedding...

March 6, 2012

> *Jeremiah 29:11-14 NKJV*
>
> *For I know the thoughts that I think toward you, says the Lord, thoughts of peace and not of evil, to give you a future and a hope. Then you will call upon Me and go and pray to Me, and I will listen to you. And you will seek Me and find Me, when you search for Me with all your heart. I will be found by you, says the Lord, and I will bring you back from your captivity...*

These words from the Lord to those in captivity are good words for all of us today.

Worked on a new resume today... was hired by NSVH as Chaplain without one, but now they need one... do you know how many pages that takes for someone my age... ran out of ink on the printer... hard to make it shorter than a sermon...

Tomorrow begins the first of eight infusions by IV of iron sucrose (Venofer®). Because of what is happening in my stomach, I have become very anemic which may be why I have had some times of extreme exhaustion for seemingly no reason. Each injection takes about an hour. Will keep them up until surgery. Haven't heard from my surgeon on surgery schedule. I really don't like needles...

Enjoyed my first day of my first full week at NSVH as Chaplain. Very busy day. Worked till noon, drove to Henderson and spent an hour "pumping iron" into my veins. Very unnerving to sit in a room with 10 others all getting some form of chemotherapy. I had more hair than all the men and women together. I guess I am the rookie there. I drove back to NSVH to participate in a panel discussion on ethical end of life procedures. It is a new journey for me. For those following my treatment schedules, my surgery has been set for March 20. Doctors will proceed by what they find...

March 7, 2012

Psalm 139:23-24 NKJV

Search me, O God, and know my heart; Try me, and know my anxieties; and see if there is any wicked way in me, and lead me in the way everlasting."

Technology is so amazing. I just got a call from my missionary friend Mark K. who lives in Hong Kong, and he sounded like he was next door. Amazing that man 7500 miles away can talk with me and then we can talk together with our Heavenly Father who is just a prayer away. Mark truly has an international prayer ministry...

March 8, 2012

Isaiah 40:28-31 NKJV

Have you not known? Have you not heard? The everlasting God, the Lord, The Creator of the ends of the earth, neither faints nor is weary. His understanding is unsearchable. He gives power to the weak, and to those who have no might He increases strength. Even the youths shall faint and be weary, And the young men shall utterly fall, but those who wait on the Lord Shall renew their strength; They shall mount up with wings like eagles, they shall run and not be weary, they shall walk and not faint.

If my memory is correct, today would have been my sister Norma's birthday. I miss her since she passed away last fall. I pray for comfort for her children and grandchildren as they remember her today.

March 9, 2012

Matthew 6:8 NKJV

…For your Father knows the things you have need of before you ask Him.

I have felt so good today it is kind of strange… thanks for the prayers… working in the yard, cleaning the garage and eating (that's the best) …

March 10, 2012

Matthew 20:32

So Jesus stood still and called them, and said,
"What do you want Me to do for you?"

Here is a pointed question Jesus asked two blind men long ago, but I think it might be that we all have an answer that we need to give: Jesus said the Father knows what we need before we ask but instructs us to ask anyway. Jesus knew they were blind, but he wanted them to put their faith into words.

I feel like that question is being asked of me right now. If I had the choice between being healed from cancer or having the chance to bring the kingdom of God to those I might never have the chance to - by not being supernaturally healed, which should I choose? Some may say I can have both choices…but do I? Which is the best? What is more important? It is kind of like the fiery furnace in the book of Daniel…three men could have been spared the fire, but would have missed the best of God's plan… just something to chew on…

(Another good day…thankful for nice weather, great wife, good family and lots of wonderful friends.)

March 13, 2012

2 Peter 1:5-8 NKJV

But also for this very reason, giving all diligence, add to your faith virtue, to virtue knowledge, to knowledge self-control, to self-control perseverance, to perseverance godliness, to godliness brotherly kindness, and to brotherly kindness love. For if these things are yours and abound, you will be neither barren nor unfruitful in the knowledge of our Lord Jesus Christ.

It is interesting that through the faith we have in God, we can, with all diligence add character qualities to our lives that in return seem to amplify our faith and our knowledge of God.

Tomorrow I will conduct the third chapel service of my new career as

Chaplain at NSVH. The group that meets, I am calling the Holy Roller's Church, as they all come in their wheelchairs and worship the Lord and so far, stay awake while I bring a message. They are a great bunch of men and women who served their country because they knew they should. I hope I can serve my Lord as faithful as they served their commanders... I think these people energize me because I am still like a kid to most of them...lol...

March 14, 2012

Psalms 19:14 KJV

Let the words of my mouth, and the meditation of my heart, be acceptable in thy sight, O Lord, my strength, and my redeemer.

Great morning at chapel. Talked about Psalms 19:14 and James 3 and believe they listened. Looking at the clock wishing it would stand still. I have to go to the cancer center in a few minutes and have an iron infusion; not bad, but I sure don't like needles, especially when they have to try three times to get a vein in the back of my hand... takes an hour and before it is done it tastes like I am eating rusty nails, but in two days I have lots of energy... just in time for the next step... Romans 8:28.

March 15, 2012

Acts 4:10, 12 NKJV

Let it be known to you all, and to all the people of Israel, that by the name of Jesus Christ of Nazareth, whom you crucified, whom God raised from the dead, by Him this man stands here before you whole. Nor is there salvation in any other, for there is no other name under heaven given among men by which we must be saved.

Today was my last day for some time at Nevada State Veterans Home. Getting everything lined up for my grand opening (surgery) on Tuesday... I sure don't want to go through this... but unless there is a notable miracle, it is my best choice. In staff meeting today, the staff at NSVH gave me a banner card, signed by all, hoping and praying for me. I am overwhelmed by the kindness being shown to Fran and me during this time by so many.

—

The countdown to the grand opening is beginning...

I will be admitted for surgery on Tuesday, March 20, 2012, mid-morning. The surgery could take up to five hours. Someone from my family will keep this updated as often as possible.

March 17, 2012

Many have said they are praying for me and I am grateful... I believe in miracles... the supernatural invading the natural world with good. I have seen walking, living, breathing examples of God healing people when there was no medical explanation. So, I would ask you who are willing to pray for me, that when the surgeon does the pre-op scope in my stomach on Tuesday that there is nothing but healthy tissues to convince the surgeon that there has been a miraculous change. I would be ecstatic if that is the case. However, I will also be at peace if there is another way God brings healing. Anxious to be in church in the morning soaking in the presence of our Lord.

In October 1995 Fran and I started Boulder City Assembly and began a journey that has involved so many. I was 50 years old when we launched the church. At 66, I believed it was time to retire, and on January 1, 2012, the church gave us a wonderful day of honoring our ministry and pledged to keep going. The church has been and is a vibrant, growing congregation. Today they chose a new pastor to lead the church in true new beginnings. I am so proud of the church and am so pleased with their choice of pastors. I feel kind of like I did when my last grandson was born. So awesome to see this new beginning.

March 19, 2012

2 Timothy 1:12 NKJV

... nevertheless I am not ashamed, for I know whom I have believed and am persuaded that He is able to keep what I have committed to Him until that Day.

My four kids (two sons and two daughters) and eight grandkids are all here to encourage us and try to find ways to help us make it through the next few days. We had a wonderful time of family prayer here tonight and have had lots of friends agreeing in prayer for me. I will win in this with the help of the One I committed my life to over 50 years ago. I may not understand the why of cancer, but I understand and know the "WHOM" I believe in.

March 20, 2012

Psalm 103:1-5 NKJV

Bless the Lord O my soul and all that is within me, bless his Holy Name! Bless the Lord, O my soul, and forget not all His benefits- Who forgives all your iniquities, who heals all your diseases, Who redeems your life from destruction, Who crowns you with loving-kindness and tender mercies, Who satisfies your mouth with good things, So that your youth is renewed like the eagle's.

Today is the day the Lord has made... I will rejoice and be glad in it!

Thanks for all the prayers, good wishes and words of pun and wisdom... yea though I walk through the valley... I will fear no evil... pray for Fran.

———

Family Updates

- Update from Fran, Duane's wife: Today is the day. Duane is going in at 10:30 A. M. and surgery will start around noon. The surgery will be three to four hours long depending on what the surgeons find and decide is the best course of action. All of us are hoping that there will be an obvious miracle that will make this surgery unnecessary. We are all believing that God causes all things to work together for good for those who love God and are called according to His purposes and that this will be for our good and God's glory. Duane is overwhelmed with the show of support and love shown to him and his family during this time.

- Family Update: Our dad was just taken into surgery at 12:45 P. M. While a bit nervous, he was still joking and had an upbeat outlook. The surgery team will provide regular updates to us, and we will post any information as we hear it. Thank you all again for your prayers and support.

- Update from the family: Dad (Duane Jordan) is in surgery that started at 1:30 P. M. Will update when we hear something. Thank you for your prayers - Fran and family

- Update from the family: Dad (Duane Jordan) is out of surgery and recovering. The surgeon found that the tumor was larger than expected and did not remove anything. The next step will be to meet with the oncologist for options. This is certainly not the outcome we were expecting; however, we know that God is still in control and we are still praying and hoping for a miracle. Romans 8:28- Thank you for your continued prayers. - Fran Jordan and family.

March 21, 2012

Dad (Duane) is still recovering in the hospital. He was able to get out of bed, walk a couple of steps and sit up in a chair for a while this morning. He's pretty sore and very tired but is in good spirits cracking a lot of jokes. Thanks so much to everyone for your kind words, thoughts, prayers, friendship and love. - Fran and Family.

March 23, 2012

Fourth Day Post-Op: Dad/Duane is still recovering but getting stronger every day. He went for a walk this morning.

He's been receiving liquid nutrition through his feeding tube, but the surgeon was just in and gave orders for a soft diet. Pain management has been an issue as the drip medication has been removed. We spoke on the phone with an oncologist and will be meeting with him the end of next week.

Fran, the kids, and grandkids have been great nurses and given encouragement and positive support. Fran, Rob, and Jon have all stayed through the night with him. A real plus has been that daughter Jen (Nurse Ratchet, as she calls herself) is a nurse at this hospital. It's been a big help. (Daughter Suzi helped compose this.)

Thank you for your continued prayers and wishes. The entire family appreciates it so much.

March 24, 2012

Duane got up this morning with a goal: to go home. His pain medication management was finally under control, so he actually got the best rest since going into hospital. As soon as he was able, he washed his hair, walked all the halls, got back in bed and waited for [the] surgeon who soon came in, assessed the situation and signed discharge forms. In a few hours, Fran and family had Duane in the van and were on their way home.

Rob and Jon had set up a new TV in Duane and Fan's bedroom, and so they now have HD and surround sound. The girls had prepped the house, the smell of fresh food was very apparent as Duane and Fran came into the house. What a blessing to come home to such a great atmosphere. We, Duane and Fran, are so loved and feel it and know it. It is so good to be home, but tomorrow morning there will be new challenges when we talk with [the] surgeon and oncologists and recovery... thanks for all your prayers and best wishes.

March 25, 2012

I am home and am rejoicing that I have delicious food to eat (without having a commode right by table). I also have had time to read all the messages that you all have posted. I will forever be blessed by all your words. I will reply to each of you as I can.

Had lots of firsts during this time, one of them being the patient and not the visiting pastor or chaplain. Another first that I hope is the last, was again trying to assure the doctors and nurses that my plumbing was working. Don't want to be too graphic, but I was rejoicing with being able to use in-house plumbing and was in the restroom with my fancy hospital robe sitting down holding my cell phone so if I needed to call Fran for help I could. I saw a nice chest pocket in the robe and decided that it would be easier to keep the phone in the pocket than to hold it, so I stuck it in the robe pocket and realized in a second that there was no bottom to the pocket when I heard a splash. Fran was the hero and found a way to fish it out... if I could have flushed it down, I would have done it because I would probably be unable to use the phone knowing where it had been. I have to get a smarter phone this time. Hope you get a laugh out this tragedy. Lol

March 26, 2012

Not sure if you heard or not, but I am home, on lots of meds and trying to find the next step. God did stop the surgeon from removing my stomach, and that is good news for me as now God will do the healing another way. The bad part is there is no way of healing other than a divine miracle and that I have a lot of pain and life changes from the surgery - but it is beginning to even out. More news on CarePages as I can. Not up to visits right now but that will change.

Update: I have two appointments tomorrow: One with the surgeon who made me hurt so much and another with an oncologist who wants to make me sicker... lol. Then I will have some educated knowledge on what I am really facing. Then I will rush to the Throne of the One who has the answers.

You may be like my wife and family who are truly finding it hard to watch this cancer fight without being frustrated at the incredible outpouring of love and prayer so many have directed to God in the belief I would be or will be healed and yet seeing little evidence of any answer. Again, the "why" is still not the issue, nor need it ever be, as long as I know the "Who" that is ultimately in charge of life. There is little doubt that all of us will come to a time when our life is over. I have found with an assurance that when the time comes, we need a plan in place that will last through eternity.

I don't want to suffer or die sooner than later, but at the same time I do not want to miss one moment of joy or peace at the expense of hours or days of despair, anger or doubt in the One whom I have found so much joy, satisfaction, protection, direction, and hope in. I am going to fight the good fight, I will keep the faith in my Lord and Savior Jesus Christ till that day I walk by sight. Without a test, there is no testimony. Please do not get angry at God because bad things happen to good people. I know in whom I have believed... hope you do too.

March 27, 2012

This is the patient writing: I have survived surgery, I am home enjoying my family and a wonderful bed. I am still working with pain management trying to find the best timing and quantity for pain meds. Almost have it under control. I had two doctor appointments today, and so had my first shower (there is a story in that too, of course).

My surgeon was first at 9:30 A.M. He showed me on a drawing what he had found in making the decision to back out of the surgery. Before surgery, I had asked him if he were to do the endoscopy and find no sign of any cancer would he not do surgery. He said, "No, I would still have to go in and make sure there was no evidence of cancer outside the stomach."

He did the endoscopy and what he found was much evidence of the spread of the tumor from the midsection to the top part of the stomach. At one point, there was penetration of the stomach wall, and then they found a tumor under the heart, in the diaphragm and then where the esophagus went through muscles in the chest cavity. In other words, there was evidence of serious growth that may have been happening for some time.

He was very upfront with us and said I was looking at months rather than years. He said my two choices of treatment were chemo or not having chemo. Whichever way there would be no cure.

We got out of the appointment at 10:50 A. M. and had to be at the oncologist by 11:00 A. M. Just made it. He said the same thing except from his point of view. He advised a cancer treatment program called FOLFOX... that would start within two weeks and would go for two months of treatments and at the end of it, there would be a determination made about the effectiveness. If none or little, I would probably suspend the therapy. If it worked, we would continue and also apply for a UCLA integrated trial therapy that would use cutting-edge research in an attempt to find more effective treatment for cancer treatment. This would be financed by UCLA.

The doctors both said there is little hope with what is available through them. The oncologist said they were willing to work with me if I found alternative methods I felt could be good. They would help schedule testing to see how effective they were.

The bottom line is I will probably not live to be 80 years old and maybe much less without a miracle. As you pray, I ask that you pray that my time will be best used for the Kingdom of God and that Fran and I become fearless as we face the future. Love you all.

March 28, 2012

Matthew 6:33 NKJV

But seek first the kingdom of God and His righteousness,
and all these things shall be added to you.

It is such a great day to be alive! Our family has had so much laughter at me getting back to normal bodily functions this week. From the phone in the toilet to just enjoying food again. Hope I never take for granted again the mundane things we do every day with intake and discharge... lol. God has indeed made us marvelously. We have been so blessed by our kids and grandkids being here this week. What a joy my family and friends have been. By the way, I got a new cell phone today... hope it is smarter than the last one.

Decided I need to make a bucket list... had an invitation to come to Kenya, maybe that will be near the top... Spend time with grandkids is up there too... what would you do in your circumstances if you were told you had months rather than years to live?

March 29, 2012

Lamentations 3:22-27 NKJV

Through the Lord's mercies we are not consumed, Because His compassions fail not. They are new every morning; Great is Your faithfulness. "The Lord is my portion," says my soul, "Therefore I hope in Him!" The Lord is good to those who wait for Him, To the soul who seeks Him. It is good that one should hope and wait quietly... For the salvation of the Lord. It is good for a man to bear the yoke in his youth.

I had a great outing today: Went to the nearest clothing store to buy some new shorts as the weather is so beautiful and needed to be able to walk outside in comfort. I helped my granddaughters wash the jeep I got fixed before I got fixed. It was fun but then their mother, Jenny, wouldn't let me help anymore... what a meany! ... lol still thinking about the bucket list... looks like I will be starting chemo soon-believing for a miracle... through whatever means God uses.

March 31, 2012

Should be in bed, but that is what I have been doing so much lately. My wife's brother-in-law and wife stopped to see us today as they are headed towards Oregon. Al and Cheryl have been such awesome friends and supportive of Fran and I getting married almost 25 years ago. Fran was married to his brother Stan who was killed in a car accident in 1986 and Fran and I married in 1987. It is hard to accept someone else being married to your brother's widow, but they opened their hearts and arms to me. In fact, the entire Tatro family became my family too through the years. Al prayed for me today before he left. I will always cherish what he lifted to our Father on my behalf. Thanks, Al and Cheryl.

April 02, 2012

It has been two weeks since surgery, and I (Duane) am doing pretty well. All the necessary bodily functions are working as designed. The pain from surgery is almost gone... the staples are out, but I still have a feeding tube. Fran and family are struggling with how to deal with the prognosis. To say that I wasn't also struggling would be untrue, but I think it is easier to accept for yourself than for others...

I am walking forward with the decision to try chemotherapy to see if it will enable me to have some control over the cancer. The doctors have said there is no cure for this cancer, but maybe we can slow it down. Regardless I am trying to understand what it means to "number our days or to redeem the time." I have a meeting with the oncologist Wednesday, April 4 to discuss the plan. They are scheduling a "port implant" soon so I can begin treatment.

There have been several friends who have cooked meals and brought them to us, and that has been a real blessing. So many are praying so I know that God is in control. Will update the chemo as soon as I know more. Thank you for your prayers, interest, and concern. Love you all!

By the way, I did get a new phone... being very careful when I put it into any pocket from now on. My son, Rob and his family were with us for a total of 16 days and left to go back to the Salem, OR area. They were all struggling to leave the nice warm weather to go back and face the rain and cold. Suzi and her three children arrived on Monday, and they are here through tomorrow. Jon and Rebekah and Jenny and Mike are nearby whenever we need them. They all have been such a blessing. I went to church last Sunday (we don't yet have a church home since retiring from our church), and I actually stood for the 15 minutes or so of worship. Trying to remember to be cautious and wise as I deal with my body... Looking forward to tomorrow as we gather more information from our oncologist. If you come for a visit, be assured I may fall asleep and be aware that I will not entertain you on purpose.

April 04, 2012

It was back to the oncologist office today looking for answers, making decisions and getting more lab work done. I was offered the chance to be in a trial study that incorporates chemotherapy with a new trial drug for the type of cancer attacking my body. The trial is conducted through UCLA, and my treatment will be administrated through them so I will have a very special team walking me through this. There are pros and cons to this type of trial that I will learn more about later, but my care will be the best. The chemo begins on April 18 and will be every other Wednesday. Four to six hours of treatment followed by two days of home infusion with a pump.

———

Just got a call to be at St. Rose tomorrow for another Pre-op registration. On Friday morning I am having a port inserted into my chest for future chemotherapy... just a day surgery. On Thursday I have to do a barium CT. They call it a banana smoothie... not looking forward to this at all. Chemo starts then on the 18th...

Had lunch with Fran near her office today with Suzi, Mary, Abbey, and Matt. So fun to have family around. Should have gotten sick earlier... not!

———

Sue Uptain-Gillham, a great friend from Prineville, Oregon sent me a devotion today that quoted a great saint as he discussed contentment: I loved this part: "Great strength comes from a contented spirit. A fretful or fearful heart drains the soul of precious strength, expending needless energy. But the contented heart builds and conserves strength. "

Being content in my faith is a daily challenge as I find more out about stomach cancer and must make so many life decisions with inadequate information... where does one find contentment in such chaos? I believe only with Jesus, the author, and finisher of our faith...

April 05, 2012

At St. Rose Hospital again today filling out papers and having blood drawn for the umpteenth time getting ready for day surgery tomorrow. The surgeon is inserting/installing a port-a-cath so I can receive chemotherapy easier. The port fits under the skin and is hooked to a major vein so they won't have to tap a new vein every time I need chemo which sounds like a lot. The story goes on.

I did drive for the first time today since surgery and went to Veterans Home for a while to see if I could phase back into work again. Felt good to be dressed up again.

———

Easter is in a few days, the first time in 30 some years I have not been involved in planning an Easter event. We had some really fun ones at BC Assembly through the years. We rented huge party tents two different times and had great outside services... one year we rented the golf course pavilion for services and had wonderful a time... One year we rented one of the schools... each year was different, but one of the best was last year when we celebrated the resurrection in our new facility with a very full house... It was great! This year BC Assembly will have a new pastor, and I am praying there will be a spirit of unity that will let the wonder of the Easter message permeate the church and town Fran and I have loved so long. I love this old hymn: After the events of today, I have to have something more than platitudes.

> *When peace, like a river, attendeth my way,*
> *when sorrows like sea billows roll;*
> *Whatever my lot, Thou has taught me to say,*
> *it is well, it is well, with my soul.*
>
> *Refrain:*
>
> *It is well, with my soul. It is well, it is well, with my soul.[2]*

———

Psalm 104:33 NKJV

I will sing unto the LORD as long as I live:
I will sing praise to my God while I have my being.

Psalm 146:1-2 NKJV

Praise the Lord! Praise the Lord, O my soul! While I live I will praise
the Lord; I will sing praises to my God while I have my being.

I felt like a teenager (well kind of remembered the feelings). I got to drive today for the first time in about three weeks. No scheduled pain medicine for a couple of days now so I got to drive my big red truck and then Fran actually let me drive her granny van by myself. I went back to the Nevada State Veterans Home where I have been the chaplain for about a month. They welcomed me back and want me to keep working if I can. It is nice to be wanted. I put on a dress shirt, slacks, shoes and a tie and enjoyed being dressed in a way that didn't make me look like I was sick or a patient. Felt like a whole person again for a while and that I could maybe regain my life again.

Easter is such a great reminder of the commitment God made to His creation. When a person has an encounter with Him, it may be indescribable to some but it is undeniable to the one who has experienced it, and it evokes praise and adoration even in the hardest of times... and praise given lifts the spirit, gives hope to the soul and joy to the heart... That is why I love to go to church... my focus is to praise the Lord, to hasten to His Throne with the congregation and as I give praise I receive so much more from God than can be imagined...

April 6, 2012

At hospital at 7:30 A. M. had surgery at about 9:30...woke up at about 10:30, home by noon. I have a low-profile port just under my left collarbone. Went too long for pain meds and feel like I just fired a lot of rounds from a 12-gauge shotgun... Should get better soon... I was in the same Pre-op bed as before... it was like a rerun of two weeks ago, except Fran and Jonathan were the only ones there helping me through this next necessary step in fighting the cancer. God will use this for my good at some point and hopefully someone will see the grace of God in our lives.

I am back home. I have a marvelous chair that grabs me and comforts me every time I am in it, and that is where I am. I have four awesome kids, and each of them has blessed me so much in their own way. Today my youngest son blessed Fran and me so much when he came walking into the Pre-op room. Last surgery there were about 20 family members with Fran and me but this time just the two of us. We didn't know Jon was coming, but when that big handsome man walked into my room, I almost cried because he was there for us. All my kids have sacrificed to help us during this time, and Jon again proved our kids love and honor us.

———

Luke 23:44-46 NKJV

Now it was about the sixth hour, and there was darkness over all the earth until the ninth hour. Then the sun was darkened, and the veil of the temple was torn in two. And when Jesus had cried out with a loud voice, He said, "Father, 'into Your hands I commit My spirit.'" Having said this, He breathed His last.

Matthew 27: 54 NKJV

So when the centurion and those with him, who were guarding Jesus, saw the earthquake and the things that had happened, they feared greatly, saying, "Truly this was the Son of God!"

Matthew 27:59-60 NKJV

When Joseph had taken the body, he wrapped it in a clean linen cloth, and laid it in his new tomb which he had hewn out of the rock; and he rolled a large stone against the door of the tomb, and departed.

Today has been called Good Friday. We look back at the time that Jesus gave His life on the cross for us. The following is a reminder that this weekend was not about a rabbit laying chocolate eggs nor baby chicks looking so cute... it was about a price being paid for us so we could have life forever... It was Friday, but Sunday was coming.

April 8, 2012

Fran and I were invited to attend Boulder City Assembly on the first day their new pastor (Pastor Blayne) was going to be there. What an awesome time. The church looked so good, the music was awesome, the place was packed and then being hugged, worshiping, being hugged, hearing a great Easter message, my good friend Lance and I (we both have cancer) being prayed for by the church feeling the presence of God, then being hugged, and hugged some more by a church that loved us. I came home and fell asleep in my big chair, and Fran couldn't even wake me for dinner... but it was worth all it took out of me just being there.

I want to thank all those friends of mine on Facebook who posted that church and the message of the Resurrection was so good for them today... it just did something in my spirit, knowing that because He lives, we can live also... Jesus indeed is the reason for this season... When doctors say you can't live a long full life but the Gospel of Jesus Christ says I will live forever and knowing the Resurrection of Jesus proves that, gives me great reason to rejoice, and I am!

If you have ever wanted to know if there is such a person as the Proverbs 31:10-31 wife, look at the picture of my wife, Fran. Such an amazing woman of God who loves and gives with all her heart. She makes us laugh (sometimes not on purpose), has a language all her own (Franeeses), is an accomplished musician, is an awesome cook, housekeeper, nurse, and still works full time... and somehow God let me meet her when we were both widowed, and we fell in love, and this will be our 25th year of marriage. I am so in love with her...

April 9, 2012

In an hour or so I have to drink about a quart of barium sulfate suspension for a CT scan. I have such a hard time getting my mind out of the way to drink this stuff... I have been dreading it for a week... please pray for me lol... I am such a wimp... but I can do all things through Christ who strengthens me...

I turned on my TV this morning and saw one of the TV evangelists I don't often like to watch, but this was God ordained, and his message seemed focused only on me even though it was recorded. I heard a call for faith, and something in my spirit broke, and I felt the incredible presence of the Lord Jesus Christ just envelope me, and where I couldn't believe for myself, I experienced grace lifting me up to believe that all things are possible to those who believe.

I tried some manual labor this afternoon and Fran and I washed a car, charged a battery, got my truck running, and had my daughter's car fixed. I got tired, but it felt good to do something besides sit or lie around. Thinking about trying to go back to work in the morning as the Chaplain of Nevada State Veterans Home... I am kind of shaky after a month away... I had remembered about 50 names; hope I can remember even part of them.

April 11, 2012

I have tried to be as positive about my recovery as I can, but it is not always easy. I had to have a CT scan on Monday after drinking the barium. That was probably the hardest thing I have had to do... just mean... I had the CT scan and was so hungry on the way home we stopped at a McDonalds... that turned out just about as bad as the barium... Oh well. One week to go before chemo... not looking forward to it. I have experienced Amazing Grace come running when I was at the end of my strength. When I am weak, then He is strong in me... His grace is sufficient... not just enough but completely enough... thanks for your prayers.

April 12, 2012

Psalms 73:23 NKJV

Nevertheless I am continually with You; You hold me by my right hand. You will guide me with Your counsel, and afterward receive me to glory. Whom have I in heaven but You? And there is none upon earth that I desire besides You. My flesh and my heart fail; But God is the strength of my heart and my portion forever.

At about 5:30 A. M. I was hurting so bad I had to get out of bed, and I took two steps, and the pain was totally gone... I laid back down for a few moments and felt so good not to hurt... got up and made ham and eggs and toast for Fran... thank God for those little miracles of grace...

———

Matthew 6:31-33 NIV

So do not worry, saying, 'What shall we eat?' or 'What shall we drink?' or 'What shall we wear?' For the unbelievers run after all these things, but your heavenly Father knows that you need them. But seek first his kingdom and his righteousness, and all these things will be given to you as well.

I have a blind pastor friend who tells some of the worst jokes you would ever want to not hear... I think I just found some to top his; what do you think?

A group of chess enthusiasts checked into a hotel and were standing in the lobby discussing their recent tournament victories. After about an hour, the manager came out of the office and asked them to disperse. "But why?" they asked, as they moved off. "Because," he said "I can't stand chess nuts boasting in an open foyer."

A three-legged dog walks into a saloon in the Old West. He slides up to the bar and announces: "I'm looking for the man who shot my paw."

I'll tell you what I love doing more than anything: trying to pack myself in a small suitcase. I can hardly contain myself.

Laughter does good like a medicine... I tried not to, but I laughed at them... must be feeling better...

Be happy, don't worry is so from the Bible.

April 14, 2012

2 Corinthians 4:16-18 NKJV

Therefore we do not lose heart. Even though our outward man is perishing, yet the inward man is being renewed day by day. For our light affliction, which is but for a moment, is working for us a far more exceeding and eternal weight of glory, while we do not look at the things which are seen, but at the things which are not seen. For the things which are seen are temporary, but the things which are not seen are eternal.

Luke 18:1 NKJV

Then He spoke a parable to them, that men always ought to pray and not lose heart... (You can read the rest.)

[These are] some good things to think about on this Saturday morning.

One of my friends, Phil Good and family, used to sing a country gospel song, *"Feeling Mighty Fine."* Well, I did wake up this morning feeling good...it feels good to feel good... third day in a row...

April 15, 2012

Today was a very enjoyable day. We were invited to attend church with some family, and the service was going normally when all the sudden the Holy Spirit interrupted a very orderly first service, and the pastor stopped the worship team and had us sing an old song that Fran and I actually knew even though most folks under 40 did not. Simple old song, "I Have Decided to Follow Jesus." Over 30 people got out of their seats and came to make the decision to follow Jesus... then he spoke to the other 700 + people and said some of you need to decide even if you are not healed, or your life isn't turning out as you thought, that you will still decide to follow Jesus. Around 4:00 A.M. this morning I was on my knees at my couch saying the same thing to my Lord. The encouragement now from this pastor was what I needed. I would only hope that the 400 plus people who call me friend would make that same decision...

———

Google earth is so amazing. With our very close friends from Kenya, we found his family home near Nairobi. I was moved to tears as there on the computer screen I was shown, via satellite pics, the headstone in a family cemetery of a young man who lived with us for months before he lost his life in a car accident here in Vegas. I didn't think I would ever see that, but with technology there it was. My friends called their family in Kenya, and we shared an awesome moment.

April 17, 2012

Happy Birthday dear wife...thank you for all the good years we have had together...

Jesus said to Paul, "My grace is sufficient... and that His strength is made perfect in our weakness." I have come to realize that we don't always have to try to look like the strong one... some dear friends came over last night and in my driveway, all the sudden the strength was gone, and I broke down and cried for the first time since surgery... they took me in their arms and didn't say anything but "It's OK." And then when I was able, I told them I had been holding it in to protect my wife and kids, they told me that it is OK not to have to be strong all the time. That helped because tonight, Fran and I both realized we needed to let go of all we had been holding in...and we did with each other, then we began to feel the grace and the strength of the Lord filling our hearts with new hope and peace knowing that when we are weak, He is our strength.

———

Today was Fran's birthday, and we spent part of the day in our surgeon's office checking out my new port and my feeding tube (which I don't think I need, but he wants me to keep it for a while). I think the surgeon saw that I am feeling much better and he gave as positive of an outlook as I have heard from him. Not that he determines life and death, but I love any encouragement that comes from the medical world.

Thursday, I begin the program of chemotherapy which the medical world believes is the only thing I can do to prolong my life. I may or may not be on a new drug trial from UCLA but will not know that until Thursday. If the treatment program works, we should know some results within two months... I must be there for treatment for six hours and then carry home a pump that continues to induce me for another 44 or so hours... The pump is taken off on Saturday morning. I have no idea what the side effects will be. Then I wait a week and go back in and do it over again. Please pray with me that the side effects will be minimal. Thanks for checking in. You are a blessing to Fran and me.

April 18, 2012

I found out that I was accepted to be on the UCLA Randomized, Placebo-controlled Double-blind Phase Two study of mFolFox6 chemotherapy plus Ramucirumab drug product (IMC-1121B) versus chemotherapy with a placebo to see if this new drug can stop or cure the kind of cancer I have. I have a 50% chance of not being on the placebo, but if I am, I hope the research helps someone else down the line. I have been told if I do not respond to any treatment they will unmask what I am getting and if the placebo, then will try the Ramucirumab... we will see what happens... cherish your prayers...

———

I was at the Nevada State Veterans Home this morning at 8.00 A.M., the first real work day in 30 days. I remembered every name of every resident I saw; the volunteers did an awesome job, and I spoke for 20 minutes to nearly a full house in the chapel. It was good to give out hope rather than being on the receiving end as I have this last month. The people were so glad to see me that it stirred my heart knowing I am still wanted. I came home and set down in my chair and woke up over two hours later. Boy, I was tired... but at peace...

Tomorrow morning at 8:00 A. M., Fran and I will be at the Comprehensive Cancer Center of Nevada getting ready to have a needle put into the port that has been placed in my upper chest, under the skin, and begin a journey of chemo treatment that I have no idea where it will end... 40 plus hours of having very toxic medicines pumped into me...

I have found out that I am in the UCLA Research program... will see how it all happens.

There will be good (Romans 8:28) that comes from this encounter with cancer treatment... Mark 16:18 reminds me that God will protect me as I take the infusions, and God wants me to be an instrument of healing to those around me... would you pray that we have opportunity to be blessings to others?

April 19, 2012

Today was the day! We started by having 10 vials of blood extracted from my body. It looked like over a cup of blood...lol. Then we had a meeting with our oncologist and he checked me over and laid out the plan for the treatment. Our research nurse was there also. Both people are as warm and friendly as I have ever found in a doctor's office. They were informative, helpful and enjoyable to talk with.

After laying out the protocol, I asked the doctor to answer a question that some of the literature said I should ask. I asked him what stage my cancer is defined as. He said I had non-operative (I think the word was unresectable cancer) which put me a Stage 4 stomach cancer. The TNM system for staging was not available. I am not frightened by this statement, more thankful knowing that what I am doing is important for future survival. Below is the definition of staging.

Overall Stage Grouping is also referred to as Roman Numeral Staging. This system uses numerals I, II, III, and IV (plus the 0) to describe the progression of cancer.

- Stage 0 carcinoma in situ.
- Stage I cancers are localized to one part of the body.
- Stage II cancers are locally advanced.
- Stage III cancers are also locally advanced. Whether a cancer is designated as Stage II or Stage III can depend on the specific type of cancer;
- Stage IV cancers have often metastasized or spread to other organs or throughout the body.

So, this helps pinpoint what the medical establishment understands about the cancer in my body. I know that only a divine miracle of Healing is all that will sustain me after the chemo has done its thing. I am hoping, praying and believing that I will live and declare the glory of the Lord.

———

"For to me, to live is Christ and to die is gain."
– Philippians 1:21 (NIV)

The chemo treatment started in a negative way as the nurse could not get the port to let blood flow out of it and until that can happen the port is useless. She tried two shorter needles and then a longer needle (three pokes which were very unnerving more than painful).

She had me lean forward, lean backwards in a hospital recliner almost on my head, turn sideways and cough and nothing changed, then, as she had me set up and lean forward, I started praying for her to be able to figure it out and all the sudden she said, "It's working". Just had agreed in faith with all of you. The rest was easy. Should have been praying for her all along. Thanks for praying.

Then followed six and one-half hours of iron, steroids, anti-nausea, trial drug, and finally the mFolFox6 chemo...

I got to meet and talk with several people going through trying to get a handle on life vs. cancer. The nursing staff was so compassionate and fun... I am going to make a difference there...

Fran and I came home from the treatment center... I took the treatment and Fran went shopping lol... but we were both very tired when we got home. We laid down on our new California king bed, and I put some good music on in the background, and we fell asleep with the sound of music and my chemo pump churning there between us. It was just the perfect temp, needed no blankets at all, and for an hour or more it was bliss... then the phones started ringing...

Some may think I am not very intelligent going this route and to that person, until you walk in my shoes don't try to second guess my decision. I am confident that the steps of a righteous man are guided by the Lord. I am at peace with my decisions for this treatment. My God can heal with or without this medicine. He, after all, is God and is able to do exceedingly, abundantly above all I can ever ask or imagine (Ephesians 3:20). Mark 16:18.

I have got it made no matter what...

April 20, 2012

1 Corinthians 15:54-58 NKJV

So when this corruptible has put on incorruption, and this mortal has put on immortality, then shall be brought to pass the saying that is written: "Death is swallowed up in victory." "O Death, where is your sting? O Hades, where is your victory?" The sting of death is sin, and the strength of sin is the law. But thanks be to God, who gives us the victory through our Lord Jesus Christ. Therefore, my beloved brethren, be steadfast, immovable, always abounding in the work of the Lord, knowing that your labor is not in vain in the Lord.

Spent my first night with "the pump" 24 hours to go... Feeling pretty good today, going to clean the garage, take out the garbage, mow the lawn... nahh think I will take a nap, read a book, relax, read the word, take a nap, listen to the pump...

April 21, 2012

Yesterday was the worst I have felt for days... so lethargic but made it through OK. My sisters, Carol, Pat, Shirley and Lynn and brothers, Lyle and Dwight also came last night. Dwight and Lyle took me to have the pump disconnected... had to drive to the middle of Las Vegas for that. Sure feels good to get that off. Sisters had a great breakfast waiting, ate waffles, eggs, and bacon and went back to bed and slept like a log for about two hours. Heard the doorbell and my brother-in-law Lynn Tatro came in the house. So glad he and the rest came. Sister and husband Clara and Lorin will be here soon. Almost my whole family of siblings. I am blessed...

April 22, 2012

Psalm 23:4 NKJV

Yea though I walk through the valley of the shadow of death,
I will fear no evil.

What a few days I have experienced. Taking chemo is like riding a dirt bike with no brakes into an area you have never been with very little lighting... no matter what they tell you, you just have to experience by yourself, no one else can make it easier. After pumping unknowns into my body for 48 hours, I have been exhausted, nauseated, and basically very uncomfortable.

The good part is that my family, all my siblings except for one and then four in-laws (who are as much family as any could be) came to walk with me through this time. My brother-in-law Dwight is an excellent chef and has turned out some beautiful meals... I am afraid I have been the only one unable to enjoy even though the memories of those meals were pleasant even if the taste buds wouldn't agree.

We all invaded our church Sunday morning, and then after I slept most of the afternoon, we walked to Arizona from Nevada on the 900-foot-high new Hoover Dam bypass bridge. It was 100 degrees at 8:00 P. M. I am so fortunate to have family who loves me enough to come and surround Fran and me with their love. Cannot get that feeling in a pill bottle. Going to miss them... I am so holding on to Psalms 23 today.

I am believing I am walking through this and not staying...

———

Romans 8:37 NKJV

Yet in all these things we are more than conquerors
through Him who loved us.

I am having a battle with my mind in trying to hold on to hope and looking for a future when I hear the sentence of stage four cancer and feel the effects of chemo just messing me up. At times it seems like tears would be so much easier than a smile or reclusing into a shell rather than attempting to be animated and welcoming. I know that it is at these times that I do have an anchor that is going to keep my spirit and soul on the right track... regardless of the five steps of grief we all face in times like this, I am persuaded, that neither, life nor death, nor things present nor things to come ... shall be able to separate me from the love of God that is in Christ Jesus my Lord. (Romans 8:38-39) I choose to rest in the green pasture of His peace today... to lie down beside the still refreshing waters of His life... I choose to live until the last breath is breathed and then I know I will live forever... I choose not to be intimidated by my feelings but be encouraged by His word... I will be more than a conqueror through Him who has loved me so... I am going to keep the good fight of faith, going to run the race... because I know it is not over when man says it is over...

April 23, 2012

Psalm 118:17 NKJV

I shall not die, but live, and declare the works of the Lord."

My siblings have been here for several days, and I am so thankful for their support, help, prayers, and laughter. We have found things to laugh about and memories to resurrect and hope to hold on to. I slept nearly through the whole night, a first for a long time, do not feel nauseated yet... hope I don't. I am hoping to be able to go back to the Nevada State Veterans Home tomorrow for services. I am praying that all the medicine that was pumped into me is actually attacking the cancer and will enable my life to go on longer than anyone could have hoped. I am determined this morning [in the truth of God's word.]

Hope you have a blessed day!

———

Psalms 23 is my [chapter] today... with the statement of stage four cancer and a weekend of chemotherapy, I feel like I am walking through that valley of the shadow of death... but the good thing is I am fearing no evil... I know His presence is there and even in the five stages of grief, God is still the one who makes me lie down in the green pastures of His peace and leads me by the refreshing streams of living water... the last two days were very rough, but enjoyed being with my great family who tried to cater to all my needs and some of my wants.

Enjoyed going to BCA on Sunday morning and hearing the worship team lead us and then having youth pastor Alex bring a great message on Go... out of Matthew 28. He brought a great reminder that Jesus intended us to reach our world with the good news of the gospel and make disciples of those we share Christ with. He is a good preacher... proud of him. Late evening my family and I walked out on the new bridge, 880 feet above the river, 98 degrees or more and lots of friendly little black flying creatures who just would not leave us alone... I managed to walk from Nevada to Arizona...and back...

If the amount of people praying is what moves the hand of God for healing, I would be healed. However, God in His wisdom has apparently chosen to say not yet. I cannot understand it, but I know in whom I have put my eternal trust and persuaded that nothing, not fear, pain or the threat of needles shall separate me from God's very best for my life... holding on for His "yes."

April 24, 2012

Philippians 4:13 NKJV

I can do all things through Christ who strengthens me...

This is the fifth day since chemo, and I am still reeling from something making me very weak. I am fighting in my mind with the idea of ever taking that stuff again. I make myself get up and do some things, but my big chair is always waiting there with arms wide open when I come by it. I did have some improvements today, and that helped me enjoy a beautiful turkey dinner my sisters made for me...and ohh the mashed potatoes and gravy with corn were sooooo good...The first thing that has tasted really good for days...but after just a small helping I was full...wish I could've eaten it all...but what I could was so good. I have lost about 30 pounds...I am where I wanted to be, but not this way... lol. I am praying for grace as I just don't have it in myself to be as strong as I think I should be... people tell me it is OK, but I don't think quitting is ever OK. Resting may be, but not quitting. [I] saw on TV tonight a man who was rescued from the freezing waters of Alaska said every fiber of his body screamed, "Give up and sleep but I knew if I did I would die." I find in this very short battle I have had with cancer the desire to do the same thing, but I am believing [Philippians 4:13].

———

Habakkuk 3:17-19 NKJV

Though the fig tree may not blossom, nor fruit be on the vines; Though the labor of the olive may fail, And the fields yield no food; Though the flock may be cut off from the fold, and there be no herd in the stalls Yet I will rejoice in the Lord, I will joy in the God of my salvation. The Lord God is my strength; He will make my feet like deer's feet, And He will make me walk on my mountains.

Tuesday night, and still feeling the effects of chemo… thought it would be over with by now. Guess we never know how it will affect us. My brother Lyle and his wife Lynn left today, and I miss him already. It was so nice to have him here. We have done so much together through the years.

April 25, 2012

I am sure you are getting bored hearing about how I feel and what is going on in this old guy's life, but I will try to keep posting for a while as I think it does me some good to try to express what is going on in me. It has been two months since I was told I had stomach cancer, just a little over a month since I was cut open and then closed with no hope of surgery helping. It has been six days since I had my first bout with chemo and it is the first day I have been able to feel like a working human being. I have eaten well since last night and have probably been able to swallow better than any time since surgery. The "ice effect" that the chemo caused is gone today, and I have drunk cold drinks and eaten ice-cold food without the electrocuting feeling I was getting before. It was funny touching or tasting something cold and suddenly feeling like I was jolted with electricity. That is gone, and I feel a little more strength today. Still good to have two sisters and a brother in law here. Thank you for your concern and care. I am truly humbled by all the expressions of love I have received from so many. Tomorrow is a new day... God's mercies are new every morning. After a blood test tomorrow, no more doctors for a week. Looking forward to life...

———

Romans 8:11, 17, 18 NKJV

But if the Spirit of Him who raised Jesus from the dead dwells in you, He who raised Christ from the dead will also give life to your mortal bodies through His Spirit who dwells in you, and if children, then heirs of God and joint heirs with Christ, if indeed we suffer with Him, that we may also be glorified together. For I consider that the sufferings of this present time are not worthy to be compared with the glory which shall be revealed in us.

John 14:15-18 NKJV

"If you love Me, keep My commandments. And I will pray the Father, and He will give you another Helper, that He may abide with you forever- the Spirit of truth, whom the world cannot receive, because it neither sees Him nor knows Him; but you know Him, for He dwells with you and will be in you. I will not leave you orphans; I will come to you.

What a difference a day can make. It is the first day I have felt like I may live a little longer... lol. Felt good to feel good today. The awesomeness of knowing that the God who created the universe is aware of who we are and truly has a plan for our lives...

April 26, 2012

1 Peter 2:7-10 NKJV

Therefore, to you who believe, He is precious; but to those who are disobedient, the stone which the builders rejected has become the chief cornerstone, and a stone of stumbling and a rock of offense. They stumble, being disobedient to the word, to which they also were appointed. But you are a chosen generation, a royal priesthood, a holy nation, His own special people, that you may proclaim the praises of Him who called you out of darkness into His marvelous light; who once were not a people but are now the people of God, who had not obtained mercy but now have obtained mercy.

The verses I posted remind me that we who believe, call our relationship with Jesus Christ "Precious." I think as a man it was only my daughters and now granddaughters or babies that I ever used the word "Precious." But Peter, a crusty old fisherman puts it into perspective... there is a preciousness in our eternal relationship with the Savior of our souls... He is the Center, the Rock, the foundation of who we are as believers. He is better than precious metals because He has established that eternal bond with us, and the word indicates we are precious to Him... here is love, not that we loved him first... but He loved us while we were sinners and that love gave us status as we believed to be a Royal Priesthood, a people of His possession... He is "Precious" to us... I am loved.

April 28, 2012

Saturday, nine days after the initial chemo infusion, and I have had a ride that was far more than I had expected. Every day has been a challenge to do more than just a little bit of exercise outside the normal. I have felt so weakened, I did not attend Chapel last week and am so grateful for Bob Nyceck who is filling in for me... I am not sure how much more I can miss and still have a job. I am working on doing all I know what to do to feel good but does not always play out that way. Today I am hurting from perhaps overexertion by driving out to the desert and meeting some friends who were doing a steak fry in makeshift grills on rocks placed just in the mouth of a cave. The steaks were as good as you could get anywhere. A beautiful night where we watched airplanes fly over, and we told stories and then read the word and prayed together. I tried climbing around on some of the rocks and used muscles I haven't since before surgery. So, during the night my feeding tube really began to cause pain...and today seemingly worse. Two steps forward and three backward. It is back to the pain meds... I am weakened and left wondering if I will ever feel good enough to continue my duties at the Nevada State Veterans Home. Sure praying so. So much to catch up on... An old hymn sustains me today...

> *My hope is built on nothing less*
> *Than Jesus Christ and righteous.*
> *I dare not trust a sweeter frame,*
> *But wholly lean on Jesus' name!*[3]

———

I had a pillow-in-the-face time so no one could see my despair attack over all the sudden becoming so weak and unable to function with the energy I have had most of my life. Tears seemed more appropriate than smiles; surrender more than trying. After a great day yesterday, I succumbed to what I was experiencing. I have found again today, however, the moment (and really it is the second) I am willing not to give in to feelings or emotions, and that if I welcome God's strength, Grace comes running into my spirit and again faith is the victor over despair and defeat. It becomes an indescribable victory that reminds me today I may not be delivered from everything but I will have a hope for tomorrow and beyond that God is not letting go of me.

———

2 Peter 1:5-10 NKJV

But also for this very reason, giving all diligence, add to your faith virtue, to virtue knowledge, to knowledge self-control, to self-control perseverance, to perseverance godliness, to godliness brotherly kindness, and to brotherly kindness love. For if these things are yours and abound, you will be neither barren nor unfruitful in the knowledge of our Lord Jesus Christ. For he who lacks these things is shortsighted, even to blindness, and has forgotten that he was cleansed from his old sins. Therefore, brethren, be even more diligent to make your call and election sure, for if you do these things you will never stumble;

I have two sons who both share my middle and last names. I could not ask for two better men to call son. Each has their own unique gifts, but it is so amazing how they are so alike. My prayer for them is that they would find a heartfelt desire to serve God with their lives. Neither one is a pastor (yet), but I can see the hand of God on each of their lives. Thanks, Jon for helping get to the Desert Steakout even with a sprained ankle and thanks Rob (and family) for flying down from Portland to mow my lawn and wash my truck.

Rebekah Jordan I wanted my friends to know how proud of you I am for being such an incredible mother to my grandson, Caiden. I think Jon is a very blessed man to have such a beautiful and capable wife like you. My son Rob is equally blessed to have Jenny as his beautiful wife and mother of his awesome daughters. Just my night to remember my kids: My two daughters Suzi and Jen are my pride and joy. They are also beautiful, capable women any Dad would brag about. Their husbands and children make me one proud Dad and Granddad.

April 29, 2012

Galatians 2:20 NKJV

… it is no longer I who live, but Christ lives in me; and the life which I now live in the flesh I live by faith in the Son of God, who loved me and gave Himself for me."

I appreciate all the messages many of you have posted. I probably have had time to reply, but I have not really felt like it. The last two days I have had to be back on painkillers, and I don't know if it is the surgery or the cancer causing the pain. I know the pain is real and I know it really slows you down when you hurt. I am hoping it is just scar tissue and not cancer-related. I will try to see my surgeon by Tuesday. I start the chemo again on Wednesday, and the cycle starts again. I do have to report, however, that I have been able to swallow so much better since I started chemo... maybe the tumor is shrinking??? I will take this as answers to prayers.

Cancer has been a real enemy in my family since my dad died of lung cancer around 1950 and then my first wife, Mary, who died at the age of 40 and then five of my siblings as well as a number of other family members. I would imagine that just the prayers prayed for my family and I could fill most of Nevada.

Cancer kills... we all know that, as do heart attacks, all kinds of diseases, car accidents, murders, and wars. Someone, however, said, cancer and all the rest of those things I listed, do not increase the death rate at all... In reality, we will all die at some point. We will all face our own mortality at some point... and the Bible tells us to understand that we need to know there is a number to our days... No one knows what that amount is unless we take our own life. 99. 9% (guessed at that statistic) will never do that as we are programmed to love life. And I do... I love to be alive...

I love to be alive... right now my backyard is so beautiful with all the roses and flowers growing here in the desert... It is kind of like God just made all the bushes do double duty (probably for Fran's sake more than mine), and it is like a rose garden that reminds us of life. This cancer I know will try to take my life, but I have decided that I won't give it the credit. I have decided I will not die a moment before God says so. Jesus said He came to give us life and that, with abundance... even with a disease I am asking God to show me how to live an abundant life until the day He lets me step out of this life into His eternal life. I have preached about this for years as a truth that we believers have, and now I want to experience it. So even in pain I hope I can find abundance rather than having a pity party... if you want to pray for me, pray that life will overflow the disease... because I know goodness and mercy shall follow me all the days of my life and I will one day dwell in the House of the Lord forever and ever and ever... (Without cancer).

———

1 Corinthians 10:12-13 NKJV

Therefore let him who thinks he stands take heed lest he fall. No temptation has overtaken you except such as is common to man; but God is faithful, who will not allow you to be tempted beyond what you are able, but with the temptation will also make the way of escape, that you may be able to bear it.

2 Corinthians 12:8-10 NKJV

Concerning this thing, I pleaded with the Lord three times that it might depart from me. And He said to me, "My grace is sufficient for you, for My strength is made perfect in weakness." Therefore most gladly I will rather boast in my infirmities, that the power of Christ may rest upon me. Therefore I take pleasure in infirmities, in reproaches, in needs, in persecutions, in distresses, for Christ's sake. For when I am weak, then I am strong.

I had to really talk my wife out of feeling guilty, but I was hurting this morning, and we did not attend church, but I did attend four churches online. I truly enjoyed the churches that allowed the focus to be on Jesus and worship and relating to the congregation as if they were really there... A couple of the pastors set the clock aside to allow ministry to be real... probably really messes up the minds of those concerned about the next service... heard more sermons today than I have for a long time... Paul says there is a purpose to the preaching of the Word even if the world thinks it is foolish. The messages I heard today were powerful and challenging.

There are some things in our lives we can determine the outcome by making godly choices and seeing God make a way of escape for us even when it is hard, and the decision to do right costs us something. However, when I have chosen poorly, I still find the mercy and grace of God at work just as they work when what is happening is not because of choices.

Those are the things in life where we just seem to be the victim, and we cannot change the circumstances and the situations in any way by any decisions we make. Those are the times we can decide to accept the grace of God (His peace, power, and presence) that promises will be there through the unthinkable, the unfair and the unknown… check out the scriptures [above].

I have an appointment in the morning with my surgeon as I have been in constant pain for a few days in the area he had inserted a feeding tube when he did surgery last month. I sure hope there is a simple fix other than removing it… I think I just fainted thinking about that (not really). I would be feeling pretty good if not for that.

April 30, 2012

For the first time in 35 plus years, I am not pastoring, but I wanted you to know that Fran and I have committed 9:00 P. M. as our time of praying for our family and others… If you would like us to pray for you, send us a message, and we will include you on our list and believe that Hebrews 11:6 is a promise that God will answer a diligent prayer:

> *But without faith it is impossible to please Him, for he who comes to God must believe that He is, and that He is a rewarder of those who diligently seek Him.*

———

I had the appointment with my surgeon, and he examined the feeding tube, and it looks like a small area of infection. I am taking some antibiotics for a week and will see if that changes anything. If not, the tube will come out. When the doctor asked me how I was eating, and I told him I am swallowing so much better, he said, "You are doing a lot better than I expected at this point…" I take that as answers to all your prayers.

Tomorrow is the start of Round Two… sounds like a fight and guess that it is… I will still be standing… even if it hits me hard. I ask you to pray that I will be able to minister to at least one other person who is going through what I am…

My brother, Lyle called and said he heard a song that reminded him of me and so if you get a chance to listen on YouTube or iTunes for a song by the Sidewalk Prophets called; *"Live Like That"* I think you will hear what the heart of God is for us no matter what is going on in our lives…

May 1, 2012

Tomorrow is the day I get violated again... (Chemotherapy). Six hours in the clinic and 42 hours with a pump... there are some positive changes happening. I can eat, swallow, and enjoy it now. Had a Jumbo Jack today... I believe there are so many praying that chemo must do something good...

I mentioned that Fran and I have committed to setting 9:00 P. M. each night as prayer time for family and others and it has been a real blessing. I would encourage you, even if you have never prayed, set a time and tell someone (accountability helps) about it and then just start talking to God about someone else's needs and then yours and you can pray easily for five minutes... may go longer because once you start you begin to understand that you are really communicating with God. There will be answers to your prayers... look for them. Try it, you will like it...

May 02, 2012

I made it to the clinic side of Round Two of chemo. It went pretty good today... no problem with the port... Fran brought me chicken nuggets and apple slices while I was taking the treatment. Jonathan came just as I was done eating. Fran went back to work, and Jonathan stayed with me until they put the pump on me and then took me home where almost immediately I fell asleep. I think I'm doing well but have 42 hours on the pump. Thanks for all your love and prayers.

———

I am experiencing the following already: This is an explanation of side effects of FOLFOX.

Almost all patients getting FOLFOX chemotherapy will experience some acute neuropathy, especially with exposure to cold.

Acute neuropathy begins shortly after an infusion of Oxaliplatin. It is often triggered by eating, drinking, or touching something cold or breathing cold air. Some patients experience sharp pain in their mouth or jaw when they take a bite of cold food. Others may feel like their throat is closing and they cannot breathe, although breathing isn't really affected.

There may be tingling, a feeling of pins and needles, or numbness in the fingers or toes, especially in response to cold, but these changes disappear within days after treatment ends.

I have had all these symptoms the first round and now sooner on the second round. It is more shocking than harmful... Jesus said I would that you were either hot or cold... I am sticking with the hot, feels better... Prayer time was so good tonight... Fran's Uncle David and Aunt Norma were here, so they joined us... they even sang Amazing Grace with us!!!!!

May 3, 2012

1 Corinthians 15:58 NKJV

Therefore, my beloved brethren, be steadfast, immovable, always abounding in the work of the Lord, knowing that your labor is not in vain in the Lord.

Today is the National Day of Prayer. Wherever you live, there is probably a group of people who are gathering regardless of denomination. I believe our right to gather to pray in a public place is an important right we must not ignore. If we don't use this right, we can lose it. More than that the Bible reminds us that the fervent prayers of righteous people are effective and powerful. Our governing bodies respond little to our protest or rhetoric, but I believe unified prayer, prayed in faith, allows our God to persuade leaders to make wiser decisions based on truth rather than for power, greed, or personal interest. God said it to the people of the Old Testament, and I believe to the believers in Jesus Christ:

2 Chronicles 7:14 NKJV

"If My people who are called by My name will humble themselves, and pray and seek My face, and turn from their wicked ways, then I will hear from heaven, and will forgive their sin and heal their land."

May 4, 2012

Philippians 4:6-7 NKJV

Be anxious for nothing, but in everything by prayer and supplication, with thanksgiving, let your requests be made known to God; and the peace of God, which surpasses all understanding, will guard your hearts and minds through Christ Jesus.

Paul writes these words over 2000 years ago, and they are so easy to quote. That is until everything in your body begins to scream out, "something's wrong in here..." Faith that was strong is all the sudden reduced to an almost surrender to feeling, nausea, pain, and despair. I guess it is just the whole mix of injecting all those foreign chemicals into my body that again caught me so off guard in how to feel. From about 3:00 P. M. yesterday, there has been no strength, no desire for food, nothing that satisfies my stomach and most things taste unpleasant to me. I cannot explain it, but in the last 18 hours, there was such a draining of all I thought I had been so strongly holding to... I felt: "What's the use... if this is the best I am going to feel, then there's not much to live for." The good thing is, however when you read it again and again, there is a new sense of the Holy Spirit confirming it ain't over yet...

So today, this Saturday afternoon, I am determined to:

Be anxious for nothing, but in everything by prayer and supplication, with thanksgiving, I will let my requests be made known to God; and the peace of God, which surpasses all understanding, will guard my heart and mind through Christ Jesus.

Funny how much better I am feeling already... just proclaiming this...

———

On my way to get rid of "THE PUMP", my companion for the last 42 hours. It has gone well... I have exercised, done laundry, swept and mopped the floor and slept in between. Slept about nine hours last night, the most since surgery. Thanks for your prayers.

———

The pump is history for two weeks. Managed to go to Costco to renew cards and enjoyed their delightful cuisine (hot turkey sandwich). Now home to take a nap...

Matthew 11:28-30 NKJV

Come to Me, all you who labor and are heavy laden, and I will give you rest. Take My yoke upon you and learn from Me, for I am gentle and lowly in heart, and you will find rest for your souls. For My yoke is easy and My burden is light.

———

We started prayer right at 9:00 P. M. and what a sense of His presence filled our little living room as we prayed for family, for those who have asked us to pray and for some who might even be offended if they knew we were praying for them. Stealth intercession can move mountains.

Not to give too much info but I was interrupted by an answer to prayer that came within minutes of praying. The nausea is gone... The effectual, fervent prayer of a righteous person avails much!

May 6, 2012

I am writing these things as kind of a journal for me. I don't like to sound like a whiner, but boy this has been a tough three days... I was thinking I would fly through the chemo and be like a new man again, but it has been just the opposite... Every new smell just explodes nausea in me, and I am on edge with that far-from-normal-feeling in my stomach. Again, I begin to question what is worse... the cancer or the treatment... also begin to wonder when new things begin to manifest themselves whether it is the cancer or the chemo or the surgery... It is all pretty disheartening, but I know that with God's help I will make it through this time...

Our prayer time at 9:00 P. M. is a guarded treasure, and we were able to spend that time with two of our granddaughters tonight... I think they were a little surprised that I turned the TV off and asked them to pray with us... but they did.

The following is my prayer for all of us who need HOPE... "The God of Hope." Rest in Hope tonight...

Romans 15:13 NKJV

Now may the God of hope fill you with all joy and peace in believing, that you may abound in hope by the power of the Holy Spirit.

———

I had to add an update... I went back and read the messages you have left for me, and it has made me cry... I am so grateful for the chance God has given my family and me to show His love. Your words and your prayers offset the chemo... I wish I could answer each of you personally. That will come I hope...

John 13:34-35 NKJV

A new commandment I give to you, that you love one another; as I have loved you, that you also love one another. By this all will know that you are My disciples, if you have love for one another."

———

Psalm 94:17-19, 22 NKJV

Unless the Lord had been my help, my soul would soon have settled in silence. If I say, my foot slips, Your mercy, O Lord, will hold me up. In the multitude of my anxieties within me, Your comforts delight my soul. But the Lord has been my defense, And my God the rock of my refuge.

My wife drove me (wouldn't let me drive as I had a very rough day) to the desert looking southwest at about 7:30 P.M. just in time to see the rise of the super moon. It was so amazing there without houses, power lines or any other lights to get just a tiny glimpse of the amazing universe God has made as it declares His glory. It was a very peaceful moment for us.

James 3:17, 18 NKJV

But the wisdom that is from above is first pure, then peaceable, gentle, willing to yield, full of mercy and good fruits, without partiality and without hypocrisy. Now the fruit of righteousness is sown in peace by those who make peace.

May 7, 2012

Lamentations 3:22-26 NKJV

Through the Lords mercies we are not consumed, Because His compassions fail not. They are new every morning; Great is Your faithfulness. The Lord is my portion, says my soul, Therefore I hope in Him! The Lord is good to those who wait for Him, To the soul who seeks Him. It is good that one should hope and wait quietly for the salvation of the Lord.

Isaiah 40:28-31 (NLT)

Have you never heard? Have you never understood? The Lord is the everlasting God, the Creator of all the earth. He never grows weak or weary. No one can measure the depths of his understanding. He gives power to the weak and strength to the powerless. Even youths will become weak and tired, and young men will fall in exhaustion. But those who trust in the Lord will find new strength. They will soar high on wings like eagles. They will run and not grow weary. They will walk and not faint.

Fran and I were just finishing our prayer time when we heard very loud claps of thunder over our house... in the desert that is a treat. I think I have been more emotional than usual and was wiping tears from my eyes when we heard the wonderful sound of rain... we walked outside, and huge raindrops were splashing on the sidewalk, and the amazing smell of a summer rain was in the air. So refreshing... just lifted my spirit. I told Fran whenever I hear thunder it reminds me that God is still working even if we cannot see Him. Read Psalms 18... a cry for help and then the answer... pretty amazing word picture of God's power.

"Musing of a Cancer Fighter" found on Duane's computer

Every emotion that has ever torn at my mind, spirit, and body has been manifesting itself during these few days following chemotherapy. Fear, loneliness, doubt, despair, rejection, lust, jealousy, anger, unforgiveness, revenge, hatred, unthankfulness, judgmental attitudes, and those are just the nicer things.... I have had to deal with each one as they have hurled themselves against my mortal being. Not only do I fight each of these fiery darts, I feel like I am the only one who ever goes through such things. I struggle at night when I try to sleep with things that remind me of the lyrics in the song "I Dreamed a Dream" from the musical Les Miserables. Part of the song talks about the tigers tearing your hopes into shreds; and that the dreams had been destroyed by life. How different life turned out to be than what was once dreamed. A person could drop into hell and the abyss of broken dreams if it were not for the power of God that is available to even the newest, weakest, or most beat up Christian...I remind myself that I have been given a portion of faith... It does no good to think more highly or lowly of myself but to think with a soberness into the word of faith... I do have a God supplied faith.

2 Corinthians 10:3-5 NLT

We are human, but we don't wage war as humans do. We use God's mighty weapons, not worldly weapons, to knock down the strongholds of human reasoning and to destroy false arguments. We destroy every proud obstacle that keeps people from knowing God. We capture their rebellious thoughts and teach them to obey Christ.

Today, I have put into practice the act of capturing the rebellious thoughts that have become strongholds of human reasoning... boldly proclaiming that there is no weapon formed against me that will prosper... none! I am an eternal spirit in a human body:

2 Corinthians 4:16-18 NKJV

Therefore we do not lose heart. Even though our outward man is perishing, yet the inward man is being renewed day by day. For our light affliction, which is but for a moment, is working for us a far more exceeding and eternal weight of glory, while we do not look at the things which are seen, but at the things which are not seen. For the things which are seen are temporary, but the things which are not seen are eternal...

2 Corinthians 5:6-8

So we are always confident, knowing that while we are at home in the body we are absent from the Lord. For we walk by faith, not by sight. We are confident, yes, well pleased rather to be absent from the body and to be present with the Lord.

It is walking in the light of such words that brings HOPE to the hopeless. These words are alive and sharp, penetrating even through the despair of illness...

Duane Jordan, remember,

Isaiah 53:4-6 NLT

Yet it was our weaknesses [Jesus] he carried; it was our sorrows that weighed him down. And we thought his troubles were a punishment from God, a punishment for his own sins! But he was pierced and wounded for our rebellion, crushed for our sins. He was beaten so we could be whole. He was whipped so we could be healed. All of us, like sheep, have strayed away. We have left God's paths to follow our own. Yet the Lord laid on him the sins of us all.

May 8, 2012

I have said it before, but what a difference a day does make.

Last night as my wife prayed I began to realize the nausea was subsiding... I went to bed but couldn't wait to get up this morning to see if I were still doing better. I took a long shower and fixed my wife some breakfast (still have the cold problem, tried to open the orange juice bottle...) took Fran to work, met with my nurse daughter who was just getting off shift and had breakfast with her. It was a wonderful time with just the two of us. Haven't done that for years. I was so excited that I was feeling good that I ordered a Taco Omelet. It was huge... must have weighed three pounds... I ate about 1/4 of it and took the rest to my daughter's husband. It was so good!!!!!!

Later I was able to visit the Homestead (assisted living home) where I had ministered since it opened 12 years or so ago... The people I had not seen in two months welcomed me so warmly. They sang "In the Garden" with me... what a blessing to me... If I am feeling as good tomorrow, I will attend the chapel service at Nevada State Veterans Home where I am Chaplain on leave of absence. It was a very good day... best out of the last 14. I will take it...

I come to the garden alone,
While the dew is still on the roses,
And the voice I hear
falling on my ear
The Son of God discloses.
And He walks with me, and He talks with me,
And He tells me I am His own;
And the joy we share as we tarry there, none other has ever known.
He speaks, and the sound of His voice
Is so sweet the birds hush their singing,
And the melody that He gave to me
Within my heart is ringing.
I'd stay in the garden with Him,
Though the night around me be falling,
But He bids me go; through the voice of woe
His voice to me is calling.[4]

———

Matthew 6:34 NKJV

Therefore do not worry about tomorrow, for tomorrow will worry about its own things...

John 10:10 NKJV

*...I have come that they may have life, and that they may have it
more abundantly.*

Chemo has changed the chemistry in my body, and I still cannot drink or
eat anything cold. I was feeling so good today I thought I would test it and
dished up some Rocky Road ice cream...big mistake... the first bite was
like frost crystals exploding in my mouth and throat... orange juice out of
the refrigerator is undrinkable. Room temp or hotter is the key... I used to
love a Pepsi with ice, but it now is so revolting to my system that there is
no temptation to try. But praise God I am feeling so much better that I
cannot even think about chemo again... but know that is the path I chose.
I had at least three God ordained (just out of the ordinary) situations that
I must believe He is watching out for me because of the prayers you have
been praying. Jesus said, "I have come that you can have life and that
more abundantly..." I experienced that more abundantly today. Jesus said
don't worry about tomorrow, so I won't. Prayer time was great tonight.

———

I have always seemed to find chances to say yes to people in need. As I sat
in the restaurant, I saw a couple who looked hungry walk by. I knew I had
to help them and did... then I stopped by the office of BCA (the church
I retired from), and the secretary handed me an envelope from a family
I had officiated a wedding several years ago, and they forgot to pay the
pastor. There was a generous check and an apology for forgetting... giving
and receiving in a few moments... Wow! You think God might really
know and care about us? Fran is sure to get a Mother's Day card now... lol.

I drove Fran to work so I could go with her to a doctor appointment for
her in downtown Las Vegas. In an area of over a million people, I changed
lanes to make a right turn and Fran's cell rang. It was our daughter-in-law,
Rebekah. She was right behind us... with our six-month-old grandson. We
were able to babysit Caiden while she got a new phone at the Apple Store.
It was just a delightful time sitting on a bench in Town Square... temps
were perfect...

Caiden was laughing making his new-found voices. So funny. Then
we ate at Red Robin... the chemo has changed the chemistry of my body,
and I cannot eat or drink anything cold... so my meal was Chicken taco
soup and hot chocolate... the waitress sure looked funny at me... Fran and
I believe this was at least the third God ordained thing we saw happening

today... This was one of those "life more abundantly" days Jesus mentioned in John 10:10.

May 9, 2012

I got up with great anticipation for another great day, made coffee and orange juice, and was hungry for a piece of toast and peanut butter with blackberry jam. Enjoyed that, did the dishes and cleaned the kitchen after Fran left and started hurting really bad where my gastric feeding tube is... so I decided to take half of one of the pain pills I had and then realized I had one more antibiotic tablet I was supposed to take... within a half hour my day started tumbling the opposite way and dizziness and nausea set in and did not leave for most of the day... what a difference a day does make... I lay on my bed and listened to praise and worship music for a long time... the peace was awesome even though there were side effects from something... tonight after prayer I am feeling better again... This song truly was an anchor in times past and just trying to sing the song today gave me new added hope... Do you remember it?

> *Great is Thy faithfulness, O God my Father,*
> *There is no shadow of turning with Thee;*
> *Thou changest not, Thy compassions, they fail not*
> *As Thou hast been Thou forever wilt be.*
> *Great is Thy faithfulness!" "Great is Thy faithfulness!*
> *Morning by morning new mercies I see;*
> *All I have needed Thy hand hath provided—*
> *Great is Thy faithfulness, Lord, unto me!*
> *Summer and winter, and springtime and harvest,*
> *Sun, moon and stars in their courses above,*
> *Join with all nature in manifold witness*
> *To Thy great faithfulness, mercy and love.*
> *Pardon for sin and a peace that endureth,*
> *Thy own dear presence to cheer and to guide;*
> *Strength for today and bright hope for tomorrow,*
> *Blessings all mine, with ten thousand beside!*[5]

Great Is Thy Faithfulness
Words: Thomas O. Chisholm
Music: William M. Runyan© 1923, Ren. 1951 Hope Publishing Company,
Carol Stream, IL 60188,
www.hopepublishing.com. All rights reserved. Used by permission.

When I was grieving the death of my first wife, this song became my anchor, I woke up singing it almost every morning for months... it still feels like an anchor of faith...

May 10, 2012

Again, last night at prayer time I began feeling much better... slept well and got up feeling so good... no nausea! I asked to postpone my next chemo because Boulder City Assembly (my former church) has asked me to be there on Sunday the 20th. Our district Superintendent James Braddy will be there to help honor my wife and me with a lifetime title of Pastor Emeritus because we founded Boulder City Assembly. It is a wonderful gesture that the church and the new pastor are doing. We are humbled by this. I knew if I took the chemo I would be wasted on that Sunday. The oncologist just called and said that would be fine to reschedule... I am so stoked. Makes me feel better already that I get a reprieve from chemo...

I drank some cold orange juice with ice in it for the first time since surgery. I didn't push it, but for a few sips, there were no adverse reactions. My pickup was at my son's house which is about four blocks away. I made my longest walk since surgery, but it was good. Got to play with my grandson for a few minutes... It felt good to get back in my old truck that I hadn't driven for weeks. I was able to visit two different hospitals (about 20 miles apart) with some friends having a worse time than I am with cancer and treatment. It was a very meaningful time for me and hopefully [for] my friends as we prayed together and shared our faith. I cannot imagine going through cancer and the treatment with no confidence in God. Christian believers are so blessed. For me to live is Christ, but to die and be with Christ is better... (Philippians 1:21). We don't live with a death wish, but we live knowing life does not end at death. If you do not have that confidence, you can... read John 3:16 and see yourself as one God so loved... then respond in belief and with faith that God does hear your words and will give you everlasting life.

People who have had to take chemo understand when those like me say, "I had a good day." I had a good day. If I listed all I could do today, you would think I was bragging. I have a beautiful old red Dodge 4x4 club cab with a three-inch lift, killer sound system with a DVD 10-inch screen and great exhaust... Today was the first time in weeks I have been able to drive. Driving on the freeway, it sounds so good at 80 (people drive that fast in Vegas on the Nevada autobahn). Went to two hospitals, not for appointments but to pray for two friends with cancer having a worse time than I am... the presence of the Lord was evident blessing each of us as we prayed. Without my faith in Jesus Christ, life as I have been experiencing it, would have little meaning or purpose, but with Him, I have confidence beyond cancer and beyond death.

May 11, 2012

One of my granddaughters is 16 today. I remember that time of life as being some of the best times as school was out just a couple of weeks after my birthday. I had my first two cars before I turned 16... a 1941 Chevy pickup which I loved but my brother talked me into trading it for a newly painted 1948 Plymouth 4 door with suicide back doors... but the greatest thing, even more than girls, is I went to a summer Bible camp in Bellevue, Idaho and had an encounter with God that never diminished and then believed I heard a prompting from God to pursue becoming a pastor... 50 years later I am so satisfied with that decision I made that summer. I remember I still did a lot of stupid things, but the grace of God always pulled me back to that fateful summer encounter.

I have a grandniece, Katie and a grandson who will be graduating from high school in a short time and a grandnephew, Jason who is graduating from BSU and I am so proud of who they are and what they have done. Knowing just these young Christian adults plus some young people I have pastored that are graduating gives me lots of hope for America even with all the bad press we hear today. I applaud those who set their sights high and achieve it.

May 13, 2012

Philippians 1:19-22 NKJV

For I know that this will turn out for my deliverance through your prayer and the supply of the Spirit of Jesus Christ, according to my earnest expectation and hope that in nothing I shall be ashamed, but with all boldness, as always, so now also Christ will be magnified in my body, whether by life or by death. For to me, to live is Christ, and to die is gain. But if I live on in the flesh, this will mean fruit from my labor; yet what I shall choose I cannot tell.

Yesterday, I denied the cravings. I had to sit down in my wonderful, loving, comfort zone that is called my big chair (really big recliner) and just continue to act like I felt bad... I could tell I needed to get some exercise as I was always just sitting.

I ate a hearty breakfast and was focused on doing something I had wanted for months. Over a year ago, on a fluke, I bought a 19-foot Bayliner boat and only took it out on the lake once. It was stored at my daughter's house all that time. My son, Jon, and I went and got the boat and Jon backed it into my garage...

My youngest son and I started working again on the boat. It was hot in the garage, and since cold has been my enemy I enjoyed it, but my son was sweating profusely. I watched him rewire all the inner parts of the charging system, and the bilge pump and whatever else needed to be redone. I was always there to give him advice whether he wanted it or not. I would come in and rest at times, but all in all, it felt good to get dirty and fix things. We worked on it for an hour or so before I got winded. Then went out later and put some new switches in... I truly enjoyed the time feeling like a man again.

It was late evening, and we felt like we should at least try to see if the starter system and all worked. Jon said, "Are you tired?" And I said yes, almost to the end... but I really want to see what would happen if we tried to start it. Lots of details still happened, but we pushed the boat out into the driveway, hooked a hose to it, and cranked it over, and after almost 18 months the engine exploded into life and made us want to go to the lake. When it started, we were grinning from ear to ear... I [felt] as normal as any feeble old man could... I [had] another treat, I was able to eat some cold watermelon... first cold I have enjoyed for weeks. I am so blessed... answered prayers for sure.

Jon cleaned things up while I collapsed into my chair but with a really good feeling of accomplishment. Still, some to do before the lake, but I had again begun feeling like more than a victim of cancer but like a survivor of cancer...

Just read this from another friend, thought it was good:

"Just because you are unhappy with your life doesn't mean you have to try and make everyone else unhappy with theirs."

Caiden, our six-month-old grandson, stayed with us for a few hours last night. Every time I would talk with him he would get the biggest grin and focus with his blue eyes on me... I think he likes his grandfather. So I had a blessed day... had to pace myself, but for chemo takers, you know what it is when you almost feel alive again. Praise God for the moments!

It was a good day yesterday, I tried a bite of ice cream again, and there was no reaction from the cold... but maybe because the first cold I have put in my stomach for a while I got a little nauseated. My digestive system is not working normally, not sure what is causing that, but must make sure I monitor it. This morning, I ate a bowl of cold cereal, the first since chemo started... that was a small miracle for me. I am still excited about no chemo next week. For those who read the Bible, Philippians 1:19-26 is becoming my theme scripture... believing life here is still for a reason.

———

Today was Mother's Day and tomorrow is my 67th birthday. It was a wonderful day of honoring my wife and my adult daughters and daughters-in-law for the wonderful mothers they all are and hearing a good sermon at church. Was wonderful to be able to worship with other believers today.

All my kids are here for Mother's Day as well as for my birthday, and I am really blessed!!!! It was non-stop friends and family for the rest of the day. Fran and I got to spend the day with all our kids and a few of our grandkids. My oldest son came from Portland with his youngest daughter, and my oldest daughter drove from Phoenix with her youngest daughter. And the icing on the cake (that I haven't seen yet) is Michelle Dana, a friend of my daughter Suzi and my family who was part of the first church I ever pastored (Riggins, ID) flew in from Colorado just to see me (and the rest of the family). What a joy we have had tonight remembering Riggins and catching up on so much of life. Michelle had so many great stories to tell about her family and especially, her son Chris. I am up way too late, but it was just hard to stop talking... Riggins was almost 28 years ago for my family, but that little community still rules in our hearts.

Before I forget to do it, thank you for all the wonderful Happy Birthday remarks made by you all... I know I have much to be thankful for on this birthday!

I read some interesting Proverbs today:

Proverbs 24:5 -6 NKJV

A wise man is strong, Yes, a man of knowledge increases strength; For by wise counsel you will wage your own war, and in a multitude of counselors there is safety. God gives us wisdom and that wisdom, if we use it, makes us strong and helps us increase in strength... (I believe wisdom to get out of my chair and labor to accomplish something is giving strength...

The wise counsel I believe I am getting from the medical team is helping wage a war on cancer, and with many counselors there is safety.

Proverbs 24:10-11 NKJV

If you faint in the day of adversity, Your strength is small. (The prayer) Deliver those who are drawn toward death, and hold back those stumbling to the slaughter...

As I read 10-11, I believe God's wisdom has told me to get up and get going on living... then asking God to deliver those who have given up and not fighting for life. When chemo is all you see, and in the infusion room with 20 or more people in different places in their battle with cancer there seems almost a death march of giving up and just surviving one more day. I am asking God to deliver me from a mindset like that and to keep me from a death wish... and give me a life wish. Thanks for all your prayers.

May 14, 2012

Psalm 116:1-8 NLT

I love the Lord because he hears my voice and my prayer for mercy. Because he bends down to listen, I will pray as long as I have breath! Death wrapped its ropes around me; the terrors of the grave overtook me. I saw only trouble and sorrow. Then I called on the name of the Lord: "Please, Lord, save me!" How kind the Lord is! How good he is! So merciful, this God of ours! The Lord protects those of childlike faith; I was facing death, and he saved me. Let my soul be at rest again, for the Lord has been good to me. He has saved me from death, my eyes from tears, my feet from stumbling.

It has been a wonderful day. All my four kids and about half of my grandkids were here to watch a young 67-year-old man blow out candles on a cake. And I did... German Chocolate cake... think Suzi made it... so good. My wife, Suzi, and friend, Michelle, made my favorite dinner: Tacos!!!! Homemade taco casserole and all the fixings... my taster is back... It was soooo good to enjoy eating again... I even drank a little cold soda. Probably going to gain some weight back.

I believe God is answering your prayers and is causing the chemo to shrink the tumor (praying it is gone).

Got some wonderful gifts... One friend brought me some ice cream money for the time when I can eat ice cream again. Tonight I had a small scoop of Rocky Road, and it was so good (no reaction to cold). No chemo till the 24th... but again I am grateful for the prayers you have prayed and the miracle of being able to swallow again and that the side effects of chemo are easing or not there. I had no reaction to the cold drink and a little bowl of ice cream I ate.

My sons got the boat ready but ran out of time to take it out to Lake Mead today for my birthday, but soon. Thanks for all the wonderful birthday gifts...

In just a few moments I will be working on my 68th year of life on this planet. I found out that the founder of Facebook, Mark Zuckerberg and I share the same birthday. He is a billionaire, but his wealth could not buy the blessings I have had poured out on me by family and friends on this birthday. I was blown away by the fact that at least 15 of my nephews and nieces took time to wish me happy birthday and say some very kind words. I expect my immediate family to do that but for nephews and nieces to send greetings is way cool.

I am so grateful for my wife who loves me so much she will go beyond the call of duty to try to make me comfortable. If Wally Pearson is reading this, we also share this birthday. A wonderful retired Air Force Chaplain and was the chaplain I replaced at the NSVH.

May 15, 2012

Matthew 6:25-27 NIV

Therefore I tell you, do not worry about your life, what you will eat or drink; or about your body, what you will wear. Is not life more than food, and the body more than clothes? Look at the birds of the air; they do not sow or reap or store away in barns, and yet your heavenly Father feeds them. Are you not much more valuable than they? Can any one of you by worrying add a single hour to your life?

Today, if I had not had a feeding tube and had to clean and take care of it, I could have forgotten that I have been sick. I have felt so normal today. I even think that it was my age that made me want a nap today, not the cancer or chemo. I have enjoyed this day so much. Our lawn never got mowed because my sons and I were too focused on getting a boat running so today as I looked at the tall grass, I assessed my strength and knew I could do it. Even when it was almost 100 degrees, I started the mower and mowed the lawn without a problem. I was able to eat whatever I wanted today and to really experiment I had a couple of scoops of ice cream, and it was so good. I sit here tonight with joy knowing that your prayers and the grace of God have brought me to have such a pain free, nausea free day. I don't know about tomorrow, I must live from day to day, but I know who holds my tomorrows and I know He holds my hand... there are many things about tomorrow I don't understand...but I know who holds my tomorrows...

Michelle Dana has been our guest for a few days. She was one of Suzi's best friends in school in Riggins, Idaho where I preached my first sermons, conducted my first wedding and funeral and tried to act like I knew how to be a pastor. Michelle and Sean have two children, and their son Christopher was injured during surgery and has been on an epic journey trying to regain his ability to walk. We watched a moving video where he tells his battle to overcome a very unfair accident. He has chosen not to let bitterness or anger over his loss rob him of a daily hope in life and in his faith in Jesus Christ. Through his faith, he has become an inspiration to thousands through this unwelcomed turn of events, and it is clear that this scripture is being played out in his life daily...

Romans 8:28 NASB

And we know that God causes all things to work together for good to those who love God, to those who are called according to His purpose.

God does not cause bad things to happen, and sometimes he chooses not to keep us from bad things because of the overwhelming good that can come out of such circumstances (even cancer). Thanks, Michelle for coming and thanks for sharing your son's victories with us... Her daughter, Mary does not often get the limelight, but it sounds as if her courage and love for her brother have been a powerful asset to him.

May 16, 2012

John 14:1-3 NKJV

Let not your heart be troubled; you believe in God, believe also in Me. In My Father's house are many mansions; if it were not so, I would have told you. I go to prepare a place for you. And if I go and prepare a place for you, I will come again and receive you to Myself; that where I am, there you may be also. And where I go you know, and the way you know.

Today was to be my chemo day but it is postponed till next Thursday, and just the thought of that has made my day so much better. I went to work (as Chaplain) and enjoyed the chapel service our volunteers conducted this morning. We had 29 people in the chapel, and it seemed that everyone was thrilled to see me and I hope they felt the same from me. After about three hours there I drove to Henderson to have lunch with my wife. Then home. I was wiped out and needed my chair (lol) and enjoyed a quiet afternoon by myself (I felt bad because Fran really was the one that needed the quiet afternoon and she was working). Like I have said the last few posts... it feels so good to feel good.

One sad note, I just found out that one of my friends who I prayed with last week passed away on Monday. The last thing I said to her was, we will see each other in heaven, and she said I could count on that. And I will...

Thank you for all your love and prayers... I know God is hearing you... and answering.

———

Psalm 90:12 NKJV

So teach us to number our days,
that we may gain a heart of wisdom.

James 4:13-15 NKJV

Come now, you who say, "Today or tomorrow we will go to such and such a city, spend a year there, buy and sell, and make a profit"; whereas you do not know what will happen tomorrow. For what is your life? It is even a vapor that appears for a little time and then vanishes away. Instead you ought to say, "If the Lord wills, we shall live and do this or that."

Today has been the fifth day in a row that I have felt like I am going to live. I went to work today and enjoyed the chapel service. I believe there are some positive changes happening in my body and I believe God is working with and through the chemo. We were praying for many of you tonight.

Sunday will be a special day for Fran and me, and I hope, Boulder City Assembly of God, the church we founded... the church and our District officials are bestowing an honor on us: Pastor Emeritus which means there will be a heart connection between the church and us for the rest of our lives.

Smile? Do you know how many old people it takes to change a light bulb? Only two... one to change the bulb and another to keep talking about how good the old one was...

I have found the older I get, the better I was...

May 17, 2012

Psalm 1:1-3 NIV

Blessed is the one who does not walk in step with the wicked or stand in the way that sinners take or sit in the company of mockers, but whose delight is in the law of the Lord, and who meditates on his law day and night. That person is like a tree planted by streams of water, which yields its fruit in season and whose leaf does not wither—whatever they do prospers.

I am so amazed that God has given me the opportunity to be alive. Today was an incredible day and still going at 1:30 A. M. Up at 6:00 A. M. driving daughter to the airport, minister's breakfast at 8:30, attended the funeral of a wonderful nurse and friend and feel so sorry for her husband. At my office till noon, drove to Valley Hospital to see a friend who just had surgery, and he asked me to sing Amazing Grace in the recovery room which I did with the help of another friend.... home to fix garage door that was wanting to stay open, joined family from Oregon and Idaho for dinner and kind of a reunion and sat on our deck till almost 1:00 A.M. talking with my pastor-brother-in-law and his son who is part of YWAM, and just got back from Brazil where he was for two months near the Bolivian border. Thank you, Lord, for strength and blessings. What a difference a week makes!

May 18, 2012

Romans 8:28,35,39 NASB

And we know that God causes all things to work together for good to those who love God, to those who are called according to His purpose... Who will separate us from the love of Christ? Will tribulation, or distress, or persecution, or famine, or nakedness, or peril, or sword? ... But in all these things we overwhelmingly conquer through Him who loved us. For I am convinced that neither death, nor life, nor angels, nor principalities, nor things present, nor things to come, nor powers, nor height, nor depth, nor any other created thing, will be able to separate us from the love of God, which is in Christ.

Today is like a pre-cancer day. I have again had lots of energy... but the question always comes creeping into my mind, "What purpose can I find in battling cancer? Why does it have to be me... Why couldn't I have had a different road to journey in my retirement years…?" When I think these things, I believe the Holy Spirit helps me remember my faith in Jesus Christ... I am persuaded, convinced and am determined that nothing and no one can separate me from the Love of God and His purpose for my life...

May 20, 2012

Today we (Fran's sisters and husbands, Betty and David (from Portland), Bob and Joyce from Twin Falls, Idaho, their son Ryan who just got back from Brazil and our good friend Jamie from across the street) had the privilege of seeing almost a full solar eclipse from our driveway. We had welding shields and saw the amazing path of the moon coming in front of the sun. We also watched it with a paper with a pinhole in it and saw the image portrayed on the wall of the house. It was a great experience that topped off a great day. But as I realized the immensity of what we were seeing I thought of this passage from the Psalms:

Psalm 19:1-4 NIV

A Psalm of David.
The heavens declare the glory of God; the skies proclaim the work of His hands. Day after day they pour forth speech; night after night they reveal knowledge. They have no speech, they use no words; no sound is heard from them. Yet their voice goes out into all the earth, their words to the ends of the world.

This was written before telescopes, but yet it makes perfect sense. I am convinced that the faith we have in who the Bible says God is, is solidified when we see the universe unfold before our eyes...

———

What a great day we had... our former church honored us with the title of Pastor Emeritus. Our District superintendent, Jim Braddy brought an incredible message on vision and honored Fran and me during his message. Then he awarded us with a plaque of recognition of service in Boulder City. Then the church bestowed on us the title, and they have a picture of us that will be in the foyer of the church, so maybe years from now somebody will remember who we were. It was a very touching presentation. Pastor Blayne Corzine has been very gracious to us.

I have not taken chemo since May 2, and I am feeling so good but am aware there is an enemy that may be working in my body, so on Thursday, the procedure begins again. I believe your prayers and the knowledge of the doctors have allowed me to know life again. I have eaten without problems. I am in better shape that way than before I had surgery. Something is working, and I know God is in the very center of it... I am blessed, and much of that comes because of the prayers of many friends and family.

James 5:16 NKJV

Confess your trespasses to one another, and pray for one another, that you may be healed. The effective, fervent prayer of a righteous man avails much.

May 21, 2012

I still have my feeding tube and it is just the right level for an 8-10 year old to hit with their head when they give me a hug. Happened at church Sunday and I still feel a little pain...but the hugs were worth it...

For many, many years I had a secretary who was such a great help to me as I pastored the church. Harriet M. now is secretary to the new pastor at BCA and is working well with him. Tomorrow is her birthday...she is worthy of a phone call, a text or a birthday card if you know her...

——

I told some of my friends who are experiencing worse effects from cancer and treatment than I am right now that I feel almost guilty because I feel so good... Today after 10 different house guests have left and gone home (loved them all), I swept, mopped floors, deep cleaned our bathrooms, painted baseboards in the bathrooms (cleaned them so much the old paint was coming off), installed a handrail in our shower, did several loads of laundry, hung clothes up, did two loads of dishes, greased the tilt mechanism on the boat, checked the gear oil and helped two teenagers and a friend working on a car in my garage with a lot of good advice. I am hoping chemo will not send me reeling again, but if it does, at least I got a lot of stuff done today that Fran won't have to. Other than the above, I just rested today... life is good.

There are so many people I am finding out about who have cancer. I know all I can do is whisper a prayer, but this is the prayer I hope each of them will pray for themselves.

Paul in Romans 15:13 (NKJV) prays:

Now may the God of hope fill you with
all joy and peace in believing, that you may abound in hope
by the power of the Holy Spirit.

I believe when hope abounds in my life as it is right now, it is by the power of the Holy Spirit... it sure isn't something I personally made happen, but I have learned to strengthen myself in the Lord. When I take chemo on Thursday, I pray I will speak of hope more than sickness.

May 22, 2012

I worked five hours today at the Nevada State Veterans Home... the time away made me forget so many things, but with the help of the great staff there, I was able to start getting a grip back on what I had forgotten. I will be bringing the message tomorrow at the chapel service... I haven't done that for a long time. I am proud to be part of a community that exists to serve those who served our country. Most of these men and women have stories that should have been written down... I hope I get the chance to hear some of them... This weekend is Memorial Day... a good time to remember...

———

I sit with people who are taking chemo and by their actions and their words it seems clear they do not know what a faith in God can be. I look at it like a guy hanging on to a little tree on the side of a sheer cliff and trying to figure out what his next move will be, knowing his options are few... when right beside him is an elevator with the door open, with Jesus standing there, asking him to let go of the tree and step in... But he won't because he is not religious, and he isn't sure the elevator is really there. If I did not have a faith in Jesus Christ going through what I am going through, I would have to cling to any little twig of hope I could find... and in this world, there are few... but God is the God of hope!! I feel like I am in that elevator and am so safe even though it is a long way to the bottom of the cliff (or top). It is a blessed assurance... unshakeable, solid, and unchanging; I know what it feels like to be held. Does that make sense to you in what you are going through?

I prayed for a number of people tonight in our prayer time that are facing mountains in their lives... and they truly need grace and mercy... I love the following scriptures as they speak to us directly about trust and God's leading...

Proverbs 3:3-8 NKJV

Let not mercy and truth forsake you; Bind them around your neck, write them on the tablet of your heart, and so find favor and high esteem in the sight of God and man. Trust in the Lord with all your heart, and lean not on your own understanding; In all your ways acknowledge Him, And He shall direct your paths. Do not be wise in your own eyes; Fear the Lord and depart from evil. It will be health to your flesh, And strength to your bones.

May 23, 2012

Today was Chapel day... it is the first time I have spoken in public for weeks, and my voice is still a little weak, but it was a joy to talk about memorials, memories and remembering, and to help us all remember what God has set as a memorial for us (the cross, the Lord's Prayer, etc.). These people, most of them have wheelchairs, make the effort to come to chapel and then they tell me they are praying for me... I feel very humbled to know that people who have things harder in their lives than I do consider it a privilege to pray for me...

I had the privilege of speaking to some 28 people at the veteran's home who gathered for chapel and talked about the memorials in our lives that help us remember what might be easily forgotten. As a nation, we have constructed memorials of wars and seasons of conflict that our nation has been involved in. They remind us of where we came from and hopefully point to where we should go. The memorial of the Lord's Supper, the Cross as well as the Word of God points us to what was done for us and points us to the way we should go. The Lord's Supper reminds us that God so loved the world that he gave his only begotten son that whoever believes in Him should not perish but have everlasting life. The Cross reminds us that our freedom from sin was not free... The Word reveals God to us and helps us remember who He is and how much we need Him.

Memorial weekend is coming up, and the following scriptures make me realize that many have gone before me without falling from their faith, and if they can so can I...

Hebrews 12:1-2 NKJV

Therefore we also, since we are surrounded by so great a cloud of witnesses, let us lay aside every weight, and the sin which so easily ensnares us, and let us run with endurance the race that is set before us, looking unto Jesus, the author and finisher of our faith, who for the joy that was set before Him endured the cross, despising the shame, and has sat down at the right hand of the throne of God.

———

Philippians 4:13 (NKJV) says:

I can do all things through Christ who strengthens me...

I used to think I had to do all things and then God would strengthen me but I am realizing the "all things" refers only to the things God has called me to do. I believe chemo is something God laid before me to do and tomorrow I will quote that verse as I start 48 hours of it... Cherish your prayers...

May 24, 2012

It was chemo day... the nurse drawing my blood samples inserted the needle with no problems, I didn't even feel it, but she said she hit scar tissues and the tiny tube would not go in the vein. Then it was a desperate moving back and forth trying to get it in... But in it went and soon she had removed seven vials of blood.

My oncologist is a wonderful man who took about 45 minutes with Fran and I and answered all our questions and was kind and understanding. A data collector from the UCLA trial program was also there asking questions and giving advice. It was a very positive experience. We were led to the "room," and there were dozens of people, all ages receiving all kinds of chemo. The nurse that had such a hard time getting the port to work on my first round, was my nurse, and everything went so well. The iron infusion was first and very quickly made me taste something I imagine is like rusty nails...Six hours to go, I began to get anticipatory nausea... and they had a nice little pill for that... I spoke to several people during the day, and all were facing challenges all different from mine: One lady and her family wished me luck, and I said that was good but prayer is what I believe in. I then found they were Christians and we promised to pray for each other.

Fran came from her office at lunch with a ham and cheese sandwich and we shared a few chips. It tasted good. She is such an incredible wife and friend. About one hour and 45 minutes more chemo before the pump would be attached. Already my taste buds were changing...and not for the good...Getting sleeeeeepy. I was in that room longer than anyone, I was the next to last one to leave. I am coming back in the morning for hydration which will perhaps help with the side effects from the chemo. My son, Jonathan, picked me up and I enjoyed that time together.

———

Home with my pump... determined to feel better... went with my son to get a year's pass for my boat and pickup for Lake Mead so the family can use it even if I can't. Because of a mix up with a new employee, they needed cash and not a debit card but we only had $14, we turned around and went to a nearby Hacienda Casino and used the ATM. I thought I would really stand out having a pump hanging from my shoulder and lines running into my chest... but there were these people with oxygen tanks and masks gambling, and so I just fit in with the old guys, just didn't take time to gamble... chemo is a big enough gamble. Got the pass finally, went home and sat down to watch the news at about 5:30 P. M. and woke up at 6:30... Fran had come at 6:00 P. M. and tried to wake me but I just slept... it is that chair of mine... it grabs me and tricks me into rest and sleep... feeling good right now... PTL

———

I am writing extra tonight because I want to put down some things that I don't want to forget. Fran fixed for me her world famous (at least in my world) chicken noodle soup. While doing that my son-in-law Mike stopped to see us and we had a good time of listening and encouraging him in his battle with health. Fran fixed the soup, and I ate two bowls, and evidently just before 9:00 P. M., I fell asleep and never awoke until around 11:00 P.M... I slept through our prayer time. I think Fran decided I was doing what I should at that moment. I am on my way to bed with my wife, my chemo pump, and very little discomfort. I am convinced that my God is answering your prayers for me at this time of my life. I am persuaded that I will live a full life as I delight myself in Him. He is the author and the finisher of my faith and tonight I fix my eyes on Him knowing He will keep me... I am persuaded that there is not one person reading this who cannot experience the same or greater hope in God as I have... To be able to tell you this tonight is worth every needle and every pain... Jesus invites all of us in Matthew 11:28-30 (NIV):

> *"Come to me, all you who are weary and burdened, and I will give you rest. Take my yoke upon you and learn from me, for I am gentle and humble in heart, and you will find rest for your souls. For my yoke is easy and my burden is light."*

I have found that rest in the midst of chaos; I have found that rest in the middle of the unknown. I have found that rest in my sickness; I have found that rest in losses I felt I could never survive... but He was there, is there and will always be there with a rest that is greater than the battle...

May 25, 2012

Isaiah 41:10, 13 NIV

So do not fear, for I am with you; do not be dismayed, for I am your God. I will strengthen you and help you; I will uphold you with my righteous right hand. For I am the Lord your God who takes hold of your right hand and says to you, do not fear; I will help you.

Back in the chemo room this morning... getting hydration (for two hours) they think it will help mitigate the effects of chemo... two hours of saline infusions. Fran is here showing me wedding rings... our 25th anniversary is coming up soon. Kinda strange since we have 28, 36, 42 and 45-year-old children... But it is all good...

Today has been an awesome day even though I am receiving chemo and spent two hours receiving hydration through my port. We felt like we were able to spend all day with family and friends. A couple from our church in Prineville brought their pastors from Kingman, Arizona by tonight and we had such an awesome time in the Lord. As they prayed for me, I believe all the prayers of the hundreds who have been praying for me were all before the throne of God at once, and I sensed such an anointing of God that I believe there is a new beginning in my body and our ministry.

This is our hour of prayer... believing that God will touch you with a sense of His presence in your lives...

Isaiah 43:1-3 NIV

"... Do not fear, for I have redeemed you; I have summoned you by name; you are mine. When you pass through the waters, I will be with you; and when you pass through the rivers, they will not sweep over you. When you walk through the fire, you will not be burned; the flames will not set you ablaze. For I am the Lord your God..."

May 26, 2012

Up at 6:30 A. M. and on our way by 7:30 to get to Cancer Center by 8:00 in the middle of Vegas. The pump came off fine, and my pretty wife and I went to Omelet House for a Taco Omelet... that was excellent, but what a difference a day makes... the residue of the chemo began to permeate my body and by late afternoon all the good I have felt for days seemed to evaporate. But I decided I would not be the victim but try to overcome the symptoms of the medicine... it has been a hard afternoon, but still determined to conduct the service at Nevada State Veterans Home on Sunday, May 27th.

It is a battle today... the doctor said Thursday if I didn't have emotional swings it would be because I did not understand the severity of the disease. Today just for a moment I felt all my self-control evaporate and I began to weep and say, "I cannot control any of my life, I am going to die..." But just about that time I turned the TV on to Sid Roth, and he said repeat after me... and one scripture after another began to strengthen my soul. And that part of the battle was over... just like that... still feel the symptoms, but I do not feel defeated.

John 8:32 NASB

*"...and you will know the truth
and the truth will set you free..."*

Pump free today, but oooh what an impact chemo has on the human body... cannot describe how it invades every part of your being and then tries to take over your emotions and something tries to take hope away... but Romans 10:17 says,

"faith comes by hearing and hearing by the word of God... "

It was what I heard from the Word that evaporated fear and brought hope back in today... still feeling symptoms, but am going to make it... I can do all the things that Christ tells me to do... but not much more than that... lol. Fran and I will be at the NSVH for chapel service tomorrow...

Talking about Abraham:

Romans 4:20-24 NIV

Yet he did not waver through unbelief regarding the promise of God, but was strengthened in his faith and gave glory to God, being fully persuaded that God had power to do what he had promised. This is why "it was credited to him as righteousness." The words "it was credited to him" were written not for him alone, but also for us, to whom God will credit righteousness—for us who believe in him who raised Jesus our Lord from the dead.

May 27, 2012

Job 5:7-9 NIV

Yet man is born to trouble as surely as sparks fly upward. But if I were you, I would appeal to God; I would lay my cause before him. He performs wonders that cannot be fathomed, miracles that cannot be counted.

I have been reading in the book of Job, and chapter five is an incredible reminder of human nature... Job's friends believed that Job had done something to deserve what he was experiencing... and they were telling him what he should do...

What they are telling him here is true, but there is little knowledge of the depths of suffering Job is going through... I believe they want him to do what they say, so they can feel better about themselves. Job did call on God many times, but God allowed him to go through what he went through. I feel that way today... I have come to the place that I believe there are those who would rather turn away towards something else than look at the ongoing battle of survival many people go through. I know I have done that. "Just get healed or get out of the way... I don't have time for your sickness..." Now the shoe is on the other foot and all I have time for is my sickness... It is my life whether I want it to be or not. Job walked through the unknown while suffering and chose not to turn away from the God he loved... though he slay me, yet I will serve him. It is an act of the will, and an act of the conscience to worship one who could heal but hasn't... the good about Job is that God did heal him and did restore him... that's my hope...

———

Fran and I had a blessed time ministering at the Nevada State Veterans Home this morning. It is the first time we have conducted an entire service for a couple of months. We gave out flags as we sang America the Beautiful. They held the flags as a precious gift. It was rewarding but when it was over a bed was all I could think of. Chemo is my worst enemy. I felt I had a handle on the treatment and so went forward with my plan to minister at the Veterans Home. About 3/4 the way through, I could only stand by holding onto the pulpit... The last amen was so welcome. (Even though I was directing the service.) It has been bed and sleep most of the afternoon and evening. Fran and I felt we must pray and we did and what a source of encouragement there is in prayer.

I still believe my redeemer lives... and He has not forgotten me...

May 28, 2012

Fran and I were blessed to take care of our six-month-old grandson this afternoon. Jon had to go to work and Rebekah was sick. We know again why God gives little guys to young parents... lol. He is a joy. In between my trips to the boy's room, Caiden did his best to entertain Fran and me. It was really a good diversion from sitting there feeling sorry for myself. And I have lots of reasons to feel sorry for myself today. How simply inhuman this cancer treatment is. I do think I am still better in most ways except for nausea.

———

For three days I have suffered a treatment illness that sucks the life out of me. I am still alive, but strength is almost gone. I have no other recourse but to call on the name of the Lord... One verse I am standing on is John 7:37-39:

> *That out of my innermost being shall flow*
> *rivers of living waters...*

I am believing for those living waters to flow out of me. It's life to the rest of my body... not just for me but for those whom I meet...

———

On December 24, 1965, I received a letter that informed me that I was being drafted into the military during the buildup of the Vietnam War. A few weeks later my first wife and I learned that she was pregnant with our first child... I found I could try to join the Air Force and I did. It was four years versus two years but still proud of the choices I made as a 20-year-old young man. Although I never saw combat overseas, I was part of the ADC (Air Defense Command) that stood ready to defend US airspace from any enemy threat. Maybe unknown to the public, thousands stood ready 24/7 to protect the borders of our country. Having the chance to look and read and touch the names on the Vietnam Memorial in Washington DC of the thousands of my peers who gave their lives while we served our country makes me keenly aware that we have so much to be grateful for on this Memorial Day, 2012.

I think Secretary of Defense Panetta just gave one of the best speeches honoring Vietnam Vets that I remember ever hearing. Chemo made me more emotional than I am usually am, but when I heard Secretary of Defense Panetta give such a factual moving speech about Vietnam and then heard our President read a speech, that I hope was from his heart, on Vietnam. I was very moved.

President Obama said that our troops coming home from Vietnam should have been treated with the respect due them and not the shameful way many were. His words were like medicine to an open wound. I was stationed not many miles from Haight Ashbury in San Francisco in the late sixties, and it was dangerous for us to be in the city by ourselves. We had short hair so no matter if we had uniforms on or not we were easy to pick out of the crowds of protestors. It was a strange time...

Hearing our President acknowledge the abuse on our military during the time we were serving our country, and then later hearing a very leftist commentator telling his version of protest, drugs, sex and drinking within miles of my base and laughing and joking about it made me realize that it is time for the nation to welcome home the Vietnam Vets... and for those who opposed the soldier to understand the shame they brought to our country. It was a good day for our military... and for the fallen from every generation.

May 29, 2012

Matthew 6:9-15 KJV

After this manner therefore pray ye: Our Father which art in heaven, hallowed be thy name. Thy kingdom come, Thy will be done on earth, as it is in heaven. Give us this day our daily bread. And forgive us our debts, as we forgive our debtors. And lead us not into temptation, but deliver us from evil: For thine is the kingdom, and the power, and the glory, forever. Amen. For if ye forgive men their trespasses, your heavenly Father will also forgive you: But if ye forgive not men their trespasses, neither will your Father forgive your trespasses.

Today was the sixth day since chemo... and I guess this is the cycle... seven to eight days before I feel good again and then it starts over. But as I said to Fran, if the chemo is keeping the cancer from growing and maybe even shrinking it, it may be better than the alternative.

A very good friend from Kenya, Father Kasio was in my home telling me of a situation in his life, and I said, "What are you going to do?" In a very quiet, yet strong voice, he said. "My Father will take care of it..." On that day I realized I had a huge family, for there are a lot of us who call our God, Father.

———

I am speaking at the NSVH for chapel tomorrow. There are awesome volunteers who are there helping and makes the day so much easier. I am speaking on being content. I found this statement by Ben Franklin, paraphrased says: *"A poor contented man is rich, and a rich discontented man is poor."*

Great strength comes from a contented spirit. A fretful or fearful heart drains the soul of precious strength, expending needless energy... But the contented heart builds and conserves strength.

Today was a very hard day for me... I had an emotional meltdown as the future seemed too dim and I felt so poorly equipped to be able to continue this journey that I never chose. Fran called me, and I broke into tears telling her I didn't know if I could make it anymore. She was so worried and asked if she should come home from work. I told her I would be OK and she reluctantly ended the call. Then an old friend called who is also going through a tough time, and something was said that made me laugh and laugh and soon the dark cloud of concern evaporated. I managed to install a new garage door opener today even though it felt like I was dragging around a dead body. I rested a lot but got it working. Fran came home early, and she helped me finish it. Focus is everything. Fixing your eyes on Jesus, the author, and finisher of your faith.

May 30, 2012

So much unknown in this battle. The place fear takes over in one's life is where the unknown begins to seem greater than the known. The unknown is something no one can completely say they know what the outcome will be regardless of their faith, hope or vision.

I think of cancer, chemo, faith, hope, and fear actively at work in me at the same time. I don't know if the cancer tumor is causing my symptoms today or if it is just the chemo that is doing it... My faith says, God will not abandon me, He will not let cancer kill me. My Hope says I am getting better, and I will survive this, and if I don't, I will spend eternity in heaven. My fear says the cancer is growing and I will not survive because I see many others also fighting this monster and not surviving. My fear says even if I take all the chemo, my life as I knew it is ended. My plans for retirement are tossed to the wind. Fear amplifies each symptom and builds on the unknown. I do not know what the outcome of my treatment will be and that unknown robs me of the peace of hope and faith. Fear is the great thief of the soul.

But then on the other side, hope and faith are amplified by the known. "I know in whom I have believed and I am persuaded that He is able to keep that which I have committed unto Him."[6] I know that there is no weapon formed against me that will prosper... I know that until I have fulfilled my purposes for my generation, I will continue to live... I know that neither death nor life can separate me from the love of God that is in Christ Jesus. I know my Father will take care of me... I know that when I pray, the Creator of the Universe somehow listens and responds. I know that love conquers, subdues and casts aside the fear of the unknown. I know Jesus said from the cross, "It is finished." and every prophecy in Isaiah 53 is mine, and every promise in the New Testament is also mine. I know that for me to live is Christ and to die would be gain (Philippians

1:21) but I know for this moment it is important that I remain to finish the race that is set before me (Acts 20:24), keeping my eyes on Jesus, the Author and the perfector of my faith (Hebrews 12:12).

———

Today I spent three hours as the Chaplain at NSVH. We had the second largest gathering in the chapel in 10 years. The folks were so energized in their singing, reading the Word, and listening to me preach. It was a great service, people sang with great conviction, and the volunteers are so amazing as they care for these wonderful folks.

I spoke on the Power of Contentment. I think I shared some of that last night. We ended with the Lord's Prayer, and I was amazed at the intensity of the people as they prayed. The Vets are great people. As I led the Lord's prayer, I was so blessed to hear their heartfelt devotion to "Our Father" as we prayed together. Then one of the volunteers asked everyone to pray for me. Here I am supposed to be the minister and the people ministered to me. It was a wonderful, priceless moment.

Amen.

May 31, 2012

I know I keep repeating myself on what chemo, cancer and whatever else, is doing in my body... I know those who check this site every day or every once in a while, are probably ready to move on and I don't blame you. For me, however, I am writing these things so I can go back and see where I came from. My family may at some time in the future get to read all my ramblings, and hopefully, they will see the words of a man who prayed for healing and justice but also a man who would not give up on his faith no matter how he felt. I am not doing this to impress anyone, but even Paul the apostle told people to follow his example as he followed Jesus Christ. If I can do this through cancer, then maybe someone will make a choice to also follow their faith.

Last night and tonight were very hard. I thought I had developed a sore throat from preaching so passionately yesterday, but the sore throat and sniffles turned into a very intense soreness and running nose. It was miserable. Not only that, Fran called from work in the early afternoon and had evidently got food poisoning and got very sick at work and came home. She was out of commission for almost 24 hours (flu?) There was no one here to feel sorry for me, and in fact, I ended up having to help her and get things for her. I have been so used to her helping me I almost was offended that she needed me... (Real Christian man). Tonight, we both felt better and got some KFC dinners and went up on a plateau overlooking Boulder City to have a little picnic. We used to go up there often to pray for our town. Felt different not to be a pastor but felt we should pray for the town and the church we started. We also prayed for a revival of our own souls. Later in our living room, we worshiped with music on our iPhone and the presence of the Lord was so apparent.

———

Psalms 3:3-5 KJV

But thou, O Lord, art a shield for me; my glory, and the lifter up of mine head. I cried unto the Lord with my voice, and he heard me out of his holy hill. Selah. I laid me down and slept; I awaked; for the Lord sustained me.

Sometimes I really love the old King James Version. The poetry and the rhythm of the verbiage... "I laid me down and slept..." The Lord sustained me...

Today, these 24 hours that we have to breathe in and breathe out, breathe in and breathe out, this same period of time that everyone else has is a gift from our God. One scripture says, "This is the day that the Lord has made, I will rejoice and be glad in it..." By choice, by the act of my will, regardless of how my body feels, or what my circumstances are, I have the choice to rejoice or to be grouchy, grumpy, complaining and looking for a pity party.

Today, by the help of my God, I choose to rejoice and be glad... In fact, as Paul, the apostle says, "Rejoice in the Lord and again I say rejoice..." By the act of my will, God will strengthen my resolve to worship him, to be thankful, not remorseful or whiny... to understand that God is there with me no matter what. So today, regardless of what I feel, I choose and determine to rejoice...

My brother, Lyle, and his wife, Lynn, arrived at our house last night from Portland, Oregon at about midnight. So good to have my brother here who has such a kindred spirit. He and his wife have been there for me most of my adult life, and here they are again, staying for a few days. I know this time is God ordained.

My garage gets used by a quite a few people from changing the oil to changing engines. One side effect is most of the guys forget to take their old oil with them. I had about five gallons of used oil in containers and found out that AutoZone Store would take it. I also had a bad battery, and they took that too and gave me $5. 00 credit card. Not a bad deal. Did a lot of recycling today.

June 02, 2012

I skipped a day because I just did not have a lot to say about anything as I was struggling with the weight of trying to make sense of my symptoms in light of what might happen in the near future. In other words, I was feeling a little apprehension about what my life would be in the- near-future and in the long-range. I was not finding too many good pictures of the future (my future). There was a whisper in my mind, "How will Fran make it if I die." "What if she cannot take care of you, where will you end up?" Those were only two of the many that were flooding my mind.

After a good day of feeling physically good for the first time in eight days, I heard a word in my heart:

2 Corinthians 10:3 -4 NLT

We are human, but we don't wage war as humans do. We use God's mighty weapons, not worldly weapons, to knock down the strongholds of human reasoning and to destroy false arguments.

I began, in the spirit of prayer, to stand against fear and to hold on to what I know and who I know. It gave me victory today to speak of life, a future and purpose for my life. I, therefore, will not allow (today anyway) the spirit of fear to invade my life. I will embrace the wisdom and the leading of Almighty God to show me how He will help me take care of those things I was worrying about. By the way, this is a daily battle, "give us this day... "His mercies are new every morning..." but I must grasp His

Grace and apply His Wisdom to my situation even when I don't feel like it.

This was my miracle day. Rob and his family and Lyle, my brother and his wife Lynn came to spend a couple of days with us. I began feeling better last night and today was just wonderful. My sons and I hooked up our boat and headed for the Lake (five miles away). Fran and three of my granddaughters joined us, and we had a ball on a rough lake. We found a calm cove and everyone but Fran and I jumped into the 85+ degree water and had a blast. I took so many pictures. Loading the boat should have been easy, and I was standing in two feet of water with my phone and wallet in my pocket... but we needed to back in a little deeper to reposition the boat on the trailer, and not thinking, I stepped into the deeper water and baptized the camera end of my droid. Maybe old guys shouldn't have smartphones because that wasn't smart. So here I go again... battery out, phone in some rice... see what happens... But what a great day just to be alive and not feeling sick... got a little weary, but it was worth it. My family and your prayers are such a strength to my wanting to win my battle with cancer...

Prayer time is precious time... family and friends we prayed for you tonight. My brother and his wife joined us and such an awesome renewal of God's love, and grace flooded my soul... and the room...

Matthew 18:20 NKJV

*For where two or three are gathered together in My name,
I am there in the midst of them.*

1 Corinthians 15:58 NKJV

Therefore, my beloved brethren, be steadfast, immovable, always abounding in the work of the Lord, knowing that your labor is not in vain in the Lord.

I never chose cancer, and I do not know what caused it, but out of the ashes of my plans has come a new desire to be in the center of God's plans for my life. He indeed knows how to make me lie down in green pastures... while He restores my soul for His purposes... I am really sensing this is about more than a battle with a disease, it is about my relationship with Him and those He loves.

June 3, 2012

2 Chronicles 20:15-17 NKJV

...Thus says the LORD to you: 'Do not be afraid nor dismayed because of this great multitude, for the battle is not yours, but God's. Tomorrow go down against them. You will not need to fight in this battle. (You will not have to fight this battle) Position yourselves, stand still and see the salvation of the LORD, who is with you, O Judah and Jerusalem!' Do not fear or be dismayed; tomorrow go out against them, for the LORD is with you."

Life is a battle...we find ourselves always facing something that takes an extreme amount of energy or faith, but there are times when I have experienced God whispering to me, "Don't worry about this battle, it is not yours.... you will not have to fight this battle." And all my worries and fears are meaningless as suddenly I see an incredible shift in what I thought the outcome would be...God made it happen. The scripture above is how I know that God will do it if we are willing to position ourselves in the right place and let Him do it...try it, you will like it.... I have a sense He is doing that with the cancer that is attacking me...

———

Not that I am counting, but I have two more days of freedom from chemo, until I start it again. It starts on D-Day, June 6th, which also happens to be Fran and my 25th wedding anniversary. What a present! So hard to believe we have come so far so quickly and now have four children and nine grandchildren. Fran was and is my treasure! I am blessed.

———

This is from my friend who is a cancer survivor:

R. E. S. T. - Relinquish EVERYTHING and Submit Totally;
T. R. U. S. T. - Totally Rely Upon the Savior's Timing.

———

Sundays are always a challenge for me. Having retired from pastoring a church, Fran and I are attempting to know which church we should make as our home church... When you have pastored most of your adult life, there is never a church as good as the one you pastored (my opinion of course), so it is hard to find a place to fit in. We love Boulder City Assembly but feel we need to give their awesome new pastor the room to grow into everything God has him to be (without our influence), so even though we are welcome there, we are doing what is right and only visit occasionally. So again today because of company we needed to find a very early service somewhere so we could go to church and get to the airport on time. We did, and we enjoyed a service where we knew none of the songs and I was one of the oldest in attendance... lol but I am sure the best church will be the church we become involved with in serving not in just watching.

June 4, 2012

I am so blessed today. No pain, very little side effects left from chemo and I think the tumor is being affected because of being able to eat just about anything without problems.

Fran is such a good cook. She made stir fry tonight, and it was sooo good... I don't know how cooks think up a meal and make it happen. I can do tacos and eggs and peanut butter sandwiches. Lol

Today was an eventful day, and I am so glad God gave me the strength to handle what came my way. So many people have such hurts that can either consume them and make them bitter or can build them up inside to be stronger than they ever were before.

It comes down to choices. I told Fran tonight, I fight anger... the Bible says to be angry and sin not and with God's help that is where I am, not sinning because of anger... I told her that as a human I probably have a right to be angry about the turn of events in our lives.

Cancer is causing more problems than just physical... it touches every other area of our lives... the best plans I had after retiring from the church have evaporated along with my good health... I could be angry and if I chose I could wallow in my anger, bitterness, disappointments, and self-pity... but as I told Fran, I have chosen not to allow anger be the controller of my emotions, life, and future.

I am not bragging, I am just telling you that each time anger tries to invade my mind and spirit I have a choice... to let it stay in the crockpot of self-pity and simmer to a boil or I can choose to say no to that emotion and say yes to the God of Hope who fills me with peace and joy as I trust in Him so that hope abounds in me by the power of the Holy Spirit.

This is not mind-over-matter or some kind of self-realization, it is a God-empowered gift as I choose... the moment I say no to what I know is self-destructive, I sense a renewed energy to find joy in the midst of chaos.

———

My friend, Steve Slater recommends a book called *"What to Do on the Worst Day of Your Life"* by Brian Zahnd. I plan on getting the book and reading it. I hope it has lots of chapters because I have entitled a lot of days as the worst day of my life.

Age has advantages, because looking back on experiences I termed the worst, God has somehow changed them around to be the best, and I have learned that God does work all things together for good for those who love Him and are called according to His purposes: Romans 8:28.

For those who don't buy into God being involved, someone told me a long time ago that if you eat a live toad the first thing in the morning, nothing can get any worse that day... Never tried it... sounds true, but I like the Bible's way better...

June 5, 2012

Ephesians 3:17-19 NIV

"...so that Christ may dwell in your hearts through faith. And I pray that you, being rooted and established in love, may have power, together with all the Lord's holy people, to grasp how wide and long and high and deep is the love of Christ, and to know this love that surpasses knowledge—that you may be filled to the measure of all the fullness of God."

What an amazing afternoon and evening. Fran and I used a welding shield and binoculars and saw that little black dot on the face of the sun as Venus passed between the earth and the sun. As I tried to digest what I was seeing, it again humbled me to realize a planet bigger than the earth was like a pencil dot on the sun... the immensity of the sun was so evident and to think it is the exact distance from earth to allow life to exist here. Then on this earth, I am not even the size of a pencil dot, and the Creator of the Universe knows my name...

Then on the way home from taking Fran out for our anniversary dinner, the moon appeared on the horizon as big as the super moon was a few months ago. It was so beautiful and bright. The meal was my last time to enjoy food for a while before I start the next round of chemo in the morning.

———

26 years ago, I lost my childhood sweetheart and wife to breast cancer. 25 years ago tomorrow, I married the widow of another Assemblies of God pastor who died in an auto accident. Fran and I have suffered much but have gained even greater. For you romantics, I remember, after meeting Fran and going on one of our first dates sitting in my brother's office and with tears telling him I am in love again and it feels so good. Fran has been my treasure (I sang her a song by that title at our wedding). We have learned to laugh together, cry together, to disagree in love, to love God together, to worship, sing and pray together. Not too many people have had such blessings twice in life. We have lived the Romans 8:28 life.

My heart aches for Fran as she feels so helpless to change the fact I have a life-threatening challenge. But she is there, every day, praying and believing for a miracle. Before she got home today, I got long stem roses for her, and since it is our Silver Anniversary, I got her a silver electric can opener (it is a very nice one, but it was more of a joke than a serious gift, and she got it but loved the gift). We have promised each other new wedding rings for our 25th but just haven't picked any out (that we can afford, lol). Since I start chemo tomorrow, we chose to enjoy our anniversary meal at the Claim Jumper... it was super good, and we had a great night... thanks for reading this far... love you all.

———

Fran and I are celebrating our Silver Wedding Anniversary, and we had a rare evening without cell phones. Mine died and am waiting for a replacement, and at the restaurant, I asked Fran for hers, and she handed me her phone and the battery was dead. She smiled and said, "Oh well, we will just have to talk to each other..." I grabbed a salt shaker just to feel like I had a phone...We had a delightful time remembering how we met, where we lived and how God had blessed us both with two great marriages... We are still very much in love, and both respect the love we had in our first marriages before our spouses died and allow room for those memories. Romans 8:28.

June 6, 2012

On my way to Portland, not Oregon, to the cancer center where they puncture the port in my chest to begin 48 hours of chemo... if you can pray for me... not a fun time... but Romans 8:28.

———

The chemotherapy room was filled with about 20 people all receiving treatment for some kind of cancer they are fighting. No interaction, but there were smiles when I would smile at someone... The treatment went so easy. Fran stayed with me till it started, and then it went till almost five in the evening, and I am wearing a pump for a total of 42 hours. I decided that just like anger is a choice, so is cursing the treatment. So, I am not cursing the treatment this time but am praying it will do what the scientist and doctors think it should. Some of my worst symptoms of the cancer have gone away, so your prayers and the treatment are working together for good.

———

2 Kings 5: 9-14 KJV

*So Naaman came with his horses and with his chariot, and stood
at the door of the house of Elisha. And Elisha sent a messenger unto
him, saying, Go and wash in Jordan seven times, and thy flesh shall
come again to thee, and thou shalt be clean. But Naaman was wroth,
and went away, and said, Behold, I thought, He will surely come out
to me, and stand, and call on the name of the Lord his God, and
strike his hand over the place, and recover the leper. Are not Abana
and Pharpar, rivers of Damascus, better than all the waters of Israel?
May I not wash in them, and be clean? So he turned and went away
in a rage. And his servants came near, and spake unto him, and said,
"My father, if the prophet had bid thee do some great thing, wouldest
thou not have done it? How much rather then, when he saith to thee,
Wash, and be clean?" Then went he down, and dipped himself seven
times in Jordan, according to the saying of the man of God: and his
flesh came again like unto the flesh of a little child, and he was clean.*

Do you remember in 2 Kings 5 the story of a great leader from Syria who
had severe leprosy? One of his slave girls was from Israel told him about a
great prophet named Elisha who could heal him.

I see myself in this: Naaman cursed the method of healing. He wanted
a quick miracle... not to humble himself to dip in a muddy river... With
wise counsel, he changed his attitude and embraced the method and was
healed. Today I choose to not curse chemo but to pray it will do the work
the doctors hope it will do...

As I prayed, I asked God to help living waters come from me and that
Fran and I will give thanks in all things for this is the will of God in Christ
Jesus. I choose to rejoice... even when I don't understand...

June 7, 2012

Day two of the chemo pump. Each time I hear the pump make its
wheezing noise as it pumps more chemicals into my body I am reminded
to pray that God will cause its purpose to do as He wills. I am experiencing

all the doctors said I would, as far as side effects, but since deciding to bless rather than curse, I have had such an easier time even though I am weak and somewhat nauseated. You should have seen me this morning trying to help Fran get some things out of the fridge. The reaction to the cold was so sudden I almost dropped a bag of lettuce. At least it wouldn't have broken. I had to put Fran's potholder gloves on to get the rest out of the fridge. I must have been funny to look at.

I get the pump off tomorrow at 2:00 P. M. and that is always a relief. Some more family is visiting this weekend... we look forward to those who love us enough to come and visit, it truly is a blessing.

———

Habakkuk 3: 17-19

Though the fig tree may not blossom, nor fruit be on the vines; Though the labor of the olive may fail, And the fields yield no food; Though the flock may be cut off from the fold, and there be no herd in the stalls— Yet I will rejoice in the Lord, I will joy in the God of my salvation. The Lord God is my strength; He will make my feet like deer's feet, And He will make me walk on my high hills.

I am thankful for life... and am thankful for the hope we can have in our God. The above scriptures have long been an encouragement for me: ... because it is written from the sense of being aware bad things happen even though we wish they wouldn't, but in everything, there can be the resolve, the persuasion not to let the events overcome our joy and relationship with the Lord.

Even with chemo doing its thing I will rejoice in the Lord... I will joy in the God of my salvation...

June 8, 2012

Isaiah 40:28-31 NKJV

Have you not known? Have you not heard? The everlasting God, the Lord, The Creator of the ends of the earth, neither faints nor is weary. His understanding is unsearchable. He gives power to the weak, and to those who have no might He increases strength. Even the youths shall faint and be weary, And the young men shall utterly fall, but those who wait on the Lord Shall renew their strength; They shall mount up with wings like eagles, they shall run and not be weary, they shall walk and not faint.

I am waiting...

Today was to be a great day with the removal of my chemo pump. My attitude has been positive toward my chemo but this morning getting ready to go get the pump off I noticed my left arm was really swollen. Just as I found this, I got a call from Fran who told me our van had stalled and would not start. My son Jon picked me up, and we drove to Henderson to find Fran. Fuel pump or something wrong. I asked Jon to take me to the Cancer Center where, when they saw my arm, scheduled an ultrasound and found a blood clot in my neck... all the time Jon is arranging to get our car towed. My doctor advised me to take the blood thinner shot in his office, and then I will have to take them daily for months... He said it was the cancer causing the clotting... regardless it just wasn't a good day. Thank God for my family who lives here, they really came through for me today. Fran's brother and his wife arrived here from Missoula this afternoon, and they are such a help already. I am in a lot of discomfort but am convinced that He who has begun a good work in me will complete it...cherish your prayers...

After a very tough day, finding a blood clot, my wife's car breaking down and a lot of discomfort this scripture brings me hope and peace.

June 9, 2012

Romans 8:35 -39 NKJV

Who shall separate us from the love of Christ? Shall tribulation, or distress, or persecution, or famine, or nakedness, or peril, or sword? As it is written: "For Your sake we are killed all day long; We are accounted as sheep for the slaughter." Yet in all these things we are more than conquerors through Him who loved us. For I am persuaded that neither death nor life, nor angels nor principalities nor powers, nor things present nor things to come, nor height nor depth, nor any other created thing, shall be able to separate us from the love of God which is in Christ Jesus our Lord.

Rough day today... in bed most of the day...

———

This is one of the most difficult days since I had surgery. Very stressful because of pain in so many areas of my body. It appears I will have to have injections in my abdomen every day for some time to dissolve and prevent blood clots. Not liking that at all, but know there are some of you that already have to do that... however, I am still feeling that fear factor towards needles... My bed is my friend today. Jesus said:

John 16:33 NKJV

"...In the world you will have tribulation, but be of GOOD cheer I have overcome the world..."

Tonight I am remembering an old chorus we used to sing taken from the words of Jesus in John 7:37-39. I am praying those words... *"Out of your innermost being shall flow rivers of life..."* This he spoke of the Holy Spirit, so I am singing and praying the song: "I've Got a River of Life..." That is the focus of my faith... life, not death flowing from what the Holy Spirit is doing in me...come Holy Spirit I need you... make the lame to walk, the blind to see, set the captive free, I've got a river of life flowing out of me...

June 11, 2012

I have been through so much agony the last three days, and I have found the bottom line is I do not know how to be healed by faith or by the supernatural. I have taken authority, spoke words of life, spoke to the mountain in my life, rebuked the cancer, have fasted, prayed, and had hundreds of people praying for me, and still, the answer seems to be "no," or not now, or hold on...and so I do. I have found it is faith that I have left when every other word seems to be no. I am learning to stand still and let God be God. If it is not my will but His be done, I must let Him work out his plan for me in His time and in His way. I will always confess that Jesus is my healer... I will always confess that by His wounds I have been healed... but so far that has not happened this time. For me to live is Christ, but to die is gain... I believe it is better I stay here much longer so I will look and plan in that direction. But if my life is cut shorter than I planned, I know in whom I have believed. Death is not a threat, but a doorway to eternity.

The last few days I thought I was getting very close to that doorway and I had to deal with my mortality and recognized if God is all I have left, I have more than enough... I am feeling better tonight, but it takes a lot of human effort to move... but I am moving... that is good... love all of you.

———

Romans 8:31 NKJV

What then shall we say to these things?
If God is for us, who can be against us?

Mark 11:23 NKJV

For assuredly, I say to you, whoever says to this mountain, be removed and be cast into the sea, and does not doubt in his heart, but believes that those things he says will be done, he will have whatever he says.

I love seeing the Facebook entries of young men and women just getting ready to start on new careers, adventures, and challenges. That probably is the hardest thing about being older, you know that days of dreaming are limited. Yet I believe that God is not done with us until the day He takes us home. Hoping for a lot more dreams and challenges for my life...

June 12, 2012

Just wanted to share these scriptures. I think I have before, but they are renewed in my spirit tonight...

Proverbs 3:1-8 NKJV

My son, do not forget my law, but let your heart keep my commands; For length of days and long life and peace they will add to you. Let not mercy and truth forsake you; Bind them around your neck, write them on the tablet of your heart, and so find favor and high esteem in the sight of God and man. Trust in the LORD with all your heart, and lean not on your own understanding; In all your ways acknowledge Him, And He shall direct your paths. Do not be wise in your own eyes; Fear the LORD and depart from evil. It will be health to your flesh, And strength to your bones.

I hope you know that those who post on this CarePage are giving such amazing words of comfort, hope, and encouragement that I find courage from. If you would allow me, someday I would like to compile these posts into a book that perhaps could help others know what to say or to know how to listen to those facing challenges that are bigger than life. The messages that you post are great blessings, the prayers that are prayed by those who never post are being heard and acted on by the Giver of Life. I cannot tell you how anxious I am every day to hear what you say. I am posting two posts today again for my sake to record what has transpired today.

———

Today the pain continued to radiate up my esophagus area into my head as well as into my shoulders. It is wonderful that if I lay still, I felt no pain, but it is hard to stay that way all day. The oncologist told me yesterday it was probably from the chemo. (The last visit he told me it was the cancer, so don't know what to blame, just know it is hard to handle).

I believe in angels. Two have been staying at my house since Friday. Fran's brother Dan and his wife Dawn have been here and asked for a list of what they could help us with. They have pulled weeds, planted flowers, painted baseboard and some of our outdoor furniture, cooked meals, prayed with us, loved on us and just have been a gift of God to us. So, a few times I got up just to let them know I appreciated them. We are so blessed to have family that love and care. The timing of their visit was so God ordered... Fran could not have made it through this rough weekend without them...we will miss them.

This afternoon I lay back down after lunch (my appetite seems to be improving), and I slept for several hours. I woke up when Fran came home and asked me if I had given myself a shot... (Supposed to do so near 4:00 P. M.). I had not, but I did then... Never hurt much at all. The anticipation is worse. Fran looked at my feeding tube and said it wasn't looking good. Two stitches had finally come out, and it lets stuff leak out (gross, sorry). Taking a shower is usually the best way to clean it. Taking the dressing off in the shower I found the tube had come nearly all the way out... and in a few moments, it fell out of the tiny hole in my abdomen. I was in shock of what to do.

I had Fran call the surgeon, and they told me to stick it back in and if not comfortable doing it myself to go to ER... I am not a mountain man, so we ended up in ER for almost three hours in the coldest room in Nevada... The doctor actually shoved it back in, gave me a shot with a foot-long needle for pain (seemed that long); put a stitch in my skin and tied the tube in. They then ran dye into the tube and x-rayed it and found it was in the right place... but it took another hour to get dismissed. A young nurse came by and gave both Fran and I a heated blanket, and we felt like heaven had come down... After being dismissed going out in the 90-degree weather felt so good... I even put a coat on. During the afternoon, my sister-in-law, Dawn had a dream and saw some amazing visions of God healing me, and she and the family there prayed for me, and God has given me the strength to make it through ER and then to have part of a steak dinner at Applebee's. It was very good. Am I healed? I hope so, I will try to live like I am... I believe Lord but help my unbelief. At least for tonight, I feel better than I have for six days. Looking for good rest tonight...

———

I was at the cancer center yesterday to get a shot in my belly for a blood clot, and the cute little nurse told me I was going to do it... funny how a person half my size can make me do what I don't want to do. Jenny, my daughter, had given me the last two and never even felt them. I knew I had to so I pinched, poked and plunged in a couple of seconds... the nurse was down on her knees watching me and was so surprised I did it so quickly...the pinch and poke never hurt but the plunge stung big time... Another nurse came over not knowing I had already shot myself and asked me if I was going to be able to do it... When I told her I had already done it, she said, "Oh darn, I wanted to watch you do it." ...had to laugh about that one. Good to have at least one thing to laugh about...

June 13, 2012

Romans 5:1-5 NKJV

Faith Triumphs in Trouble

Therefore, having been justified by faith, we have[a] peace with God through our Lord Jesus Christ, through whom also we have access by faith into this grace in which we stand, and rejoice in hope of the glory of God. And not only that, but we also glory in tribulations, knowing that tribulation produces perseverance; and perseverance, character; and character, hope. Now hope does not disappoint, because the love of God has been poured out in our hearts by the Holy Spirit who was given to us.

Life is so much better today... hope is much stronger today... a friend sent an email with these verses in it... some might enjoy reading it again.

I wonder if Job ever felt like saying, "Don't brag on me today, I don't want to be a target anymore?" Tonight I feel like that.

I hope you noticed the word feel. I feel like that. Job confessed his feelings and some were far deeper than I would ever go (maybe?). I think like Job my faith in God is intact, I have an eternal hope but the combinations of so many things that takes more energy than I have, makes me want to quit trying to hold on to the hope of tomorrow. I don't want to go to bed because if I sleep, I have to wake up to something else in my life or body that may not work right. Survival is my only job right now, and I don't like the work!

My vision for my life is so limited that I am not sure I can see it. Job came to such feelings and voiced them... yet he also came to a point that he said with conviction, *"though He slays me yet will I trust in Him... I will maintain my ways, He shall be my salvation"* ... and later he said, *"I know my Redeemer lives. " (Job 13:15,16; 19:25)*

There is a place where we voice our feelings, but at the same time we utter the prayer of David, *"May the words of my mouth and the meditations of my heart be acceptable to you O Lord, my strength, and my redeemer." (Psalm 19:14)*

So, at these low points I remember that I wrestle not against flesh and blood but against principalities and powers bent on my demise (especially my faith and hope), and that God gives us weapons that are not of our making but are mighty from Him to demolish strongholds of the mind and the power to take those very thoughts of hopelessness captive and the power to cast them out of our lives.

If you read this, you have seen a battle waging in me that has just been won by taking hold of a word of faith. Job said in his weakness, "I know my Redeemer lives..." Saying "I know" breaks the power of feelings and he personalized his relationship with God as He said, "my." Such simple word spoken energize faith and wins the battle of the mind...

When we have exhausted our hoarded resources, and we think the battle cannot be won, that is when God's grace is poured out, and He gives more grace than we need to win... and He gives, and He gives and gives again...

Say it in your heart, I know... my God will never leave nor will He forsake me... I know... in whom I have believed. My faith is built on nothing less than Jesus Christ and righteousness...!!!

June 14, 2012

Something happened to me last night that has not happened ever that I can remember... I could not go to sleep... I was told by the cancer treatment center that taking a certain allergy medicine would help keep the joint pain down and I seem to have either allergies or reaction to chemo or a cold, so I took one of those non-drowsy pills and at about 2:30 A. M. I was as wide awake as I was when I got up the previous morning at 6:00 A. M. I woke Fran up at 5:45 A. M. and have been awake all day long... If this is what speed does to you, no thanks. But what has happened is that I had lots of time to think, meditate and pray. It was not wasted. But I feel the sleep coming and may be asleep before I finish the next word. My son, Rob, came from Portland today and I picked him up at the airport... we had a wonderful hour or more talking about the Lord and what God is doing in his life and in mine. I have been blessed even though no sleep...

I found myself in that low place last night, not caring if I came out of the despair. But God somehow penetrated my mind, and in an instant, the battle was won. I am willing to allow God to use my circumstance to help a struggling friend find hope in the midst of despair. Anyone going through similar situations will find that God does not leave us even when we don't care. He is faithful... *Now faith is the substance of things hoped for and the evidence of things not yet seen...* (Hebrews 11:1 KJV) holding on to that. I am looking for that sweet sleep.

June 15, 2012

Psalm 23:6 NKJV

Surely goodness and mercy shall follow me all the days of my life and (then) I shall dwell in the house of the Lord forever!

Sleep is sweet... I enjoyed every minute of it. So bizarre not to sleep for a whole 24 hours and not even feel sleepy, but I slept last night about eight hours and woke up refreshed. My son, Rob, was here today. I helped him mow my lawn and weed whack it. He did the work, and I watched. Good combination... My energy level is still diminished so much.

Today I went to a new hair cutting place in town, and I struggled to walk in and act lively enough [so that] the girl cutting my hair would think I was OK. She asked me how I was as I sat down and looked in the mirror... staring back at me was this old looking man who was vaguely familiar. The girl asked me how I was and I said, "Well I am alive, does that count?", and she said, "That really counts." I let it go and then asked her about her training and who was the first person's hair that she had cut. She said, "My father." I asked her, "Were you nervous?" She said, "Not really but my Dad was." We laughed. I asked her, "Do you still cut your father's hair." She said, "No, he died three weeks ago." I then knew why she had responded about being alive is what really counts. I asked her what caused his death, and she said they don't know... his heart just stopped, but she said, "I really want to know why."

I tried to talk to her like a dad and said, you may not understand the why even if you find out, but the important thing is to know Who you can turn to in times like this. She knew I was talking about God and said, "I know." I gave her a tip more than the haircut cost in honor of her dad and Father's Day. I then quit whining so much about my condition... I am alive, and I am loved by a great family and lots of friends... I will live till I die, and when I die I will go on living...

June 16, 2012

Today, my brother Lyle sent to all the survivors of our father, a wonderful thesis one of our sisters wrote about our Dad. It said some of what I put in the previous post about a legacy. Just for my sake, I write this post about my dad. On this Father's Day, I want you to know about my father.

I was named by a man named Floyd Everett Jordan: my dad. He was a father to 11 wonderful children (I am bragging), he was never a rich man, but he did everything he knew to do to help provide for his very large family.

When around 47 he became aware something was very wrong with his health. He had spray painted lead-based paints during World War II and commercial painted often during his adult life which may have contributed to the diagnosis of his illness. Doctors said he had lung cancer. I can only imagine the incredible shock to my mom and dad.

As he looked at his large family, he became aware that unless he was healed, he would not be there to help care for his wife and kids. I remember vaguely going to faith healers like A. A. Allen and Oral Roberts and many people coming to our house to pray for him. But the cancer progressed. I was only five, but I remember playing with my toy trucks by his bed and always wanting to be close. Hopefully, I brought him joy.

I have one distinct memory that no one can confirm that happened before my dad died. Weeks before his death, while playing with my toys around his bed, I remember that he called me and pulled me onto his chest and wrapped his arms around me and prayed for me. He asked that God would put in my heart a desire to fulfill what he felt he should have done and that was to be a pastor. I believe though cannot confirm that he also prayed for my younger brother, Lyle, the same way. I am not sure what he prayed for my sisters, but I know it was good.

I have always looked at his illness from my point of view. But now that I am fighting cancer I have seen it from his point of view a little better. Cancer does take lives. It does leave families in shatters. It is full of pain. It does make people very sick.

My dad had to face all that while looking at his kids come in and out of his room, the younger ones clueless with what was happening in our dad's mind, body and spirit. My dad died a few months after I turned five. I know I did not understand, but it was not good.

I remember my mom trying to hold up under the weight of no husband, no money, and a huge family. What I do know, from 62 years of life later, is that my father left my family and me a legacy that will last through eternity. He had a faith in Jesus Christ that has affected his children, grandchildren, great and great-great grandchildren and the story goes on.

It was hard, but cancer was not the end. My dad is part of what Hebrews 12:1 calls the great cloud of witnesses who have already conquered death through life in Jesus Christ. On this Father's Day, I want to be like my dad. I want a legacy of faith to outlive anything like cancer that threatens my life or anyone else. I want to be like my dad and leave what cannot be taxed by the government, spent by squabbling heirs, or stolen by thieves. I want to leave to my loved ones the faith I have in the God that will not abandon me to death but has promised me life and that more abundantly both here and in the place Jesus said He is preparing for those who trust in Him.

At the age of 16, at an Idaho church youth camp, I felt, heard, thought, was impressed by something so real that it has not left me even today. It was a call of God to respond to His call to pursue being a pastor. I was not sure what all that meant, but in my heart and spirit I said, "Yes." It was years later that the memories of that night and what happened in my father's bedroom merged together and I know God answered my dad's prayer. (My brother is also a pastor). I think both of us could say tonight, "We want to be like our Dad. We want what God has done in us to explode in our kids..." and God is doing that... Happy Father's Day.

———

If you ever have been in a twelve-step program, when it is your turn to speak you say, "I am so and so, and I am an alcoholic..." It is an admission of your problem.

Tonight, I introduce myself again: My name is Martin Duane Jordan, and have been diagnosed with Stage IV stomach cancer. I am actively fighting it with prayer, the best medicine I can find and usually a spirit of hope.

———

Here is a little update on me: Each chemo round I have said it was the worst ever... this time it has been that for sure. Not complaining just stating facts. But I am still alive. I have another day to savor life as it comes even when I am almost too weary to embrace it. I am so loved by my family and friends (at least they say and act like they do) so I am at peace.

One negative thing, I sure am not liking mirrors lately... there is a tired looking old man always staring at me... he looks kind of familiar but not sure... what does that mean? Please pray for my wife... she is carrying a load that really is more than she can carry...

June 17, 2012

Proverbs 24:10 NKJV

If you faint in the day of adversity, your strength is small.

Father's Day today: It was a good day. Even though I slept little last night, I was up wanting so to go to church to worship. We were welcomed so warmly at BCA and enjoyed worship and a good message. I also appreciated the message Pastor brought. All my kids expressed their love for me throughout the day. So it was a good day. After church, I got to eat some of my favorite Mexican food with one son and family and then later enjoyed strawberries and shortcake with one of my daughters and family.

Tomorrow is the day I have been dreading for some time when I get to ingest two pints of a barium smoothie in just 30 minutes. I will endure it because the CAT scan that follows will determine if the cancer is growing, shrinking or no change. That will determine the next course of treatment I will pursue. While I was so sick for so many days, I wanted to end anything that had to do with medicine. I was complaining to Fran that treatment lately has meant either pain or humiliation (putting on the robes etc.). But this morning when I opened my Bible there was a verse just kind of standing out to me, and on a note page I had written something about that verse a long time ago that really got me thinking about my daily attitude towards my treatments.

Jeremiah 12:5 NKJV

[The LORD Answers Jeremiah] "If you have run with the footmen, and they have wearied you, then how can you contend with horses?"

I again realized that God calls us to be contenders of our faith...He empowers those who by faith are willing to go into a storm rather than retreat from one. He gives strength to those who have no strength, but he still asks us to do something: wait, believe, ask, embrace, and pursue... God seems to empower the desire to rise above whining, complaining or just plain giving up. Paul says, "In my weakness, I am made strong..." That is a faith statement...Adversity is something we all contend with... but if we let it conquer us when it is not that hard, how will we face the greater challenges? How will we contend? It will be realizing that our real help comes from the Lord.

June 18, 2012

The scriptures I used last night from Proverbs and Jeremiah really helped me see that I must take the initiative towards my treatment, my family, my faith and whatever I am doing... do as unto the Lord.

So, I got up this morning determined to take the barium and aggressively chugged the first half of a mocha flavored barium smoothie... Hopefully this is not TMI, but unfortunately, my stomach didn't agree with my mind, and I parted company with the smoothie in a few moments. I called the cancer center, and they said do the rest of it through my feeding tube. My daughter Jen, who is an RN, got off the night shift at a hospital and stopped to help me on her way home. To me, it was really funny to have my daughter pumping this fluid in my stomach and hearing my stomach rolling and gurgling as almost a quart eased in. The good part is that I couldn't taste a thing. I had the CAT scan with iodine contrast without any issues... It was so good to be free for the rest of the day and to feel almost human again. Wednesday I should find the results of the CAT scan and will move forward with an assurance that He who has begun a good work in me will complete it...thanks for all your wonderful words of encouragement and for your prayers...

Forgot to say that I felt so much better today (getting close to next round of chemo) but needed to cut some dead palm fronds and some that were rubbing on our house on a tall palm in our side yard. Got the 12-foot ladder and put it on the tree and managed to do it without much effort with my sawzall. Picking up the 10 or so branches was a little harder. A thermometer close to the tree in direct sunlight said about 125 degrees... but it felt only like 103 or so with the wind blowing. I remembered the times when I would grab a tall glass of cola filled with ice and guzzle it after a workout like that, but chemo has taken that joy away... the best I can have is cool water. Not complaining, just explaining. My big chair sure felt good for a little while...

June 19, 2012

Psalm 121:1-8 NIV

I lift up my eyes to the mountains-Where does my help come from? My help comes from the Lord, the Maker of heaven and earth. He will not let your foot slip - He who watches over you will not slumber; Indeed, He who watches over Israel will neither slumber nor sleep. The Lord watches over you - the Lord is your shade at your right hand; The sun will not harm you by day, nor the moon by night. The Lord will keep you from all harm - He will watch over your life; The Lord will watch over your coming and going both now and forevermore.

If you read my Facebook today, you noticed that I went back to the surgeon to either fix or remove the feeding tube. I have not used the tube since surgery except yesterday to take barium. In and after ER the other night after it came out, the doctor reinserted it and sewed a stitch in that came out in two days, and it gave me pain every day.

I was in the room waiting for the surgeon, and he came in and looked at me a moment and said, "You are really looking good!" (Never said good looking). He said, "You were so pale and drained-looking last time." I took that as good news. (He should have seen me on Friday or Saturday). We talked about the tube, and both came to the agreement it would be better to take it out (a faith move) and hope it is not needed for a long time (never is soon enough for me). It is the first time in months that I have not hurt or been hurt at a doctor's office. He pulled that sucker out, and I never felt a thing. It feels good to be free of that irritant...After three months of that thing, it is wonderful to have it gone. Hopefully this a positive step forward.

Tomorrow I should get the results of the CAT scan, and I believe it will be a positive report so I will be continuing with chemo. That means seven to ten days feeling like death warmed over. In my selfishness, I want to quit, but if it is doing good, I am doing this more for my family than I am for me. If it was for me, I would be, "No way." But if Fran can be spared losing her husband for a long time, I will take my medicine... I have endured for this long so I can do it some more. I am not wanting to sound heroic, but love has a way of making you willing to laying down your comfort or life for whom you love. After all, what is a little discomfort and pain when God gives us grace like rain when we need it? Cherish your prayers for strength when the needles start coming again...

June 20, 2012

Today was Decision Day according to a CAT scan report. I just got the good news that the CAT scan shows that the cancer has not grown, is hard to see and there is no evidence of it being in lymph glands. In fact, there is little evidence there are any abnormalities except from the surgery I had and the feeding tube...

So, I am believing that God is causing the chemo to do what it is designed to do. I am in the third hour of chemo... there are four bags dripping or being pumped into me. I can feel the effects in my body. 45 hours to go but if this stuff is working, I can handle it.

Our oncologist took almost an hour detailing that the cancer is not progressing. With very frank discussion between the doctor, Fran and I, he told me that some of my symptoms could be coming from taking him too literal about the cancer causing the blood clot... He meant it is because of cancer all these things are happening, not that he meant the cancer had reached the place of the blood clot. He said, with the blood clot, the feeding tube coming out, spending time in ER, not sleeping for 36 hours and the pain I experienced would be enough to cause anyone to be overly concerned that I was losing the battle to cancer. He did all he could do to encourage me that it appears we are winning this battle.

I had come in the office quoting the scriptures in Proverbs and Jeremiah to myself and then shared them with the doctor. Those scriptures helped me be ready for either a good report or a negative report, and the chemo went well.

The lady sitting beside me is a Christian, and we both talked of the wonder of God in the healing process. I think everyone heard us, but that was OK. Each person who came around me was just wanting encouragement, and as soon as I started, it came right back at me.

Fran is such a valiant wife... what a gift to me... she has been there for me at every turn (except giving me shots: she can gut a chicken and change Caiden's diaper but can't give me a shot without freaking out... lol). Friends brought us dinner tonight and then prayed for us with authority. Two local businessmen (a doctor and a contractor) who do not attend my last church came and prayed for me on Monday. They displayed such a spirit of compassion and faith. The battle is not mine even though I feel like the battlefield, but I know God is doing a good thing in me that He will complete.

I think most of you will get an evite from my daughter through me about my 25th wedding anniversary. I know most of you cannot come, but thought you might like to be reminded that Fran and I have been living a Romans 8:28 life. If you don't know what that means look up the verse (google it) and read it carefully. We just believe even when hard things happen God causes good to come out of it.

Getting rid of my food tube was a good move. Food is edible, my throat works, and I don't have the pain of the tube. I am tubeless in Boulder City.

It has been a good afternoon even with the chemo pump, and some friends brought us a great dinner... I had seconds and dessert. 39 more hours of chemo... a friend of mine is in the hospital taking chemo and gets out at about the same time I get the pump out... he texted me something that made me laugh... we get out at the same time and then feel like dog droppings. That wouldn't have been my pastoral way of saying it, but it is really kind of what this stuff does for you. But Fran and I prayed tonight for me and all the people I know on chemo this week asking God to cause every molecule of chemo to do what the researchers and doctors intended them to do (hopefully that would be to heal us).

——

Psalm 91:1-8 NKJV

He who dwells in the secret place of the Most High shall abide under the shadow of the Almighty. I will say of the Lord, "He is my refuge and my fortress; My God, in Him I will trust." Surely He shall deliver you from the snare of the fowler and from the perilous pestilence. He shall cover you with His feathers, and under His wings you shall take refuge; His truth shall be your shield and buckler. You shall not be afraid of the terror by night, nor of the arrow that flies by day, nor of the pestilence that walks in darkness, nor of the destruction that lays waste at noonday. A thousand may fall at your side, and ten thousand at your right hand; But it shall not come near you. Only with your eyes shall you look...

There are so many psalms of hope in the book of Psalm in the Bible...I am learning about dwelling through this challenging time of cancer. I am praying God will speak through this to you.

——

2 Corinthians 12:8-10 NKJV

Concerning this thing I pleaded with the Lord three times that it might depart from me. And He said to me, "My grace is sufficient for you, for My strength is made perfect in weakness." Therefore most gladly I will rather boast in my infirmities, that the power of Christ may rest upon me. Therefore I take pleasure in infirmities, in reproaches, in needs, in persecutions, in distresses, for Christ's sake. For when I am weak, then I am strong...

I don't know if chemo qualifies for what the scripture I am posting says tonight, and I don't know if I have come to the place where I have pleasure in my suffering, but I like the scripture of His Grace being sufficient.

But if rejoicing brings strength, then I will try... I rejoice that the chemo, even though there are so many side effects, seems to be empowered by God to bring a good report that the cancer is not winning.

The cold neuropathy took a new twist today. I was looking up towards the top of our fridge, and my face was being blown on by the air conditioner vent when suddenly the inner part of my nose began to get super sensitive (like just before a big sneeze is coming on) but it went miles beyond that, and it felt like needles inside my sinuses and then I couldn't breathe through my nose... I knew it was cold causing this and I think I ran, at least hurried, outside... sure glad I live in a hot climate. It was near 100 degrees. After taking a few breaths in the heat, the symptom disappeared... other than the weakness being back big-time and the nausea coming and going, I am doing well. Arlene, our family friend who is a nurse, came today and gave me my injection. Sure helps when nauseated not to have to do it yourself and I never felt a thing... she is good. It feels so good to have the feeding tube gone. 12-13 more hours on the pump... hallelujah!!!! Then I have three weeks until my next chemo...

———

Lamentations 3:22-25 NKJV

Through the Lord's mercies we are not consumed, Because His compassions fail not. They are new every morning; Great is Your faithfulness. "The Lord is my portion," says my soul, "Therefore I hope in Him!" The Lord is good to those who wait for Him, To the soul who seeks Him.

June 23, 2012

The report was good about the cancer not advancing, but that never stopped the chemo from doing its work on my body. Friday night into late Saturday was about as bad as it has been in this fight against cancer. I am confident I will recover in a day or so, but right now there is very little good to hold on to. But, in the middle of all the discomfort, there are always bursts of good that makes me know that love is the greatest power on earth.

I hadn't been able to eat for about 36 hours, and neighbors from across the street who have two precious little kids brought me some chicken soup. I ate a bowl of that and within a little while knew I was going to make it again. Then Arlene, our friend who is a nurse came and again gave me a shot even though I had told her I probably could do it today... she came and brought a wonderful dish of fresh fruit. I forgot about it until just a few moments ago. I had been in bed asleep for hours and got up for a few moments. I wandered around the kitchen knowing I needed something but could not think what and remembered the fruit. Even though it was cold and stung a little, for about five minutes all I could do was eat fruit. It was like my body was craving it. So, two times today someone just happened to bring the exact food I needed. I perked up so much after eating the fruit it was amazing. Fran said it reminded her of when Elijah was traveling, and the angel woke him up and said, "Eat for the journey is too great for you..." God just works through his angels in amazing ways. I have a new sense that I am going to overcome this chemo and cancer! Heard tonight, doctors give the diagnosis, but God gives the prognosis... be blessed.

———

This round of chemo is done, but the results of it live on with a vengeance in my body. But hope is the center of our existence. I have hope this too shall pass. Thank God for the angels who came this week just because they wanted to bless. No one asked them to fix a meal, fix chicken soup, give me shots, or bring a wonderful fruit dish, but they did, and I am blessed.

June 24, 2012

1 Corinthians 16:9 NKJV

For a great and effective door has opened to me,
and there are many adversaries.

Psalm 118:24 NKJV

This is the day the Lord has made;
We will rejoice and be glad in it.

Sundays at home are a new thing for this old preacher. I always enjoy going to church to worship the Lord. But today was not a day I could make it. Fran went by herself. But I enjoyed a day of hearing from many speakers and convinced God was trying to tell me something. One speaker said these words: "Every setback is a setup to a comeback." At one point, he even used an example of a person who had cancer. Then another speaker spoke of the incredible miracles of God opening doors to ministry even when there was no possible human way. Great doors of effectual opportunities but with adversity. (1 Corinthians 16:9).

Although adversities are not caused by God, He will use the things that are thrown against us to draw us closer, take us deeper, lift us higher, and to give us clearer vision. The adversity of cancer, even at my sickest point, will produce a victory at some point in the future, if not today. Vision is what we see that may not be seen by anyone else. If our vision is masked, then hope is lost, and the reason to go on is limited. Opportunities, adversities, and vision are given new meaning when we live with a passion going after that which we know is God's best. It has been a day of nausea but yet a day of being engulfed by the presence of the Lord even when I slept in my big recliner. I plan on getting up tomorrow, sick or feeling good and saying with passion, this is the day the Lord has made... I will rejoice and be glad in it...

June 25, 2012

What a joy to wake up and be thirsty for a hot cup of coffee. My oldest son and family gave Fran and me a Keurig machine that brews all types of hot drinks. I made a cup of medium roast in just a minute or so, and the first sip was wonderful. I dreamed of Krispy Kreme glazed donuts... these are probably not the best for me but just being able to have a hunger for something is a huge leap forward. It means the cancer and the chemo are retreating.

I try not to curse the chemo, and I tried to have a really good attitude towards it, but that was last Wednesday... today just spelling the word brings a rush of nausea. The nausea, headaches, and weakness are so pronounced that it is difficult to describe but remember having a bad case of the flu and multiply that several times. I am so glad I have three weeks till the next scheduled treatment.

Fran and I prayed tonight for wisdom and faith to know if I should continue the treatment. When the cure seems to be as bad as the illness, it makes it hard to wrap one's mind around it.

A friend called from California today and asked how I was. I told him, "I am going to live if I don't die, but if I die I will live anyway." He said, "No, how are you?" I answered that is the truth, I am sick, but that's how I am. It really is...

1 Timothy 6:12 says to *"fight the good fight of faith and lay hold of eternal life to which you were called..."* I don't think I have always fought the good fight of faith, but I know I have fixed my eyes on Jesus, the author, and finisher of my faith... I believe I had laid hold of eternal life... surely goodness and mercy have followed me all the days of my life, and one day I will dwell in the house of the Lord forever. Jesus said, *"In my Father's house are many mansions, and I go to prepare a place for you..."* (John 14:2)

No matter what the cancer does, I know in whom I have placed my hope, trust, and faith. I don't know any more than you whether I have months or years left, but I love this scripture from Proverbs. This is one of my favorite scriptures that has brought me peace for a lot of years:

Proverbs 3:5-6 NKJV

Trust in the Lord with all your heart, and lean not on your own understanding; in all your ways acknowledge Him, And He shall direct your paths.

I choose to trust Him to direct my paths...

June 26, 2012

The chemo is wearing off... got up Tuesday morning without nausea... It was good. Two friends about my age came by, and we talked and laughed and then went to A&W for a Coney dog meal... It actually tasted good. Was worn out when I got back but satisfied it was a sign the chemo is waning. I have no solid info on what cancer is or isn't doing, but I feel a quiet peace in my spirit tonight, and it reminded me of an old hymn we used to sing: You will show your age if you remember it.

> *Far away in the depths of my spirit tonight*
> *Rolls a melody sweeter than psalm.*
> *In celestial like strains it unceasingly falls*
> *O'er my soul like an infinite calm.*
> *Peace, peace, wonderful peace,*
> *Coming down from the Father above!*
> *Sweep over my spirit forever, I pray*
> *In fathomless billows of love!*[7]

There are several other verses, but you get the point. Peace is not something you manufacture, it is not a sign of surrender to your circumstances, it is not a passivity towards trouble, but it is a gift that God gives to the one who will receive it. I believe to receive it you have to walk in forgiveness of your own life as well as forgiveness towards others. There has to be an understanding of who God is and that He is the rewarder of those who diligently seek Him... The following scripture is very short but chew on it, meditate on it and see what it says to you.

Isaiah 26:3 NKJV

*You will keep him in perfect peace, whose mind is
stayed on You, because he trusts in You.*

A good day when a cup of coffee tastes good, and I get to drive my pickup to the dump. It has been almost a month since I drove my pickup... I think I am getting better! A friend brought us fresh grilled salmon and rice tonight... wow was that good... I woke up this morning feeling good... After five days of misery, it feels good to wake up to life!

I saw all the pictures of the fires burning and remembered a time a long time ago in Riggins, Idaho.

I had just started pastoring in Riggins, a little town in the mountains of Idaho. Wildfires were burning all over the area, and some of the members of the church had homes being threatened. A retired Army Chaplain had a beautiful home in the timber and stood on a Sunday morning and asked if we could pray for rain. I was so new, I blurted out, "I don't have the faith for that, will you pray?" He did, and it rained the next day... God can do it again. I think I have a little more faith now... like a mustard seed size of faith... wonder if that would be enough?

June 28, 2012

Just when you think things are going better, all the sudden it "hits the fan." I woke up yesterday with the hopes that I was really going to feel good and by 9:00 A. M. the chemo reaction hit with a fury and I was sick all day long. I didn't even have the strength to write on this CarePage.

I got up this morning cautiously optimistic that it was going to be a better day. I was able to cook breakfast for Fran and myself and even drank some grapefruit juice. Then, as I was drinking a cup of coffee, suddenly remembered I was supposed to conduct a memorial service at the Long-Term Care at the BC Hospital for a friend who had died of cancer... then I got a call to reinforce that.

I had been so sick that I had not finished preparing so I had to shower, shave, iron a shirt, get ready, and write a memorial service before 10:30 A.M. Ever get an extra measure of grace? Got it today...I made it there by 10:00 A.M. and the service was wonderful (my opinion) although many others said it was great. I saw so many good friends that

I hadn't seen for weeks. They made me feel so loved. Somehow I had the strength, the words, the music, and a wall behind me to lean on. God is so good...I believe God gave me a special grace to do what I had to do in that moment...now I am worn out, but I am, so thankful to be alive and to have the chance to still make some difference with my life. I love this little portion of scripture from James 4:6 *"But He gives more grace..."* even when His grace is sufficient He is willing to give us more for those times we couldn't do it in our own human strength. Hold on friend, joy comes in the morning...

———

Yesterday was a reality check. In my battle with cancer, it has taken its toll on my being able to fulfill my duties as the Chaplain of the Nevada State Veterans Home. They were so willing to let me stay until I got better or realized I couldn't do it anymore. So hard to say, "I can't," but it was necessary for the good of the Home. Yesterday it became abundantly clear I was no longer able to fulfill my role as Chaplain if I continued taking chemo. Chemo right now is all I know what to do... I walked around the chapel and sat in my office, but I knew it was time. So, I gave the director my letter of resignation. It was hard to think about closing the door on two different ministries in six months... but being a person who believes God directs the steps of believers, I am believing that there is a purpose and a reason for each door closing. So amazing how life can change so quickly. This was a Romans 8:28 moment again. I am still a very blessed man... Whoever the next Chaplain is, it will be a great door of opportunity for him or her.

As I walked out of the door of the NSVH I looked up and asked, "What now Lord?" and one of my favorite scriptures came to mind:

Romans 8:28 NASB

...We know that God causes all things to work together for good to those who love God to those who are called according to His purposes...

Then I found this verse:

Psalm 138:8 NKJV

"The LORD will perfect that which concerns me; Your mercy, O LORD, endures forever; Do not forsake the works of Your hands."

I (as will you) live one day at a time. I am anticipating living life to the fullest I can each day. I hope that in your walk through life you will look for the best and go for it.

June 29, 2012

All of my children are in town with their families to help Fran and I celebrate 25 years of marriage. What a great life I have had with Fran. Our kids have planned quite a celebration for Saturday. After my first wife died I was certain I would never see a 25th wedding anniversary, but Fran and I have done it, and I think pretty well. I am a very blessed man. If I had life to live over, I hope if faced with the same circumstances I would marry her again. I embrace the truth of Jeremiah 29:11 (NKJV).

For I know the thoughts that I think toward you, says the Lord, thoughts of peace and not of evil, to give you a future and a hope.

I have seen God give me a future... and I am still living it.

Today I have had the strength and stamina to do far more than I thought I could. Of course, a two-hour nap helped a lot. It has been a blessed day...

June 30, 2012

Psalm 23:6 NKJV

Surely goodness and mercy shall follow me all the days of my life and I shall dwell in the house of the Lord forever!

Today has been a stellar day. All my kids and grandkids and about 50 people gathered to help us celebrate 25 years of marriage.

I was so surprised and so moved that a couple who have been friends from the very first church I pastored drove all the way from the San Diego area to be with us. Rich and Judy are just two of the finest people I know. They knew and loved my first wife and mourned with me when she died, but when I was so blessed to meet and marry Fran, they embraced her like a friend they knew all their lives. A Christian song from the 80's was called "Friends." The song talks about how we are forever friends if we both have the Lord as Lord of our lives. Truly they have been those kind of friends.

But more than that, neighbors and friends we have met here in Boulder City came, and just plain blessed us. My kids did such a wonderful job of honoring their parents. Boulder City Assembly was so kind letting us use their facility... but the very best was that Fran, my wife of 25 years was even more beautiful today than ever. I was so proud to be her husband.

I again had the strength and grace to make it through today. Some wondered if I really had been sick (except they can see I have lost weight) but it truly was the grace of God that got me through the two hours of talking with all my friends. At the close of the two hours, I was tired I could hardly walk to the car and Fran and I came home, and I collapsed on the bed for about an hour. Then all our kids came to our house... it was so much fun. Grandson, six-month-old, Caiden captured the hearts of everyone today. He is such a great kid... again tonight, I must say, I am a blessed man.

July 1, 2012

Thank God for good days... each day is a blessing when there is strength to live through it. Woke up after three hours of sleep this morning and could not get back to sleep, so I set up watching about four sermons on YouTube and got so blessed. Put the earphones in and listened to worship music and must have fallen asleep and slept a few more hours. Church was good this morning at BCA. Then had lunch with Oregon and Arizona family before everyone had to take off... went home and slept. Each day between 4:00 & 5:00 P. M. I have to give myself a shot... just never gets easier thinking about it, but doing it is really not that bad. Doesn't hurt more than a sting and then that goes away... but I still would rather not do it. Two of my granddaughters are going to spend the summer with their dad and are leaving tomorrow for Texas. As if we haven't had enough the youngest one just had a birthday, so we celebrated her birthday and their going away at IHOP (her choice). We had a fun time there and then it was also our youngest son's first anniversary, and since we still have house guests to help, we volunteered to watch their son Caiden who is six months. He was a marvelous kid tonight and went to sleep easy and slept till his parents came and got him. Heading for bed, thankful for a day that was full of blessings and hope.

I believe with the extra week off from chemo I will find several days with new life and energy. There is an old song that says,

> *"I don't know about tomorrow, I just live from day to day... I don't know about tomorrow, but I know who holds my hand..."*

One of my kids told me today that the surgeon who operated on me had told them while I was in the recovering room that he expected me to survive only six months to a year. I am excited to prove him wrong. I hope you will walk with me through these next few months and witness the miracle of life... Paul said [in Philippians 1:21], *"For me to live is Christ, but to die is gain..."* Like any believer, we are in a win-win situation. *"... whoever believes in Him shall not perish but have everlasting life..."* (John 3:16 NIV/NKJV).

———

Matthew 5:4 NKJV

"Blessed are those who mourn for they shall be comforted"
... and more...

Check out the photos of our 25th Anniversary celebration on the photos page. I have a beautiful bride and some really good kids... I am blessed and know it. I truly believe God wants each of us to believe we can live a blessed life in Him. Blessed even when we have losses... the beatitudes in Matthew 5 speak to that...

———

Psalm 90: 1-2 NKJV

Lord, You have been our dwelling place in all generations. Before the mountains were brought forth, or ever You had formed the earth and the world, even from everlasting to everlasting, You are God.

In anticipation of feeling better, I have decided to go to Oregon with my oldest son Rob. I am leaving tonight and will be there a few days. I am excited. It is the first time I have traveled outside of Las Vegas area since February. I believe God has touched my body to give me strength for this time. It will be good to see cool weather, green mountains and hopefully the blue Pacific.

July 2, 2012

I am in Oregon, traveled with my son and three granddaughters. First time out of town since learning about the cancer and then my surgery. It is good to be as far away from chemo as I can be... feeling very good considering where I have been. Thanks for all your prayers and good wishes. Got in late last night and got up early this morning to pouring down rain and 52-degree weather. Rob is a maintenance supervisor at four airports for Horizon Airlines. Medford was one of the four, and he needed to drive down to take care of some equipment problems, so I rode with him. As usually is the case, a one-hour job turned into a seven-hour job... and at 5:00 P. M. we are still here... but it is beautiful and green, and the weather in Medford is so nice... We drove from Salem to Medford, and the scenery was breathtaking. Trees, rivers, meadows, rain and blue skies. Fran is coming tonight, so we spend the Fourth together. On our way back...

July 3, 2012

We got back to Silverton just in time to see a spectacular firework display with a lot of family and friends I hadn't seen for a long time. The only downside was that it was 52 degrees again but clear skies. I felt so good today and realized again this is what happens two weeks after chemo... tomorrow would have been my next round of chemo, but I have asked to put it off a week... I think I feel alive again... and expect to have a good week... Jesus said,

John 10:10 NKJV
"...I have come that they may have life,
and that they may have it more abundantly."

Many of my posts I did when I felt the worst but attempted to show faith and hope. For me, there is a need to remember hope is powerful at the lowest and highest part of our lives. Here I am feeling good, but I still want to remember hope because it is easy to forget hope when nothing seems wrong. I want to remember the intensity of my prayers and not lose the passion I had for God when I was so sick. I want that and more when I am feeling better... Hope does not disappoint... but builds one's faith and character. I would rather have cancer and live in hope than be cancer free and forget where my hope comes from. So, I am practicing being hopeful when I feel good because I believe the day is coming when I will be cancer free, and I don't want to forget... my hope is built on nothing less than Jesus Christ and righteousness... I dare not trust any but Jesus...

July 5, 2012

In Oregon with family. 23 family members yesterday and 19 today. It was a day of running to the airport in Portland twice to get my kids from Boulder City. Weather is beautiful. Going to the coast tomorrow morning. I love the Oregon coast. This has been my goal to be able to walk on the beach barefooted. 17 of us going. One of my son-in-law's first time to see the Oregon coast. As beautiful as it is here, my heart is still overwhelmed with awe over who the Creator is. That is where my faith is... in the One who so loved the world and me that He gave his only begotten son that if I believe I will not perish but have everlasting life.

July 8, 2012

Back home after traveling over 1000 miles by car and 2000 miles in three different airplanes. Got to walk on the beach for several hours, go through Lincoln City, Depot Bay and Newport, Oregon. Saw the beauty of Silver Falls at the state park near Silverton, Oregon... Some of the things I really felt like I needed to do before chemo starts again. The extra week from chemo was such a blessing... Most people love it when they have to get a smaller size for their pants, but it was a little sad knowing how I lost four pants sizes. Wouldn't recommend my weight loss program to anyone. One good thing about chemo, while in Oregon, everyone else was being bitten by mosquitoes but I never had one bite... I guess I must have been emitting something the bugs didn't like. Wouldn't recommend chemo as a repellent either lol.

As I left my family, my emotions surfaced again, and I could hardly stop the tears as I said goodbye to those who had made last week one of the best in 4 months. I guess a thought clouded my mind that this could be my last time to see some of these. I was told by someone that the surgeon had not expected me to live more than six months and although the test said there was little evidence of the cancer growing, the oncologist insists I must continue chemo to increase my survival. If I continue, I will have very few days of feeling good in the next months. I think the tears were knowing the hard times ahead and the thought of not feeling good for a long time. I know people tell me not to speak negative words, but after four months of sickness, I am aware that my health is not my faith.

My faith is in Jesus Christ regardless of whether I live or die... I trust in Him... sometimes I waver. Sometimes, like today, even after listening to several sermons, I get sucked back into mindsets that are like strongholds and must be broken by faith and obedience to the Word. My victories today do not mean I will not have a battle tomorrow. Any defeats today do not dictate that I will have defeat tomorrow. I am grateful that I know that His mercies are new every morning... Lots of people say they are praying for me and I believe it... I hold on to scriptures like the following:

Ephesians 3:20-21 NKJV

"Now to Him who is able to do exceedingly abundantly above all that we ask or think, according to the power that works in us, to Him be glory in the church by Christ Jesus to all generations, forever and ever. Amen."

July 9, 2012

Life is good... One more day till chemo and I begin the cycle again... Trying to win this battle with cancer. I feel very selfish in that my attention is almost 24/7 on me and my problems. Everything I write has the word "I" in it so many times it sounds very "me" centered... There are iPads, iPhones, etc. ... I feel that I am I-me... It is not my purpose to focus just on me, but that is the way it becomes because no one else can really do it for me. So, it is about me and my relationships with family, friends, disease, the medical field, and survival. What I write is about me and what I am doing or have to do. If I did not have this battle with cancer, I would be writing sermons, articles about faith and life, not about feeling nauseous, fighting blood clots, giving myself injections each day, or about how rotten chemo makes me feel. But I do have this battle and others who may read this understand because they too have their own battles that turn the attention inward. I don't think it is that selfish especially as I look at the book of Psalms or even the prayer Jesus prayed in the garden... Paul the Apostle even boasted in what God was doing in his life or about how much suffering he was going through. So, I guess it is OK to express what one is going through if the end result is to bring purpose to the hardship. Jesus asked that there would be another way besides the cross... unfortunately, that cross has to be faced... for me and others in battles like mine, the cross is faced every morning... but believing the scriptures, we are reminded that His mercies are new every morning. Great is His faithfulness...

As a pastor [the following verses were] always one of my goals for my church. Verse 4 is how I am trying to live my life during my struggle with cancer... not to be too self-centered.

Philippians 2:1-4 NKJV

Therefore if there is any consolation in Christ, if any comfort of love, if any fellowship of the Spirit, if any affection and mercy, fulfill my joy by being like-minded, having the same love, being of one accord, of one mind. Let nothing be done through selfish ambition or conceit, but in lowliness of mind let each esteem others better than himself. Let each of you look out not only for his own interests, but also for the interests of others.

July 10, 2012

One of my heroes, Pastor Mike Teixeira, took time out of his vacation to meet me on Tuesday afternoon for a short time of touching base. He too has gone through the chemo trip and now appears to be cancer free. We talked of cancer and all the effects of chemo but then turned our focus on ministry and our relationship with Jesus Christ. He is not my hero because he has conquered cancer (which is awesome) but because he has such a passion for ministering the Gospel to people. I came away from that meeting with a renewed sense of destiny... I am believing that I will again be able to pastor in some capacity as cancer and chemo become a thing of the past... Thanks, Mike for making time for me... it meant a lot...

———

I wonder if a person can become allergic to water. I am supposed to drink lots of water, and since I got home from Oregon, I have been trying to do that. However, I became nauseated constantly, and someone suggested lemon drops to help take away the nausea so I have tried them and they work a little, but decided to try lemonade... it has become the only liquid I can drink without just sipping. I can actually drink it normally, and today the nausea is nearly all gone... I think I have discovered something...

———

It is hard to describe the feelings I have tonight as I am contemplating tomorrow's start of round six of chemo. There is the mental and the physical battle in me revolting against subjecting my body to the torture of pumping poisonous chemicals into it. Spiritually I know I can do all things through Christ who strengthens me but tomorrow, faith and works have to mesh as I sit in that sterile chair and let a wonderful nurse (they are wonderful people) stick a needle into the port in my upper chest. As soon as the needle is inserted, the cocktail of chemicals flow and I sit there and try not to concentrate on all that is transpiring.

My next goal will be Friday when they take the pump off... I am not trying to be macabre or morbid, but that is the way I feel tonight.

The spirit in me is willing to do whatever I believe God says, even if the flesh is weak. I am reminded of this scripture:

Jeremiah 32:17 NKJV

"'Ah, Lord GOD! Behold, You have made the heavens and the earth by Your great power and outstretched arm. There is nothing too hard for You."

You can heal my body from the cancer attacking me; You are my strength when I have none of my own; You are my peace when turmoil wants to overwhelm me; You give hope when everyone says it is hopeless; You lift me up when I feel like I am falling; Your love empowers me to look beyond my own self and see needs of others; Your comfort to me is how I comfort others who are facing what I have been through, and Your gift of faith is what ties all these things together into a personal relationship with Almighty God, my Savior, and Lord. I can do this tomorrow (oops it is chemo-day as I end this blog).

July 11, 2012

Gloria! I got it! Ha... No Chemo today!!!!! All I wrote last night faded as I began to write about the God who can do anything. Then this morning I woke up singing "Because He Lives" which talks about being able to face whatever comes tomorrow. I used my phone to listen to it on YouTube all the way to the clinic. I was ready... they drew blood and tested it and then waited for the doctor. The doctor spent an hour or more with us helping us get our mind around taking more treatment, then he said there could be no treatment this week. My white blood cell count was too low; the protocol for the trial treatment from UCLA says I cannot sustain chemo and treatment until the count comes up. So, I believe God arranged for another week off... he gave me another week without chemo... like Elijah, the journey was becoming too great... and God provided... the doctor said it is nothing to worry about, just enjoy the week off... and I will! Thanks for praying for me... it is a good answer... the doctor believes I am going to live and though cancer will never be cured can be contained and become manageable through smaller doses in the future. The chemo and shots will still be brutal for the next few months, but I am confident God will sustain me as he did Elijah in his journey through the wilderness... In a lot of ways, it was good news... that there will be a decrease in treatments as tests prove the cancer is contained. Suffering with purpose makes suffering more sustainable.

July 12, 2012

Not that I am counting, but it has been 114 days or 164,160 minutes or 2736 hours since I had surgery and began this journey of fighting the battle with cancer.

I have celebrated this whole day of not having chemotherapy by working in our office at home, cleaning and organizing areas that I have neglected since I resigned from Boulder City Assembly. Even though my white blood cell count (absolute neutrophil count) was too low to take chemo, it is not low enough to be a grave danger to my immune system.

Having the reprieve from chemo for another week is so far very rewarding. Last night friends, Kathy and Ron brought us a wonderful meal of soup, cornbread and strawberry shortcake. What a wonderful gift.

I have been overwhelmed by the kindness of so many people. Some of my high school classmates that I haven't seen for at least 39 years sent me a wonderful handmade and signed pillowcase with one of my favorite scriptures on it...

Proverbs 3:5-6 NKJV

Trust in the Lord with all your heart, and lean not on your own understanding; In all your ways acknowledge Him, And He shall direct your paths.

Anne, who made it, said it was for me when I am recovering from chemo... Then a neighbor came over and invited Fran and me to go to a Christian retreat in Minnesota with accommodations taken care of... we just have to get there... if I am well enough we may do it... Then tonight my daughter brought us some of her specialty soup... we are blessed...

Going back to the verses from Proverbs...

Trust in the Lord with all your heart... There are times I get so divided in that "all your heart" thing... However, I am discovering grace in a fresh way... when I don't trust with all my heart, rather than pushing me away, God pulls me back from my lack of trust and faith to himself... like Peter when walking on the water got his eyes off Jesus and on the waves and began to sink... had I been Jesus I would have told him to swim or call for help... but grace (Jesus) reached out and pulled him up and into the boat. Then he asked him, "Why did you doubt?" Peter probably looked at Jesus and started to say, "Did you see how big the waves were?" ... Then he must have realized how big his God is. The Proverb says, *"In all your ways acknowledge Him..."* What a powerful exhortation... even in cancer, chemo and being so sick it is a comfort to know that any of us can see God in every area of our lives, even in the suffering. His grace truly is sufficient.

July 13, 2012

Up late... Fran and I had a date night at home... one of the first days in weeks we have been alone all evening. Chinese food and a movie... feels good to feel good.

Talking with some friends today about hard times and losses we all face and I reminded them again that God causes all things to work together for good... not saying He makes it all good the way we like it, but meaning for the believer, for every event of our lives that looks like it is all wrong, God will bring good out of it. Missionary Jim Elliot who was killed by the very people he was trying to help, penned these words when in his 20's: *"He is no fool who gives what he cannot keep to gain that which he cannot lose."*[9] For those who embrace this truth, our outlook goes beyond today and looks at what God will do at some point in the future. Fran and I have seen God bring good out of the battle against cancer... the real results may be in the lives of my grandchildren, and I may not even see all the good that God is bringing through this trial of faith... an old song by Bill Gaither, *Joy Comes In the Morning*, encourages us to hold on. We will find joy after the night is done.

———

The following is for my sake, just so I have a record of an important truth in my life.

I was blessed with two brothers. My oldest brother, Laurance, was a true hero of mine; a godly man... I loved him so much... He died over 20 years ago because of cancer. Lyle, my other brother, younger by 18 months, is a multi-talented man who can sing, play the piano, guitar and probably other instruments as well as being one of the most creative fabricators, mechanics, welder, auto body repairman, carpenter (you name it) a person could find. He is also a great preacher/teacher, a student of the Bible and has pastored for years. Like my older brother, he can fix almost anything. For men like that, cancer in a family member is so hard because there is nothing they can do to fix what is going on. They just have to watch and pray. And that is what my brother is doing for me. He is praying and watching. To have a brother who is not afraid to tell me he loves me and is a man of great faith, passionately praying for me is a gift beyond measure. I love my brother... the Bible says God is one who sticks closer than a brother... I truly understand that concept because of Lyle. We live miles apart, but he is always in my heart.

———

My mother always used to say, "Practice what you preach." I have had to live by that rule all my life especially as a pastor, and I am glad for that. It seems, if I haven't already faced and walked through what I preached on Sundays, I would inevitably face it the week after I preached. It seemed God would take what I preached and let me experience trusting Him like I hadn't before or experience some pain or hurt at the hands of another person and I would have to choose either to respond as I had preached a person should or refuse to listen to my own words... Early this morning I wrote, "Hold on... the battle is not over, joy is coming... faith is the victory..."

After feeling so good the last few days, this afternoon, nausea has begun to be my enemy again, and I felt anger rising in me and begin to ask, "How much more...?" and then remembered what I had written... I chose not to refuse to follow what I know is right, and I am holding on... maybe in the morning at church, the miracle will come... if not... I still know what victory in my spirit is...

July 14, 2012

I heard an old Chuck Girard song on YouTube tonight called, "Slow Down." Fran and I realized tonight that we have compromised our prayer time during the last two weeks and missed several days... so tonight we slowed down and at 9:00 P. M. we prayed and such a precious sense of God's presence filled our living room (and our hearts). Oh, how we were encouraged, and the nausea just went away.

In Luke 18:1 it says that Jesus told his disciples a story with the emphasis that men (and women) should "*always pray and not lose heart*" (NKJV) in Hebrews 12:3 again says to "*not grow weary and lose heart*" (NIV). There are several other uses of that phrase in the Bible, so it is obvious any of us can lose heart, which means get discouraged, give up or give in to circumstances that we battle... Hebrews 12:1-2 reminds us that many people have gone through much worse than we have but like them, we all need to keep our focus on Jesus, the author, and finisher of our faith.

Each time I read the word, "finisher", I get a mental picture of pouring a sidewalk and finish the concrete with a smooth surface and when it is cured it is a finish that we can walk, stand, ride on without hurting it... that is how I believe our faith is in Jesus Christ... solid enough to put all our trust on. I may not be able to walk on water, but I can sure walk on the paths of faith God is directing me to.

———

A day without sunshine is a wonderful day in the desert of southern Nevada. We had heavy clouds and some heavy thunderstorms. I realized our gutters had not been cleaned out since I had gotten sick... so in between storms I got my fiberglass ladder and cleaned the front and back gutters. Under a 40-foot cypress on a ladder reaching to pull the last of the leaves out when thunder roared right over my head startling me so much I almost fell off. With four tall trees in the backyard and lightning flashing, I realized being under those trees was not a good place to be... at least it was a good excuse to quit working... Long story but each time I am on a ladder I remember this verse:

Jude 24-25 KJV

Now unto Him that is able to keep you from falling, and to present you faultless before the presence of His glory with exceeding joy, To the only wise God our Savior, be glory and majesty, dominion and power, both now and ever. Amen.

July 15, 2012

If you read the Bible verses I am going to post you might understand that I believe I had strength given to me... Fran and I spent a wonderful time at Boulder City Assembly, enjoying worship and sensing the presence of God there. We were able to hear one of my favorite speakers, Dr. Sam Huddleson (assistant superintendent of the NCN Assemblies of God). He was there to officially install Pastor Blayne Corzine as the very first elected Pastor of Boulder City Assembly. We were blessed to be part of that part of the service. The pastor told the congregation that I had not been able to take chemo last week and when he said that I pumped my arms in the air and said "Yes!" He and others have felt like the low blood cell count is serious (and it may be) but I am so thankful for not having chemo. Afterward, we did what Pastor Blayne says church folk do: "When we meet we eat." And I did... lol. We spent the day with various people enjoying their fellowship. Then Fran and I cleaned our van out... neither of us had much energy lately to do that.

You who know Fran, know funny things happen to her... we vacuumed the car, and she wanted to take it to the one automated car wash in town... I had just got back from my bike ride, and she let me recover in my chair lol. She took the car and in about 10 minutes called from inside the car wash... it has stalled on her... she couldn't go forward or back up... she tried to find the station's number on her iPhone but couldn't, so I looked up the number, and she called and was rescued. Only Fran could have that much fun at a car wash...

That bike ride was the second ride since surgery, almost four months ago (over a half mile). It really felt good when I was coasting downhill, the cool wind in my face; then reality hit, I had to ride back up to get home... but I did it the whole way... felt good...

(But those who wait on the Lord Shall renew their strength).

These are verses that I am holding on to during my treatment schedule... God is my strength...

Isaiah 40:28-31 NKJV

Have you not known? Have you not heard? The everlasting God, the Lord, The Creator of the ends of the earth, Neither faints nor is weary. His understanding is unsearchable. He gives power to the weak, and to those who have no might He increases strength. Even the youths shall faint and be weary, And the young men shall utterly fall, but those who wait on the Lord Shall renew their strength; They shall mount up with wings like eagles, They shall run and not be weary, they shall walk and not faint.

———

Psalm 23: 4 KJV

"Yea though I walk through the valley of the shadow of death I will fear no evil, for thou art with me..."

This verse has had a lot of interpretations written by wiser men than I, so I don't pretend to know all David meant as he wrote this, but I do have a tremendous sense of God being right in the middle of what was going on with David as he penned these words. Chronic illness or terminal illness is a deep valley we humans at times have to go through, and there is a shadow of death cast over us because of our disease. Stage IV is a shadow or a darkness that seems to take away the light of our lives. A chronic illness like diabetes also casts a shadow that tears at hope in our lives. But by the empowerment of God's Holy Spirit David says, "In this valley and with a death sentence, I refuse to believe evil is going to win." Why? Because God is with us... A shepherd's defense or offense in that day was a staff and a rod. So, David is saying, "All the Lord's resources are on my behalf..." and what a comfort knowing that God is pouring all his resources into our lives... we fail at times to recognize that He is doing that, but as a good friend, Pastor Tom told me again just now, "God knows what's going on... he was not taken by surprise." In Jeremiah 29:11 another scripture echoes this *"I know the plans I have for you..."* I have a calm assurance that it is well, not only with my soul, but my entire being because God is with us...

July 16, 2012

It has been about two weeks of feeling good... Tomorrow is my chemo day again (if the blood tests are in the limits). As much as it would seem to be a good thing to (be) off another week, it appears the chemo has been holding the cancer at bay so I wouldn't want to avoid it too long.

Today I was able to go to a minister's breakfast for Assemblies of God pastors from all the Las Vegas area. (First one I have been to in four months). It was a good time as a young mother from Boulder City Assembly was awarded her license for ministry with the AG. She had finished four years of schooling and did a lot of hard work to get to this point, and I was asked to pray for her and her husband and another couple who also were given their credentials. There were a lot of other people that could have, but it was an honor to be asked and then to do it. It was a very full day. Fran was funny: She said, "Since you feel so good why don't you mow the lawn?" Which I did (don't think she has noticed it yet).

It was my last night before chemo, and the last time I will like food for about 10 days, so Fran and I went out to dinner... that won't happen again for some time if it makes me as sick as before. Nice to spend time with my wife and best friend. She has been struggling with what this disease and treatment is doing to me, but she daily finds that God is her strength. As the Bible says

Psalms 46:1 -3 NKJV

God is our refuge and strength, A very present help in trouble. Therefore we will not fear, even though the earth be removed, And though the mountains be carried into the midst of the sea; Though its waters roar and be troubled, Though the mountains shake with its swelling.

Even if the worst thing happens, God is still our strength, and we do not have to fear...

Just noticed it is our prayer time... will be praying for you...

1 Thessalonians 1:2 NKJV

We give thanks to God always for you all, making mention of you in our prayers...

Prayer is an effort and a discipline, but just coming back from almost an hour of prayer and worship, I can tell you it is worth it... "*They that wait upon the Lord shall renew their strength, they shall mount up with wings as eagles, they shall run and not be weary, walk and not faint...*" *(Isaiah 40:31)* There is no way to describe the feeling that I get as the chemo begins to pump into me, and even the thought of it is almost too hard to bear, but as Fran and I prayed, a new strength knowing that even though the journey is too hard on my own, God provides what is needed to get through it. The kind words and prayers of friends and family truly lifts a person's spirit, so thanks...

———

2 Corinthians 4:7-9 NIV

But we have this treasure in jars of clay to show that this all-surpassing power is from God and not from us. We are hard pressed on every

side, but not crushed; perplexed, but not in despair; persecuted, but not abandoned; struck down, but not destroyed.

One more day of feeling alive... chemo on Wednesday. It has been like I am a new man for the last few days... The chemo is working (supported by prayers) I feel better than I did before I was diagnosed with cancer. Still, don't like it but one day at a time...

July 18, 2012

The doctor said I had what is called anticipatory nausea. And I guess I did because I felt nausea coming on as I prepared to leave to go to the Cancer Center and it intensified as I walked into the lobby and signed in at 8:00 A.M. this morning. Another patient and I sat down at the same time to have our blood drawn and at first, they got us mixed up. They called me the other guy's name (Mr. Chow) and his wife got so amused that they would confuse a Chinese guy with me... it opened a door all day long to talk and laugh with them. My blood counts were perfect, and so I started the treatment and really did quite well. I slept off and on through a movie, and when I woke up, an elderly mother was there for treatment, and her daughter was sitting in the next chair. I began to talk to the women, and the daughter recognized me as she had been to our church in the past. She was the leader of a prayer ministry called "House of Prayer." She and Fran knew each other quite well. She said I was on their prayer list... the treatment really did go easy, and I got to leave before they did, so I went over and prayed for the mother and really did sense the presence of the Lord. It is a small world. I was able to bring joy to several of the patients before leaving. My feet must have looked better today because the Bible says,

Isiah 52:7 NASB
"How lovely... are the feet of those [him]
who bring good news... "

What better news than a God of Hope...

———

Isaiah 41:10 NIV

"So do not fear, for I am with you; do not be dismayed, for I am your God. I will strengthen you and help you; I will uphold you with my righteous right hand."

I've been receiving chemo now for over 14 hours, and the nausea is not as bad as before... I will be disappointed if that changes. I was able to do dishes and help with the laundry tonight. Just before surgery, I bought a Jeep Grand Cherokee that one of Fran's coworkers needed to get rid of. It had an exhaust manifold leaking, and it is a two-wheel drive, so the differential in the rear was making a bad noise. I had that fixed and just got it home getting it ready to sell when my daughter's Ford Expedition's transmission went out... Jen needed a car for work, so she took the untested jeep and drove it for three months. She got her car back today, and so did we, and we are all blessed. So Fran and I drove it to Henderson twice, and it drove very well. The Inline 6 [engine] got us to 80 so fast it wasn't noticeable. For an older jeep, it does well. I use the word blessed so often that it sounds trite, but I am blessed...

July 19, 2012

1 John 1:8-10 NKJV

If we say that we have no sin, we deceive ourselves, and the truth is not in us. If we confess our sins, He is faithful and just to forgive us our sins and to cleanse us from all unrighteousness. If we say that we have not sinned, we make Him a liar, and His word is not in us.

Nearly 2:00 A. M. and I just woke up after snoozing in my big chair for three hours. I really am believing that your prayers, by the mercy of God has made this chemo time so much easier than the past. I drove to Henderson on an errand of mercy for Fran and stopped by an AutoZone to check on buying a new light switch on the 1998 Jeep Jen had borrowed. Jen hadn't mentioned it, but the dash lights would flicker and usually go out. The switch was $79. 00 plus tax but not in stock... so I decided to go home and take it apart and see if I could fix it. I took the dash apart and the switch apart. I did all of this with my pump hanging on me. In the meantime, Jacalyn, a college student, and her friend took time to come and see her former pastor. I was so blessed they took the time out for me. Then back to work, I found that two circuit boards were loose and I re-soldered each connection and put it back together, and it worked like a new switch. I was pretty proud of myself.

I took an hour nap, and then Fran and I went for pizza at a new pizzeria with our kids, Jon, Re and Caiden and Mike and Jen... missed Kalani and Kaia big time. They are with their dad in Texas. Came home and we noticed it was time to pray... for each family member and my 560 some friends on Facebook... not all by name but by groups. I enjoy the presence of God as we pray. Makes it worth all the effort... it was a good day... even on chemo. His mercies are new every morning.

—

When my youngest son was eight years old, I gave him a toy semi-tractor/trailer (about three feet long) for a Christmas present. He fell in love with that so much that he slept with it the first two nights with the engine idling...tonight I am sleeping with my chemo pump. 46 hours... Unlike Jon, I dislike the noise and the feeling of the pump injecting chemicals... but this too shall pass.

July 20, 2012

I have said it before about chemo and cancer... what a difference a day does make...

I woke up this morning singing, "This is the Day that the Lord has made." I was going to get the pump off. The time had gone so quickly, and I had felt so good.

I drove to the Comprehensive Cancer Center feeling very confident that I would not have any problems. Like the old coffee commercial, the chemo was going to be good to the last drop... evidently, the last drop was the kicker... Because of the low readings on my white blood cells, the doctor prescribed a shot called Neulasta... to help build up my immune system. I dropped Fran off at a restaurant to meet some friends, and I drove home... by the time I got in the door of the house I knew I was in for some new experiences and began to feel the headaches, esophagus pains, nausea and general hurting all over...

This still was the day the Lord had made, but all the sudden rejoicing was not part of my thought process... all I could do was lay down and try to find some comfort... the fury of chemo has come with a vengeance... Four weeks of daily feeling better is now gone... I am confident that this too shall pass, but tonight is a taste of hell... thank you for your prayers...this afternoon rejoicing is a tremendous effort... but in Him I have life...

July 22, 2012

Psalms 3:3-4 NKJV

But You, O Lord, are a shield for me, My glory and the One who lifts up my head. I cried to the Lord with my voice, And He heard me from His holy hill.

I was in bed all day Saturday and Sunday... the only relief I could find was from pain medicine and some strong anti-nausea... Tried the Claritin but did not notice any help... my only relief was laying very still in bed or in my recliner. I got up to pray at 9:00 P. M. and I heard a song being sung on YouTube tonight that reminds me that there is hope and help even in the worst times.

My natural man wants to just get out of this suffering, but my spiritual man hears the Word... and the Word begins to lift my eyes beyond my sickness to my Hope that I know is eternal...

I am feeling the effects of this chemo so bad that I am having a problem even thinking about it so this is all for tonight...thanks to all of you who are thinking about me and offering a prayer for healing and deliverance... I could hardly sit and pray tonight... tomorrow will be better...

Vickie, my niece from Nampa, said something so sweet that it made me cry... she said she wished Facebook had a hug feature... she would send me hugs... thanks, Vickie, I sure could use some right now...

July 23, 2012

For the last few days, I have been trying to define and qualify what my life is all about. I truly have felt I have lost three days of my life in the black hole of the abyss of absolute nothingness... I spent hours in front of my TV sleeping through Fox and CNN news, James Bond movies, Pawn Stars, Jimmy Swaggart, Stanley Stupid, and a variety of sports and auto shows because I had no strength or desire to do anything else. After you do that you don't feel you can get much lower in your spirit. But tonight at 9:00 P. M. as I looked at the clock I realized it was our prayer time, and I needed it. Gathering my strength, I walked to the couch and opened my iPad looking for the old hymn "Blessed Assurance" that had been going through my mind. The closest thing I had was a secular song by Andre Bocelli called "Because We Believe." So, I played that one... and the words moved me...

Found my song on YouTube and began to weep at the chorus...

*"This is my story, this is my song,
praising my savior all the day long... "*[10]

As I began to pray in between my tears, I said, "Lord, I don't want my story to be about a man who had cancer and chemo but about a man whose story was to praise his savior all the day long..." I told Fran that she could put that on my grave... "This was his story: praising his savior..." I want my story to be about the One who came to give me life and that more abundantly. I tell those who read this about my battle with cancer, but I hope you see my story is about Jesus Christ and what He has done in and through me... I will conquer cancer, but that is only a little bit of the story of Martin Duane Jordan... his story is that he found Jesus Christ as his savior one day and was never the same...for him to live is Christ, but to die will be gain...

July 24, 2012

Thanks for all the words of encouragement... this was another day of fighting nausea and nothing tasting good. Fran cuts up watermelon, and that is about the only thing I can always eat if it is not too cold.

It is refreshing. I can tell you this is a great weight loss program... but not a pleasant one (which one is?). There was not one thing I could do today that made me feel better in my body, but I must have listened to worship music for hours as I just knew I needed a spiritual touch as much as physical. It did help. I promised Fran last night I would do the dishes this morning so she wouldn't have to. I told her I would be feeling better. I kept my promise, but it was a battle to put each dish and pan away and then reload the dishwasher. I was so tired after that little job.

Fran and I do not miss our prayer time as it is our time to pray for family and others that we promised we would. We do for others as we hope they are doing for us.

It is always a refreshing time. Do prayers ever get answered? I have to admit I wonder at times as there are so many hard things going on in so many lives. But as we open our heart in faith to our God there is a certainty that God will work all things together for the good of those we are praying for... we recognize we are not God and recognized that God sees life from His side of eternity and not our temporal side... but in almost every situation as we look back God caused circumstances, events, and people to somehow bring what becomes the best answer for the prayers prayed. Why hasn't He healed this cancer? I don't know why but there is a deep confidence that good will triumph. I am going to wake up in the morning and proclaim that this is the day the Lord has made, and I am going to rejoice in it... I will breathe in and breathe out and try to live life to its fullness.

July 25, 2012

Wouldn't it be great to be able to be in several places at once and then have the energy to do it? This weekend had so many opportunities: Northwest University 60's Alumni Reunion/retreat in Washington; invited to a Christian camp in Detroit Lakes, Minnesota; one of my daughter's birthday party; and an invite to go to central Oregon.

I know the chemo is wearing off, but it is still fighting my body... I tried to help my brother-in-law, Gene, get figs off our fig tree and became weary in just a few moments of exertion. But tonight, Fran and I decided we should try to get some exercise and we did walk about a mile which was much further than either of us intended, (if we had had taxis we would have called one) but we made it anyway... my recliner was waiting for me...

Our 9:00 P. M. prayer time is a lifeline that gets my mind away from cancer... I read tonight that Jesus said the words He spoke to us are spirit and life... (John 6:63) and tonight I just want to look at life... for so many years I spoke and preached about our dreams and how we should have a passion for life... then a doctor says the word "terminal," and my dreams and passion for life seem to wither and fade. I know I go through cycles with chemo in what I think or say, but even at my age, I don't want dreams and passion for life to die before I do. Jesus said,

John 10:10 NKJV

"I have come that they [you] may have life, and that they [you] may have it more abundantly..."

I am believing that my life is for a purpose and so even if I am struggling with chemo and cancer I believe there is an abundance of life somehow exuding from me... Jesus said that His strength is perfected in my weakness... can it be true that when I am weak His abundant life is still flowing through me? Can it be that when I am at my weakest, there are still rivers of living water flowing out of me? (John 7:37) Doesn't make sense, but by faith, I am grabbing on to this...

———

Just a hymn of encouragement to someone:

It Is Well[11]

When peace, like a river, attendeth my way,
when sorrows like sea billows roll;
Whatever my lot, Thou has taught me to say,
It is well, it is well, with my soul.
It is well, with my soul, it is well, it is well, with my soul.
Though Satan should buffet, though trials should come,
Let this blest assurance control,
That Christ has regarded my helpless estate,
And hath shed His own blood for my soul.

It is well, with my soul, it is well, it is well, with my soul.

Another old hymn to end or start your day with:

WONDERFUL PEACE[12]

Far away in the depths of my spirit tonight
Rolls a melody sweeter than psalm;
In celestial strains it unceasingly falls
O'er my soul like an infinite calm.
Peace, peace, wonderful peace,
coming down from the Father above!
Sweep over my spirit forever,
I pray in fathomless billows of love!
What a treasure I have in this wonderful peace,
buried deep in the heart of my soul,
So secure that no power can mine it away,
While the years of eternity roll!
Peace, peace, wonderful peace,
coming down from the Father above!
Sweep over my spirit forever,
I pray in fathomless billows of love!

July 26, 2012

I love good news. Today I heard from two friends who are battling cancer that they may never have to take chemo again. Each night Fran and I have been praying for them and several others who are battling terminal cancer. It is good to hear good news. As I was thinking about good news, I realized there is always good news... even in the middle of chaos. Paul said I am not ashamed of the good news about Jesus Christ which empowers us to have salvation.

I rejoiced in my friends' good news but at the same time I got hit hard again by chemo or something and today was physically a struggle... I was expecting today to be a day of physically being renewed... that was not the case... chemo still hanging on... my spirit was renewed but not my physical but the good news is that there is good news. I remembered again the following scripture:

2 Corinthians 4:8, 9, 16-18 NKJV

We are hard-pressed on every side, yet not crushed; we are perplexed, but not in despair; persecuted, but not forsaken; struck down, but not destroyed Therefore we do not lose heart. Even though our outward man is perishing, yet the inward man is being renewed day by day. For our light affliction, which is but for a moment, is working for us a far more exceeding and eternal weight of glory, while we do not look at the things which are seen, but at the things which are not seen. For the things which are seen are temporary, but the things which are not seen are eternal.

Isn't that good news?

———

Another hymn that helps sustain my faith when facing the unknown.

> *"Great is Thy faithfulness," O God my Father,*
> *There is no shadow of turning with Thee;*
> *Thou changest not, Thy compassions, they fail not*
> *As Thou hast been Thou forever wilt be.*
> *"Great is Thy faithfulness!" "Great is Thy faithfulness!"*
> *Morning by morning new mercies I see;*
> *All I have needed Thy hand hath provided—*
> *"Great is Thy faithfulness," Lord, unto me!*
> *Summer and winter, and springtime and harvest,*
> *Sun, moon and stars in their courses above,*
> *Join with all nature in manifold witness*
> *To Thy great faithfulness, mercy and love.*
> *Pardon for sin and a peace that endureth,*
> *Thy own dear presence to cheer and to guide;*
> *Strength for today and bright hope for tomorrow,*
> *Blessings all mine, with ten thousand beside.*[13]

July 27, 2012

For some reason, the chemo just doesn't want to give up, but I accomplished more today than for over a week. I got to spend time with my seven-month-old grandson and share birthday dinner with my youngest daughter. Got to watch my youngest son mow my lawn (tired me out) then helped him get our boat ready for him to take out to the lake. After collapsing in my big chair, I enjoyed watching the Olympics Opening Ceremony... enjoyed the parade of nations as athletes from over 200 nations came into the stadium. It was fun to see the pride each athlete had for their nation. It made me feel the immensity of our world but how insignificant one person could feel. I know I felt how strange it is that I can make such a big deal over the illness I am experiencing when the world is so big, and the needs are so incredible.

I see the struggles in Syria where children are dying in the line of fire as factions fight for what they believe is worth dying for. I see the pain on the faces of family members in Aurora, CO as they talk of their murdered loved ones. I see the depravity of this world and how evil seems so prevalent, and I am only one older man who has terminal cancer.

What difference can I make? I believe that somehow each of us is so important to the complexity of life on this planet. What I do touches someone else who touches someone else and on and on it goes. We can try to influence for good or evil; the choice is ours, but it seems that the overwhelming majority of this world chooses good most of the time. And I believe they do it because this world has been influenced by what one person did for it...

John 3:16 NIV

For God so loved this [the] world, that He gave His only Son, that whoever believes in Him shall not perish but have eternal life...

I am one of those "whoever's."

What Jesus did has echoed through the streets of every nation, some accept it, others don't, but what He did touched off a flame that has spread over all the earth. Somehow, we are part of that plan and as small as our part may be, we all contribute to something so huge that it is impossible to fully comprehend. We may be insignificant to the whole, but we are important to the ones we touch. I may be only one, but I am still one that can help influence the world. As long as I can do that, my life is significant.

Another old hymn that I remember singing and embracing its truth:

Grace Greater Than All Our Sin[14]

Marvelous grace of our loving Lord,
Grace that exceeds our sin and our guilt!
Yonder on Calvary's mount outpoured,
there where the blood of the Lamb was spilled.

Refrain

Grace, grace, God's grace,
Grace that will pardon and cleanse within;
Grace, grace, God's grace,
Grace that is greater than all our sin.
Sin and despair, like the sea waves cold,
Threaten the soul with infinite loss;
Grace that is greater, yes, grace untold,
Points to the refuge, the mighty cross.

July 28, 2012

Since I felt so much better yesterday, Fran and I felt we could do a short road trip. Our thermometer was reading 110 degrees at 4:00 P. M. so we decided to look for the coolest place within 200 miles. We chose Cedar City, Utah. It felt good to drive. For months, my driving has been very restricted, but as we were leaving Vegas, it was great to be driving somewhere besides a doctor's office. It is 64 degrees here this morning. Getting ready to visit a local church this morning. This is the day the Lord has made...

July 29, 2012

Fran and I always try to go to church whenever we can and so being in Cedar City, Utah we decided to attend Westview Christian Center (AG church). The people were so welcoming and kind, the worship was awesome (several Kim Walker songs). The worship leader led with a precious anointing. Fran and I were so ministered to... felt the Holy Spirit so strong and alive. The associate pastor spoke, and it was so good. It was all just what we needed.

As we got out of church we got into the hardest cloudburst we had ever been in. We turned into a Wal-Mart parking lot, and in places, the water was a couple of feet deep. Later we drove to Brian Head, rain all the way, but at 10,400 feet it was 44 degrees.... loved it... tonight Fran, and I took walks in the cool weather, saw an incredible sunset scene. What a blessed time to be with my best friend, my wife. We are cherishing these moments as gifts to us... we are both sensing we are being held by God as we walk through our battle with this cancer.

July 30, 2012

We got home from Cedar City at about noon. It was sprinkling here, and the temps were 90 and below... what a blessing. We had a great time together. I have felt very good today, and maybe the chemo is almost done... just in time for another round on Wednesday.

I am coming to the place again that the quality of life vs. the treatment is really playing with my mind. I am again praying for wisdom... I know we walk by faith, not by sight, but I sure would like some irrefutable sign that says, "This is the answer..." I would hope it would say, "I am healing you, don't take any more chemo..." but haven't heard that yet...

I know there are some who might say they know what they would do, but unless they have faced terminal cancer they might not understand the life and death decisions these are... King David many times asked for guidance... this is just one of them.

Psalm 25:4 NKJV

Show me Your ways, O LORD; Teach me Your paths...

I am trying to trust in the Lord with all my heart and acknowledge Him in all my decisions and believing He will direct my paths... I would cherish your prayers for wisdom, guidance, and healing...

These words blessed me tonight... think I hear a message in them for me... hope some of you will too...

Isaiah 40:28-31

Have you not known? Have you not heard? The everlasting God, the Lord, The Creator of the ends of the earth, Neither faints nor is weary. His understanding is unsearchable. He gives power to the weak, and to those who have no might He increases strength. Even the youths shall faint and be weary, And the young men shall utterly fall, but those who wait on the Lord Shall renew their strength; They shall mount up with wings like eagles, They shall run and not be weary, they shall walk and not faint.

——

I realized last night that I really do want to live... I want to have what I have been watching other people take for granted. I want this cup to pass from me... I don't want to suffer, be sick or hurt... I don't think I say this out of panic or being fearful... I look back, and I have been fighting with all I am to overcome this cancer. I have seen God give me strength in my spirit when in the flesh, I was so weakened. I have seen God give peace that passes my understanding. I know His grace is sufficient and that in suffering when I am weak, then I am strong, but I really, really don't want to be sick anymore. But what if I continue to be sick? What do I do then? While I am typing I have made a choice: I am deciding ahead of time that I will rejoice in the God of my salvation... and that I will be able to do what I must do as I can do all things through Jesus who strengthens me... abundant life is still mine, life still has quality even if the treatment fights quality of life in my body.

July 31, 2012

Psalm 119:114 KJV

Thou art my hiding place and my shield: I hope in thy word."

For you that have kind of followed my journey through this cancer battle, you know I have been again so ready to quit chemo and let happen what will happen. Chemo tries to kill cancer cells but kills good cells too, and all that makes a patient sicker than any stomach flu and takes away energy to the point any activity is almost impossible. Tomorrow is my next round, and I cannot tell you how much I don't want to go into the cancer center tomorrow... but after praying for wisdom, I have decided I will be there at 10:15 A. M. to conquer my fears, nausea and face this cancer head-on.

Psalm 40:1-3 NKJV

I waited patiently for the Lord; And He inclined to me, He also brought me up out of a horrible pit, out of the miry clay, and set my feet upon a rock, and established my steps. He has put a new song in my mouth Praise to our God; Many will see it and fear, and will trust in the Lord.

August 1, 2012

Did you know God uses each of us to bear one another's burdens? Saw that in action today. The cancer center was like a reunion today when I got there.

A good friend, Pastor Robert K., was with his wife Joanne who was taking treatment, and then Gloria, a leader of a prayer ministry, was there with her mom. It made for a good time of sharing our faith and just catching up. Cancer may be evil, but even like this time, good came from the battle. I saw an infomercial for St. Jude's Hospital for Children and saw those kids fighting cancer, and I know they are so sick yet are trusting the adults to do the very best for them, and the kids looked so brave. I thought, 'I can do at least as good as they are doing and I know how to trust my Father in Heaven to direct the medical people to do their very best human endeavor on my behalf.'

So, I took this treatment on as a challenge, not a doom and gloom struggle. So far it is working. I am on the pump for 48 more hours. I can feel myself getting sick in my stomach, and weaker in my body- so I know more is coming. But it is only for a season, and then I will rebound again by the amazing grace of God.

———

Psalms 39:4-6 NKJV

"Lord, make me to know my end, and what is the measure of my days, That I may know how frail I am. Indeed, You have made my days as handbreadths, and my age is as nothing before You; Certainly every man at his best state is but vapor. Selah. Surely every man walks about like a shadow; Surely they busy themselves in vain; He heaps up riches, and does not know who will gather them.

Perhaps this Psalm can bless you like it did me...

Psalms 40:1-3; 9-11 NKJV

I waited patiently for the Lord; And He inclined to me, And heard my cry. He also brought me up out of a horrible pit, Out of the miry clay, and set my feet upon a rock, And established my steps. He has put a new song in my mouth—Praise to our God; Many will see it and fear, And will trust in the Lord. I have proclaimed the good news of righteousness In the great assembly; Indeed, I do not restrain my lips, O Lord, You Yourself know. I have not hidden Your righteousness within my heart; I have declared Your faithfulness and Your salvation; I have not concealed Your loving-kindness and Your truth From the great assembly. Do not withhold Your tender mercies from me, O Lord; Let Your loving-kindness and Your truth continually preserve me.

One hour on a chemo pump with 17 hours to go. The side effects are an almost immediate, metallic taste in the mouth, weakness, nausea and more, but it is a choice to attempt to lengthen my life. Is it working? ... I hope so. Kind of like a surgeon setting a fractured bone... hurts like everything but somehow the healing comes. Hoping and praying that is what is happening in me. I have a great desire to live. The Psalmist said in faith:

Psalm 118:17, 24, 25 NKJV

I shall not die, but live, And declare the works of the Lord. This is the day the Lord has made; We will rejoice and be glad in it. Save now, I pray, O Lord; O Lord, I pray, send now favor (prosperity, healing).

August 4, 2012

The cycle started again on Thursday night as the chemo began to do what it is supposed to do... To sleep, I took an anti-nausea pill with a relaxer in it, and I probably slept better than I have for some time. I woke up this morning thinking I was feeling much better than last time, but by mid-morning it had all turned around and strong nausea and fatigue set in. I know I am in it for the long haul of just not feeling good. I am so thankful Fran is able to be with me during these times.

This is my choice to try to destroy the cancer but knowing it is also going to wreak havoc in my body. I am still convinced that even at my weakest, God's grace is sufficient to get me through.

My hope is built on nothing less than Jesus Christ and righteousness...

I am believing that the effectual, fervent prayer of a righteous person avails much. I am convinced that God is listening to the prayers offered on my behalf. Hopefully, in four or five days, I can say again, "I am feeling better..." and begin to feel alive again... I am mourning for what life used to be, but I read,

Matthew 5:4 NKJV

Blessed are those who mourn for they shall be comforted...

I am being comforted in the middle of my trial and am believing that God is causing all things to work together for good. I hope I don't waste this time and miss what God is working out...

———

Day three of chemo is exhausting... It all hit the fan this morning... Good to read about all you who are having a great weekend.... enjoy each moment and try not to whine over the small stuff. Look for the good in your family, overlook the minor things and embrace the love... Life is too short to not see the good, to miss a sunset or a shooting star because of conflict or anger. I am so blessed by my wife who is here by my side even when I am so sick...

August 5, 2012

Too sick to attend church today so enjoyed church online, then the Olympics, and later the NASA landing of Curiosity on Mars. Thought that would be the highlight of my weekend, but the most exciting part was going with Fran to a car wash. The good thing was that she didn't get stuck in it this time. Not sure what tomorrow holds but I know Who holds tomorrow.

Seven months ago, I said goodbye to Boulder City Assembly, the church Fran and I had founded. I cannot believe the change in my life since that day. I had believed that I would have opportunity to minister in a lot of different venues but had to give that idea up too because of cancer.

Today I felt more like crying out of sadness over the loss of health and my loss of hope for ministry of some kind. I have great hope for eternity and life after this life, but today was such a hard day.

Each cycle of chemo is such a powerful tool that attacks the human spirit, and it seems to devastate hopes, dreams, passions and future plans. I have believed that even when I am weak, I can be strong in my spirit, but today the flesh is weak and so is the spirit. I think I saw today what being so sick is doing to my wife.

Six months she has put up with a new drama every week. I don't cry in front of her as I know it affects her so much, and she doesn't read this post very often so I can write that if I thought crying would help I would be doing it all the time. However, I can't believe it is happening now: each time I write about my weakness, my sadness, and my despair there suddenly comes a spiritual energy that begins to lift me as I am experiencing right now. Can't explain it, but it's like God just shows up and lifts me up... out of my innermost being there seem to be those rivers of life starting to flow again... I choose to believe that Romans 8:28 is still working on my behalf... Think I can make it another day... I think I should write more often...

August 6, 2012

Psalm 30:1-5 NLV

Prayer of Thanks

I will lift You up, O Lord, for You have lifted me up... O Lord my God, I cried to You for help and You healed me. O Lord, You have brought me up from the grave. You have kept me alive, so that I will not go down into the deep. Sing praise to the Lord, all you who belong to Him. Give thanks to His holy name. For His anger lasts only a short time. But His favor is for life. Crying may last for a night, but joy comes with the new day.

This Psalm speaks what I believe is going on in my life... there is a plan, a time, a season for all we go through... I stand tonight in the assurance that it is well with my soul even though my body is struggling with cancer. I am persuaded that nothing can separate me from the love of God that I have found in Christ Jesus. He is the strength of my life, the hope of future, the peace in my spirit. Though tears flow, they are short-lived because the God of hope fills me with peace and joy as I trust in Him. Trust overcomes despair. Hope triumphs over defeat.
This is a new day!

August 7, 2012

A friend emailed me today and said some very kind words about my life being an inspiration through my struggle with chemo and cancer. I was kind of embarrassed about his words. However, I had just read in

John 6:66 where many disciples of Jesus turned away from following Him and Jesus asked the 12, "Will you leave also?" Peter again comes through in surprising fashion and answered with a question, "Where else could we go? You have the words of life..." I realized it doesn't really matter how inspirational any of us might sound, there is only one place we can go that always offers life, always offers hope, always pours out love, and always gives wisdom... and that is back to the One whose words are spirit and life. There is nowhere else I can go. As I go to the Lord and He is my last hope and resort, who else would I speak of? My doctor is a great guy, but he can offer little hope beyond months, but Jesus offers eternal hope that reaches beyond the expanse of space and time. And that hope never makes me ashamed to talk of it.

Romans 5:5 NLV

Hope never makes us ashamed because the love of God has come into our hearts through the Holy Spirit Who was given to us.

If I offer any inspiration, it is only because I am talking about the only Hope I have...

Romans 15:13 NKJV

Now may the God of hope fill you with all joy and peace in believing, that you may abound in hope by the power of the Holy Spirit.

I mustered up the energy and drove to the post office to mail a package for Fran, and after standing in line talking to a friend for about ten minutes, I walked out to my pickup. It was 110 degrees and going home was not what I wanted, so to stay cool I decided to drive to Arizona which means crossing the Colorado River on the new bridge (900+ feet above the water) and driving about a mile into Arizona and turning around (about 15 miles round trip). It was nice.

Here is something to think about:

Proverbs 3:5-8 NLV

Trust in the Lord with all your heart, and do not trust in your own understanding. Agree with Him in all your ways, and He will make your paths straight. Do not be wise in your own eyes. Fear the Lord and turn away from what is sinful. It will be healing to your body and medicine to your bones.

August 8, 2012

Tomorrow at 6:30 A. M. I get to drink that wonderful barium contrast for a CT scan. The drink is so hard to get down that I am hoping I can do it. We are hoping and praying the cancer is in check, and the scan will show that.

I cannot wish the cancer away, but by faith, I believe God can do what no other can.

Hebrews 11:1 & 6 NKJV

Faith is the substance of things hoped for and the evidence of things not seen. But without faith it is impossible to please Him, for he who comes to God must believe that He is, and that He is a rewarder of those who diligently seek Him.

August 9, 2012

Enjoyed some breakfast for the first time in nearly two weeks... amazing how good a pancake can taste when you haven't had one for months...

I valiantly drank the barium this morning. But after I got about 3/4 of it down, it parted company with me very quickly. The test went well without it. Will not find out till next week the results.

I have contacted my oncologist and told him that I will not take any more chemo for the present. I have decided that I want some quality of life back if it is possible. I have lost 40 pounds and lots of strength. I don't even recognize the old guy looking back at me in the mirror. I think I have given it a good shot, but it has taken its toll on both Fran and me. I believe my spiritual man has not decreased, but my outward man has certainly been beat up.

Like I have said, my hope in eternity has never wavered, but my hope in ever having a normal life again certainly has diminished. I pray with faith, but as of yet, faith is the only substantial thing I have to hold on to... and faith is the only evidence that I will be healed... there is no tangible evidence.

So, what is a person supposed to do? The writer of Psalm 73 basically says, "Good things happen to everyone else, but not to me..." and he fights in his spirit not to become negative because he realizes a responsibility to other people not to speak a message of gloom... he begins to rehearse in his mind what he has in God and changes his whole attitude.

I believe that when we are in the middle of very challenging situations, we must guard our heart and our mouth, so we don't tear down other people's faith or the reputation of our God.

Psalm 19:14 NKJV is a prayer.

Let the words of my mouth and the meditation of my heart be acceptable in Your sight, O Lord, my strength and my Redeemer.

Proverbs 4:23

Guard your heart with all diligence,
for out of it spring the issues of life.

Jesus said that out of the abundance of the heart, the mouth speaks... So, if I let my heart meditate on the negative part of life that is what my mouth is going to speak. If I consider faith and hope, then that is what my mouth will speak... and when I speak faith, it is easier to live by faith... I chose that faith will be what is in my heart and is spoken by my mouth...

Pastor Blayne Corzine's wife Lynn brought over a Mexican casserole last night that was so good tasting... Thanks, Pastor Blayne and Lynn... you are both awesome. Another friend, Kirstie McGuinness brought us some wonderful soup that was just right for that day. It is wonderful to have friends. Going to have lunch with some good friends from Kenya tomorrow. What a treat...

August 10, 2012

Psalm 56:3-4 NKJV

Whenever I am afraid, I will trust in You. In God (I will praise His word), In God I have put my trust; I will not fear. What can flesh do to me?

Today was a good day even though I did not feel very good. Fran and I met with friends from Kenya who became part of our family years ago, through some hard times they were going through here in my town. It is such a great story I wish I could tell it all, but our relationship and meeting with part of the family today reminded me again why I truly believe Romans 8:28. To me, it says that out of any circumstance God can make good things happen for those who love and trust him.

As you know, I had to resign my position as Chaplain at the Nevada State Veteran's Home because of my illness. I could not understand why I would have a position that would fit so nicely with what I was hoping as a semi-retirement and then find out I have a terminal illness.

Tonight, I was able to sit on a church council and see my replacement approved for ordination. I had recommended Bob, and the administration saw what we all had seen and selected him even though he had not yet been ordained.

Tonight, I saw Romans 8:28 working again... not just for my good but for the good of 170 some residents of the veteran's home. They now have a chaplain that is able and willing to serve them with great compassion and love.

My illness opened a door for a man God was calling to this position. This could not have happened without my illness. I never got this disease so this would happen, but God knew this would allow a man He positioned there two years before to be His man for such a time as this. In God's mercy, I know there is a plan for the rest of my life that He has ordained... I am at peace with that even in the midst of illness.

August 11, 2012

I am constantly made aware of things that are not normal in my body. I am struggling with nausea and digestive problems, and diet does not seem to change that. Last night I became very ill in the bathroom and could not get to bed till 3:00 A. M. I woke up this morning very weak and nauseated.

Fran reminded me that my pickup had to be smogged today or I would have to pay a penalty. I got up and drove my truck to the smog station and decided to wash it first... couldn't do it- too weak... Drove back to get it smogged and it passed, drove home, registered it online and collapsed into bed...

Fran and I were looking forward to a barbeque with a neighbor, but I was too ill. I am not sure but all the activity of yesterday may have been harder than I supposed.

This is why I have decided that I am going to suspend chemo until there is a reason to start again. I will still go in for blood tests, but I want to try to regain some of my life again. To extend the days of my life without quality is not my goal now... I want to extend the quality of life to the days of my life.

I dreamed several times today while sleeping of being a pastor again and remembered the joy there was sharing the Good News with people looking for hope. Tonight I was invited to preach at a church, not of my denomination and I will when I get stronger. That will be a joy. I may not have much to offer as a person, but I sure have a lot to offer as a messenger of God.

Thank goodness for the Olympics, the Seahawks, and the Velocity Channel. I found my anti-nausea medicine also lulled me to sleep... missed a lot of all those things on TV but slept with them going on. Hoping to go to church tomorrow... this is why I go to church when I can...

This scripture I have shared before, but I believe it speaks of where I am right now. I changed some pronouns to make it personal, but you'll understand.

2 Corinthians 4:16-18 NKJV

Therefore I [we] do not lose heart. Even though my [our] outward man is perishing, yet my [the] inward man is being renewed day by day. For my [our] light affliction, which is but for a moment, is working for me [us] a far more exceeding and eternal weight of glory, while I [we] do not look at the things which are seen, but at the things which are not seen. For the things which are seen are temporary, but the things which are not seen are eternal.

———

I am up late as I tend to sleep a lot because of the cancer treatment I am taking.

I got to hold two babies who are about the same age today, Emanuel and Allison Kasio's (who live in Kenya) beautiful little girl. Allison and daughter are visiting family here and made the effort to come and see Fran and me.

The Kasios are like family to us. The other baby was my grandson. The little girl is so petite and pretty and my grandson so hefty and handsome... no comparison in weight. What a treat and these little ones just seemed to know I am a grandpa and they were fun to be with. I look back on my meetings I had with people today and realize that God truly is working things together for good to those who trust Him. It has been a Romans 8:28 day...

August 12, 2012

Ephesians 2:10 NKJV

For we are His workmanship, created in Christ Jesus for good works, which God prepared beforehand that we should walk in them.

Fran and I attended services at two different churches today and found hope and blessings in each. Even though I was weary, there was just enough strength to do it all. It was good to see friends at church today and to be able to worship with them. I like the above verse in Ephesians... good to think about when you think you or someone else is not very worthwhile. I don't think God makes junk.

We were treated to a very wonderful lunch by our neighbor, Jamie. We were so blessed by her. So today was full, and there was "enough" energy to do it all but thank God for naps.

Remember the story of Jesus with his disciples on the Sea of Galilee in a little boat in a horrific storm?

Mark 4:39 NKJV

Then He arose and rebuked the wind, and said to the sea, "Peace, be still!" And the wind ceased and there was a great calm...

I feel like I have been there; in a storm with little relief in sight, but I also feel like God has rebuked the storm and has commanded peace to be mine. In church tonight, I realized anew that I "am at peace." I am at peace with God, with family, with friends and in my soul and mind. I have a peace that passes my understanding, it is a peace that brings a calm that cancer cannot take away. I sense a peace that so far suffering has not taken away. There is a peace that finances cannot take away. By faith, I walk in a peace that death cannot take away, but none of this peace is because I willed it or made it happen... it is because Jesus spoke peace into me that the world did not give and the world cannot take away.

Will fear come? Probably. But the Holy Spirit will remind me of the Word and where fear comes from and remind me I can be at peace.

August 13, 2012

I went to see my primary care doctor today just to touch base with him and get all my medical records in place. I had not seen my doctor for about six months. Although he knew from the records what was going on, he wanted to know how I was doing. He just looked at me for a little while and said, "You know you are going to have to just put your life in God's hands and trust Him." As I was leaving, he took my hand with both his and told me he would be praying for me.

Nice to have a doctor talking faith to his patient. For those who face sickness and hard times, it is good to remember where our help comes from.

August 14, 2012

I am always so blessed by you that decide to send a message my way. It means a lot.

Tomorrow is the day I meet with my oncologist and the reps from UCLA concerning chemotherapy. I have decided to suspend the treatment for a season. I know the doctor will really want me to continue but I know I must take some time.

I would cherish your prayers... for Fran. She has had a huge load to carry since my surgery and chemo. She is with me on this, and we are walking by faith that God is going to continue to be our strength.

Today was the first day I have had in 14 that physically I have felt that I might have a future. I know I will always have a spiritual hope in an eternal future, but to grasp the feeling that life might be able to go on for a while is a great feeling. When David wrote Psalm 23, he said,

> *"Yea though I walk through the valley of the shadow of death I will fear no evil... "*

And then Jesus asked His disciples after calming the sea why they were afraid and where was their faith... Then Paul wrote, we have not been given a spirit of fear, but of love and a sound mind... So, I know I do not have to face what I face with fear, I will walk by faith, not by sight.

Psalm 56:4 NKJV

In God (I will praise His word), In God I have put my trust; I will not fear. What can flesh do to me?

I always cherish your prayers.

August 15, 2012

Psalm 57:7-11 NKJV

My heart is steadfast, O God, my heart is steadfast; I will sing and give praise. Awake, my glory! Awake, lute and harp! I will awaken the dawn. I will praise You, O Lord, among the peoples; I will sing to You among the nations. For Your mercy reaches unto the heavens, And Your truth unto the clouds. Be exalted, O God, above the heavens; Let Your glory be above all the earth.

It has been an eventful day. So glad my son Rob and his family are here with us this week.

Rob and Fran went with me to the oncologist this morning. I took my blood tests and went in to see the doctor. He had already been forewarned that I had decided to suspend chemo for a while. We looked at the results of last week's CT scan, and it was great news. For the second time, the cancer has not progressed. In fact, at one point, they said they could not see the cancer. The oncologist was pumped, and so was I... He believes the cancer is still there but unable to grow.

Six months ago next Monday, the surgeon who chose not to remove my stomach told my family I might not live more than six months but here I am alive...

Without the chemo for a while, I want to see if I can regain my strength and try to get my life back. I will go in every other week to do labs and check on new ideas for treatment. But I am satisfied the cancer has not had a chance against all the people praying for me. I did agree to an iron infusion which took about an hour because I was anemic... It made me very nauseated again, but it was a good time as I was able to talk with another couple about having faith during a time like this... I could do little more than rest today.

But tonight I feel strength coming. I may drive to the Grand Canyon with my family tomorrow. I am praising God for this new evidence of him touching my body...

Thanks for all your prayers... God is working a miracle... I give praise to the One who is my life!

August 16, 2012

Today was a wonderful day with my oldest son's family, my wife, and our nine-month-old grandson. We traveled over 450 miles going to the Grand Canyon and back. The weather was awesome, went through lots of rain to get there and then it was cloudy on the south rim with the temps in the 70's. Our grandson was so amazing and just cooed, laughed, ate and slept. I think he enjoyed six babysitters. The canyon exuded a sense of God's creative power. Each time I see it, I am reminded of the creative power of God. The canyon is like the ocean, there is no way to explain it. I feel great peace as I look at that huge gaping fissure. Don't know why but I always sense that even in the chaos of the crowds from all over the world. David wrote,

Psalm 121:1

I look to the hills, where does my strength come from... then He answers Himself. My help, comes from the LORD.

Today I felt a resurgence of strength, physically, and spiritually.

August 17, 2012

Have you ever wondered what happens to a prayer after it is prayed in faith? My mother lived to be 99 years and nine months old and I know one of her most consistent prayers were for her children and grandchildren (and there are a lot of those). Her prayer was that each of them would come to find a relationship with Jesus Christ. It is so amazing that even several years after her death, her prayers are still being answered.

In John 17 the prayer of our Lord is recorded.

John 17:20-23 NKJV

"I do not pray for these alone, but also for those who will believe in Me through their word; that they all may be one, as You, Father, are in Me, and I in You; that they also may be one in Us, that the world may believe that You sent Me. And the glory which You gave Me I have given them, that they may be one just as We are one:

I believe this is a perpetual prayer that each generation is blessed by as the power of the Holy Spirit reveals Jesus as the true light to each person born into this world. *(John 1:9 Jesus was the true Light which gives light to every man coming into the world.)*

Why do I bring this up? First to remind you that:

James 5:16 NKJV

"The effective, fervent prayer of a righteous man avails much."

Secondly, that your prayers offered in faith for people who need healing like me or who need a miracle of some kind are effective, and I believe are lasting.

Your prayer prayed last week is not lost in space... it is there before our God and will be answered in His will and His timing. Six months ago, a surgeon sewed me up saying I probably wouldn't make it more than six months... Today I ate three good meals and tonight had a small bowl of Moose Tracks ice cream and enjoyed it. I drank a cold Pepsi (first one in six months and it was wonderful).

I believe that a prayer prayed by my brother-in-law and his wife for me in their kitchen in Montana on the day we learned something was wrong is still availing and still is effective. I am living proof of that.

I know my life is as a vapor that appears for a moment and then disappears (like you, I don't know when I will die or how) but for today I rejoice that literally thousands of people have prayed for me, and God is answering and I have good reason to believe there is still a plan in place for the rest of my life.

Remember Jeremiah 29:11:

> *For I know the thoughts that I think toward you, says the Lord,*
> *thoughts of peace and not of evil, to give you a future and a hope.*

(I believe God still has a plan for me with or without cancer).

Thanks so much for all the words of encouragement. As I ate an A&W hamburger at a truck stop on I -40 and later ate pizza and a hot wing at the Grand Canyon, I remembered the night before the surgeons were going to remove my stomach and I was praying with my wife that God would not allow it to be removed. The surgeon found cancer in other places and did not remove anything. He believed I would need a feeding tube, so he inserted it. Now six months later the tube is gone, still have my stomach and the cancer has not grown. Maybe God used chemo to cause this or maybe I needed to learn to trust Him more... no matter, I know God is working good on my behalf. I choose to give Him thanks.

August 18, 2012

Got up at 4:45 A. M. to say goodbye to my son, Rob, and his family as they headed for the airport to fly back to Oregon. They came on Monday and blessed us all week long... Fran and I went back to bed after they left and slept till about 9:00 A. M. then I had the challenge of trying to do what I did before I had surgery and chemo.

The lawns needed mowing and cleaned up. Got it all done, but I was totally wiped out afterward... I am fighting some side effects from something and felt pain in the stomach, and the nausea come back... maybe worked too hard for an old guy? lol These things always turn into a mind game wondering what is causing it.

Fran and I spent a wonderful hour in worship and prayer tonight... my iPad has lots of good worship music that is easy to listen to as we prepare to pray for those we are led to pray for.

Did you ever notice that the Psalms have many cries for help because life has just turned into a mess? The amazing part is that almost every one of them turns towards God answering the cries for help...

I read the following Psalm in the Message Bible. Maybe you can relate to these words...

Psalm 130:1-5 MSG

Help, God — the bottom has fallen out of my life! Master, hear my cry for help! Listen hard! Open your ears! Listen to my cries for mercy. If you, God, kept records on wrongdoings, Who would stand a chance? As it turns out, forgiveness is your habit, And that's why you're worshiped. I pray to God — my life a prayer —And wait for what he'll say and do.

August 19, 2012

Many of you know:

Psalm 34:19 NKJV

Many are the afflictions of the righteous,
But the Lord delivers him out of them all.

It is reality and faith put together. We all know that life is always a challenge. Looking at those who have more money than they can ever use I still see struggles and problems. People who have nothing, struggle with life in another way. Even the people who are living righteous lives have to remember that Jesus said the rain falls on the just and unjust, or the sun rises the same for everyone. We are not immune from trouble.

The word "many" means "more than one," it means a lot. That is the reality of the life side of that verse. But the faith side which is really the real side says, "God will deliver us out of them all." Beth Moore said it so well in her teachings on Daniel (condensed and paraphrased), "*Some are delivered from the fire, some through the fire and some by the fire.*" But God does deliver. Even when fighting illness, injury, broken relationships, dashed dreams, financial disasters, the righteous (one in right standing with God) can bank on God being there with deliverance of some kind.

Galatians 6:9 NKJV

And let us not grow weary while doing good, for in due season we shall reap if we do not lose heart.

It is easy to lose heart when you are hurting, but when we hold on to the unchangeable truths of God's word we find strength...

Isaiah 40:31 KJV

But they that wait (seek after, look for, hold on to) upon the Lord shall renew their strength; they shall mount up with wings like eagles. They shall run and not be weary, they shall walk and not faint.

This was another day of being able to sense life and that more abundantly. Still feel the effects of chemo in my body, but it is relenting. Thanks again for your prayers...

———

We went to BCA church today and were so blessed by the worship experience and a good message... having a Biblical name like Jordan, makes hearing preaching about crossing the Jordan a little humorous especially since I was the former pastor... lol.

We also attended their baptism service and saw four people baptized. I used to tell people I baptized that they may not be baptized in the Jordan (River), but they are blessed to be baptized by the Jordan. (Old pastor humor).

Another day of not being really sick... I enjoy being alive. It was good to realize that I get another chance to have as Jesus said, He came "to give life and that more abundantly."

August 20, 2012

For whatever reason, nothing that I eat or drink tastes good after I have swallowed it. Don't know if it is still chemo or what is still causing this. Even though there is no good taste, I know I must eat to try to gain strength. Fran wanted to go get a hamburger tonight, so we went to A&W, and I watched some men eating, drinking, and enjoying it so much. I have to admit I was a little envious. Lol. As I was thinking about this, I remembered the scripture:

Psalm 34:8 KJV

*"O taste and see that the Lord is good:
blessed is the man that trusteth in Him."*

I see a lot of people trying to find something in this life that satisfies, but so much leaves a bad taste and there never is that inner satisfaction.

This Psalm indicates that when we put our faith in God, there is never a bad taste but only blessings as we trust Him. To some, I may sound radical, but I know in this battle with cancer that my hope is built on eternal truths of God's Word, love, and grace not on something that can turn around and destroy me. My hope is built on nothing less than Jesus Christ and righteousness. He gives a peace that surpasses our understanding or comprehension. I don't understand cancer, heart disease, ALS, rheumatism, diabetes, or any other life-threatening disease, but even when these things go beyond our understanding, there is still peace offered by God... ask for it, believe for it, live in it...

———

1 Timothy 2:1-4 NIV

I urge, then, first of all, that petitions, prayers, intercession and thanksgiving be made for all people— for kings and all those in authority, that we may live peaceful and quiet lives in all godliness and holiness. This is good, and pleases God our Savior, who wants all people to be saved and to come to a knowledge of the truth.

My wife and I attempt to have a dedicated prayer time each day. I talked with one of the young men of BCA church today who is going to Reno to college this week. I told him Fran and I would not forget to pray for him. Some students don't have a prayer being prayed for them by anyone. If you are a student that would like your name lifted in prayer by grandparents who are former pastors, contact me through a message, and we will pray for you as often as we can.

I wonder how my Christian friends interpret this scripture in light of all the political trash talk that I see posted. It seems we should use more energy praying than bashing politicians, political parties or positions...

Taking our stand might be more effective on our knees believing that our prayers are effective and powerful.

August 21, 2012

I have two good friends who are so weakened by cancer that there does not seem to be much hope and that causes my heart to be troubled. They are both Christians, and they have been through much greater struggles than I have and still hold on to their faith in Jesus Christ. My heart is not troubled because of what will happen if they die, because Jesus told us in John 14:1-6 KJV to not let our hearts be troubled because He said, "*In my Father's house are many mansions*" (rooms)... you can read the rest. We have that eternal hope. But I am troubled because I have seen in the past couple of years so many Christians and good people who are being bombarded by cancer and other diseases. So many innocent children. I have a sense that God is wanting to remind the church that He still is the Healer. Jesus says in John 10:10 NKJV, "*The thief (Satan) does not come except to steal, and to kill, and to destroy. I have come that they may have life, and that they may have it more abundantly.*"

As a pastor, I have seen people discouraged when cancer attacks a loved one, a leader or a child. It is like there is a thief that is stealing, killing, and destroying and we cannot do anything about it. We have believed in life and that more abundant, but cancer and other diseases dull the truth of that.

However, I believe that God is appointing true men and women of faith who will do as Jesus said and will pray for the sick and they will be healed. They will do it not to start a TV ministry or mega church but will simply do what the Bible says. Jesus did not do it for a show. Jesus often told those who were healed not to tell anyone about what happened. As God appoints and anoints men and women of faith, I hope that my friends and I meet one of these people and will be healed. Maybe God will appoint me and you to be His representative for healing on this earth...

August 22, 2012

I am so glad I took a break from chemo, and I am gaining strength almost back to pre-surgery status. We had more rain today than I have seen in the 17 years I have lived in the desert. The rain started, and the water began to rush off the roofs into the gutters, but the gutters plugged up almost immediately. Water was gushing over the side onto a sidewalk which was a few inches lower than the bottom of the door to the guest room. Had to decide... get wet or let the room flood. Decided to get wet. We have no raincoats down here, but I found a hooded jacket and made my way out to a big rock that I could stand on and on tiptoes reach into the place where it was clogged. The drain began to work immediately, but the rain was so hard the water was about to run under the door of the room. I remembered I had a sump pump. I got it, put it in the water, and turned it on and pumped a steady stream of water for 20 minutes. Several other little disasters had to be dealt with, and I was surprised I had the energy to do them. Needless to say, I was totally soaked. Later Fran and I took a drive around town to see the damage and got home and noticed the back tire on my car going flat. I had evidently picked up a nail... but it was in my driveway.

Later as Fran and I prepared to pray together, I read this scripture:

Philippians 4:4-7 NIV

Rejoice in the Lord always. I will say it again: Rejoice! Let your gentleness be evident to all. The Lord is near. Do not be anxious about anything, but in every situation, by prayer and petition, with thanksgiving, present your requests to God. And the peace of God, which transcends all understanding, will guard your hearts and your minds in Christ Jesus.

So we began to thank God for strength to do what had to be done today; thankful for a house to stay dry in; thankful the flat did not happen on the road somewhere (it was still raining hard); I gave thanks for my wife and for family; we gave thanks for our relationship with Jesus Christ that regardless of our circumstances there is a powerful peace that God gives. I have found in life it is more rewarding by far to give thanks than it is to feel sorry for oneself. Rejoicing is far more powerful than anger or self-pity. In every situation, look for ways to be thankful...

—

Romans 13:1-7 NIV

Let everyone be subject to the governing authorities, for there is no authority except that which God has established. The authorities that exist have been established by God. Consequently, whoever rebels against the authority is rebelling against what God has instituted, and those who do so will bring judgment on themselves. For rulers hold no terror for those who do right, but for those who do wrong. Do you want to be free from fear of the one in authority? Then do what is right and you will be commended. For the one in authority is God's servant for your good. But if you do wrong, be afraid, for rulers do not bear the sword for no reason. They are God's servants, agents of wrath to bring punishment on the wrongdoer. Therefore, it is necessary to submit to the authorities, not only because of possible punishment but also as a matter of conscience. This is also why you pay taxes, for the authorities are God's servants, who give their full time to governing. Give to everyone what you owe them: If you owe taxes, pay taxes; if revenue, then revenue; if respect, then respect; if honor, then honor.

In this election year that is so charged with feelings, as Christians it is good to remember what Paul the Apostle said as he lived under a very repressive government which ended up killing him: If you read the scriptures from Romans 13, you could call Paul, naive and crazy. In light of this scripture I find it very hard to bash our President (even though I don't agree with his policies and actions) in fact, I felt very strongly last night that I should pray for him and his family, and I did. I also feel led to pray for Mitt Romney and family and do. I will use my vote to express my choice. Meditate on these scriptures... they are not my words...

August 23, 2012

I got up this morning feeling like it was going to be a great day. The flat tire on the Jeep would stay up for about 10 minutes. I had to get it to the tire shop which I figured I could do in about seven minutes if I put over 40 pounds of air in it. Started to do it but the compressor just wasn't working right. We had something here we never have, and that is humidity... had to drain the tank... got all that done, pumped up the tire and made it to the shop.

I waited about an hour then took Fran to a couple of stores in Henderson, and all the sudden everything began to change. I lost all my strength and began to get sharp pains in my stomach... I ended up laying down most of the day.

When I was told I had stomach cancer they never told me about any symptoms, so my mind raced in that direction... tried to eat some supper and again brand new pains began all through my stomach and chest area, and I am thinking this is not good.

As I am laying in my chair, I hear Fran talking to someone outside, and it is one of my neighbors who has two little kids. I walked out, and my neighbor begins telling me she has been praying for me and she is convinced I am going to get well and be healed. I am trying to agree but not feeling much faith right then... her little four-year-old daughter comes over to me and says, "Will you chase me and try to catch me?" Can you see this old guy running after a four-year-old? But I did, and she ran all around our front yard grass with me trying to catch her. Best I felt all day. Never caught her, but I tried. After about 20 minutes of that it was enough, so I said goodbye to the kids and mother, and as I go in the door the little girl shouts out, "Goodbye sweetie..." Don't you know that made my day? That's one of those times you smile inside... God knew I needed something like that to get my mind off fear and back to faith. My fear of cancer for that moment was broken by the words of a little girl...

Reminds me that John said,

1 John 4:18
Perfect love casts out all fear because fear brings torment..."

Then Paul said:

2 Timothy 1:7 KJV
For God hath not given us the spirit of fear; but of power, and of love, and of a sound mind.

When Fran came in it was about nine, and we came together to pray. Fear was not an issue, but faith and love were... After prayer, Fran started playing some old hymns and worship choruses on the piano, and it was such a blessed time...

2 Corinthians 4:16 KJV

For which cause we faint not; but though our outward man perish, yet the inward man is renewed day by day.

———

Philippians 4:4 -7 NIV

Rejoice in the Lord always. I will say it again: Rejoice! Let your gentleness be evident to all. The Lord is near. Do not be anxious about anything, but in every situation, by prayer and petition, with thanksgiving, present your requests to God. And the peace of God, which transcends all understanding, will guard your hearts and your minds in Christ Jesus.

It was a good day to be thankful...

August 24, 2012

When we find ourselves facing insurmountable obstacles, and we don't know what we should do, I find myself and others always trying to find an answer. It is like we have to say something. I read a lot of things on Facebook from the profane to the profound. We all have lots of words... I get amazed at what upsets people, and I wonder if I should respond. I believe we need to learn to speak words of life from the Bible. Look at the next few words... what shall we say?

Romans 8:31, 35, 37-39 NIV

What, then, shall we say in response to these things? If God is for us, who can be against us? Who shall separate us from the love of Christ? Shall trouble or hardship or persecution or famine or nakedness or danger or sword? No, in all these things we are more than conquerors through him who loved us. For I am convinced that neither death nor life, neither angels nor demons, neither the present nor the future, nor any powers, neither height nor depth, nor anything else in all creation, will be able to separate us from the love of God that is in Christ Jesus our Lord.

In the face of cancer or financial uncertainty, what should I say? Say the Word... remember, faith comes by hearing and hearing comes from the word of God... Rom. 10:17.

My goal for today:

Psalm 19:14 NIV

May the words of my mouth and the meditation of my heart be pleasing in your sight, Lord, my Rock and my Redeemer.

August 25, 2012

My wife and I have neglected so many things these last six months that we decided today was the day we would try to make a dent in a room that had become our collect-all-room. Mostly photos from a lot of life and sentimental items we just hadn't been able to let go of, like the last birthday card my mother sent me before she died... What do you do with things like that? Means nothing to anyone else but in your heart, you remember a person who loved you all your life.

I found a diary written by my first wife, Mary. It was about her and baby Suzi, written when leaving an airbase in Illinois and moving to a California base. I found the receipt for a Holiday Inn in Independence, Missouri and Mary wrote that I thought it was too fancy and expensive... the receipt said we paid $10.50 for the night. That was December 31, 1966. I found a Seattle newspaper I bought the day President John F. Kennedy was assassinated and on the first line the newspaper misspelled the word president. Found my diary when I was writing about meeting Fran for the first time... Things that mean a lot to me... how could you ever part with them? Unfortunately for my kids, they will have to make that decision after I depart... lol.

We really worked hard, and yet when it came to trying to sleep tonight, it seems to evade me because of the continual nausea that won't let go of me. But in my mind and heart I know that as I look back, I see God displayed in my life through the good and the bad. I am like David in the Psalms:

Psalm 37:25 KJV

I have been young, and now am old; yet have I not seen the righteous forsaken, nor his seed begging bread.

I look back and see a heritage that my parents handed down to me that has made me a rich man. Not in monetary ways, but in my spirit. I have loved life... I have found joy even in the hardest times... I have always seemed to find a way to smile and look for the good in the middle of greatest loss. Maybe an optimist, but it sure is better than always looking for the bad in life. I have never had to hate anyone... I may have hated what they did, but never the person... I have always believed God would take care of them.

Romans 12:17-19 NKJV

Repay no one evil for evil. Have regard for good things in the sight of all men. If it is possible, as much as depends on you, live peaceably with all men.

Looking at the past makes me realize time flies and waits for no one.
I like this scripture:

James 4:14 NKJV

Whereas you do not know what will happen tomorrow. For what is your life? It is even a vapor that appears for a little time and then vanishes away.

The writer goes on to say we should look at the future, wanting the will of God... and say "As the Lord wills..."

I look forward to being in church tomorrow. Not sure how chemo affects others, but for me somehow it seems to weaken faith, passion for life, and hope. That's why I love to be in church with other believers because I find hope, renewed passion for life and my faith is built up.

Hebrews 10:23-25 NKJV

Let us hold fast the confession of our hope without wavering, for He who promised is faithful. And let us consider one another in order to stir up love and good works, not forsaking the assembling of ourselves together, as is the manner of some, but exhorting one another, and so much the more as you see the Day approaching.

August 26, 2012

Several years ago, I heard a 73-year-old missionary to South America talking to about 2000 of us, weeping as he spoke because he was dealing with being forced to come home because of his age.

He emotionally said, "Oh that I had another life to live so I could continue the ministry I loved so much." He took his shoes off and asked, "Who will fill these shoes." It was awesome to see hundreds of young men and women rush to the front of the church and say they would... That was so exciting to see.

But now I realize the older missionary had to walk off the platform and go home to an entirely different lifestyle. As much as I can, I am believing that cancer will not take my life, but there are still questions. As I stood in church today worshiping, my physical strength just went away, and I had to sit down while the rest of the church stood in worship. I don't know if it is the residue of chemo still affecting me or if it is the cancer. I looked at the younger people and thought, they had so much life in front of them. Perhaps a pity party, but I was wishing I had another life to live to be able to do what I never got done. Maybe everyone has times of regret, I don't know, I just know I felt that way today. All of us have times when it just doesn't seem to make sense... but if we will let Him, God will make this day make sense...

Isaiah 40:31 NKJV

But those who wait on the Lord shall renew their strength; They shall mount up with wings like eagles, They shall run and not be weary, they shall walk and not faint. David found himself in a very hard situation, and this is what he did:

1 Samuel 30:6 NKJV

But David strengthened himself in the Lord his God.

How? Worship? Prayer? Voicing your faith... I am choosing again, to do just that...

I enjoyed being in church today, and for whatever the reason the worship leader led some of my favorite worship songs. It was refreshing. We attended Boulder City Assembly, the church Fran and I started almost 17 years ago. Through the years many people's lives were impacted by the Gospel of Jesus Christ in this church.

Two notable young people, Tara and Alex, became invaluable to the church in the area of worship leading, teaching, music and then finally in becoming our youth pastors. I had the privilege of officiating at their wedding. Weekly 20 - 40 youth would show up for youth services, and many of them found a relationship with Jesus Christ. They had an awesome ministry. Today a couple dozen youth gathered around them to pray with them and say goodbye as today was their last day. They believe God has led them in a new direction for their lives and ministry and the church graciously thanked them and said goodbye today. As I understand it does not mean an end to youth ministry at all, just a change. As Pastor Blayne Corzine leads the church, I know there are new and exciting days ahead for the youth and the church. Sometimes believers just need to be reminded what our "real life" is...

Colossians 3:1-4 NLT

Since you have been raised to new life with Christ, set your sights on the realities of heaven, where Christ sits in the place of honor at God's right hand. Think about the things of heaven, not the things of earth. For you died to this life, and your "real life" is hidden with Christ in God. And when Christ, who is your life, is revealed to the whole world, you will share in all His glory.

August 27, 2012

Romans 8:35-39 NLT

Can anything ever separate us from Christ's love? Does it mean He no longer loves us if we have trouble or calamity, or are persecuted, or hungry, or destitute, or in danger, or threatened with death? (As the Scriptures say, "For your sake we are killed every day; we are being slaughtered like sheep.") No, despite all these things, overwhelming victory is ours through Christ, who loved us. And I am convinced that nothing can ever separate us from God's love. Neither death nor life, neither angels nor demons, neither our fears for today nor our worries about tomorrow—not even the powers of hell can separate us from God's love. No power in the sky above or in the earth below—indeed, nothing in all creation will ever be able to separate us from the love of God that is revealed in Christ Jesus our Lord.

Every time I have confessed that I was discouraged, sad or worried I have found hope in the Bible, in a song, in the word of a friend or family member, so I am convinced that God wants us to admit that we are not the strong tower we think we are. So, I confess that today I felt discouragement washing over me... I feel the neuropathy creeping up my legs. I get so weak after just a little exertion that I feel I must sit down. Anything I try to eat or drink causes nausea. Today as I looked back over my day I was having trouble finding any purpose for my life. But as I confess this as I write, I again sense the encouragement of God coming back into my heart and mind. Listening to Pandora this evening and right now hearing the song "Breathe" I am reminded in my spirit that I really do need God and that He puts purpose in my life...

August 28, 2012

1 Peter 3:15-16

But sanctify the Lord God in your hearts, and always be ready to give an answer to everyone who asks you a reason for the hope that is in you, with meekness and fear;

What a difference a day makes. I almost went to bed letting my emotions rule me. I was discouraged by how I felt, but I let God intervene. Got up this morning and something had changed. Today I felt so good. The best in six months. I was determined I was not going to allow my fear of being sick keep me in my bed or in my chair... I made breakfast for Fran, mowed my front and back yards (really tired me but I kept going), did dishes, made the bed and straightened up around the house and then a neighbor across the street invited me to swim in their pool. I decided to (the first time in over six months). It was so refreshing and like a medicine... no nausea after all the work and swimming. I don't know why or how I felt better, but I give God the glory.

Tomorrow I see my oncologist again. I have decided to postpone chemo for a while longer for several reasons.

I do have a hope... my hope is first of all, eternal, but there is also a hope that makes me believe this is the day the Lord has made, and I will rejoice in it. These scriptures help me explain why I talk about the Lord in the same breath as cancer.

Romans 5:3-5 NLT

We can rejoice, too, when we run into problems and trials, for we know that they help us develop endurance. And endurance develops strength of character, and character strengthens our confident hope of salvation. And this hope will not lead to disappointment. For we know how dearly God loves us, because He has given us the Holy Spirit to fill our hearts with His love.

August 29, 2012

James 1:5, 6 NKJV

If any of you lacks wisdom, let him ask of God, who gives to all liberally and without reproach, and it will be given to him. But let him ask in faith, with no doubting, for he who doubts is like a wave of the sea driven and tossed by the wind.

At 8:15 A. M. Fran and I walked into the Comprehensive Cancer Center where I go for chemotherapy. As soon as I walked in, I felt nausea but fought it back. I was nervous also because all my life I have had a compulsive desire to try to please people. In a few moments, I would talk to my oncologist who is really, really a nice and decent man and also to the rep from UCLA who has kept track of almost everything about my physical life that he could for the trial study that I am on for a new treatment for cancer. I was going to tell them that I needed a longer break from chemo and I was not sure how that would go over with them. But before I went back to see them, the lab called me back to draw blood...I am anemic now because they took so much (seven vials) lol. I then met with the doctor and rep, and they were so in agreement with me and told me to go home and not worry about my treatments for right now; that I needed to be sure if I wanted to continue.

I am confident that God does help us make good decisions when we ask for His help...

So, in this process of deciding, I am believing I will somehow find guidance from God... In all your ways acknowledge Him...

Proverbs 3:5-8 NKJV

Trust in the Lord with all your heart, and lean not on your own understanding; In all your ways acknowledge Him, And He shall direct your paths. Do not be wise in your own eyes; Fear the Lord and depart from evil. It will be health to your flesh, and strength to your bones.

—

When I get discouraged, and we all do, we need to have a good talk with someone: David talked to himself, and it helped.

Psalm 43:5 NLT

Why am I discouraged? Why is my heart so sad? I will put my hope in God! I will praise him again—My Savior and my God!

I came home today feeling so relieved that I am taking a longer break from the drugs that are pumped into me. Fran had an appointment with an orthopedic surgeon today because of pain in her hip. I drove her there, and after examination of x-rays, he prescribed a cortisone shot and poor

Fran when she saw that three-inch needle she thought it was at least six inches. It did hurt her a lot, but she is feeling better tonight.

As we were driving into Boulder City from Las Vegas, we saw a rainbow and then as we got within blocks of our house, a cloudburst broke loose dumping almost an inch of rain in less than 30 minutes. We saw a lady dropped off at a bus stop right in the middle of this rain and gave her a ride to her home. In 60 seconds she had literally gotten soaked. I was fascinated by the huge amount of water running down the streets, and so we never went home but drove around watching the rising water in the streets and flood channels. It was so amazing.

My granddaughters (16 and 13) from Oregon flew down this evening but while on the way to the Portland airport I sent a picture of how hard it was raining. They get so much rain that I was afraid they would back out, so I told them it would be dry by the time they got here. I picked them up at 8:30 P. M., and by the time we got back to Boulder City, you could see dust where the dirt had been washed into the streets. Amazing! What a joy for Grandpa to have two of his grandkids come and hang out. I am truly blessed.

August 30, 2012

After we picked up our two granddaughters last night, we asked them if they needed something to eat, but they couldn't decide and about that time I saw a Krispy Kreme. I turned in, and we bought a dozen doughnuts, and then they gave each of us one right off the line. I had been so hungry for a doughnut that I could hardly wait to take a bite. First day in months that I could. I got such a kick out of my wife when she took a bite of that hot doughnut she almost got emotional about how good it tasted. Then on to Arby's for a classic sandwich. What a combination, but everyone was happy.

The girls and I stayed up late watching a movie. My stomach began to rebel against all that foreign food, and I had to take medicine to calm that. But today, probably a bad thing, I had coffee and a doughnut. Then toast and cereal.

I don't know if you have heard of the Stratosphere Tower in Vegas (1100 feet high). I decided to take the girls there since it had been years since I had been up there. We walked probably a half mile from our parking place to the tower to buy the tickets to go to the observation deck... would you believe it, they had to close it because of lightning. So we went to Circus Circus to the Adventure Dome (inside amusement park), and the kids won some arcade games (the youngest young lady won a whoopee cushion, and she had more fun with that obnoxious thing, lol) and rode on an incredible roller coaster they have there. After walking (more like me dragging) around for a couple hours, I told the girls I was exhausted and needed to get home. Felt so good to get back in the pickup. I drove them down the strip, and they got to see the fountains and so much more.

We live about 25 miles from the strip and when nearly home we saw the lightning and got into a horrific rainstorm (cloudburst). Where there was only dust earlier now, there were raging streams. At one place mud and gravel had washed across the freeway. It was amazing. Then as soon as we got to my town, the storm was gone. We drove by a Dairy Queen, and I asked the girls if they wanted an ice cream cone. The answer was yes. I got and ate the first ice cream cone (chocolate dipped) I'd had for probably eight months. We had a great evening. My 28-year-old son came over, and he and the girls fixed tacos for us all. We ate on our deck and enjoyed such a good time.

The girls go back home on Saturday. I have enjoyed them so much. They just seem to love me unconditionally... I don't understand it, but I sure receive it.

I was asked to do a wedding tomorrow night because the other minister had some conflicts come up. The last wedding I did was just a week before my first chemo. Jesus did his first miracle at a wedding, so maybe I will receive a miracle of healing at this wedding.

I love this Psalm. David was trying to convince God he needed a new beginning. We all do in some ways in our lives. The third verse is the key... restore to me the joy of your salvation... Restored joy can triumph over any hell we are going through... Good prayer:

Psalm 51:10-12 NLT

Create in me a clean heart, O God. Renew a right spirit within me. Do not banish me from Your presence, and don't take your Holy Spirit from me. Restore to me the joy of Your salvation, and make me willing to obey You.

All in all, it was a good day.

Psalm 91:1, 2 NLT

Those who live in the shelter of the Most High will find rest in the shadow of the Almighty. This I declare about the LORD: He alone is my refuge, my place of safety; He is my God, and I trust Him.

Here in the desert, we have to have our house and property sprayed for bugs every few months. We make an appointment, and a person comes to spray in every room in our house and then outside. Fran neglected to tell me this was the day and she forgot too. This is Fran's day off, so we were sitting on the deck eating breakfast and relaxing reading the Bible and the newspaper. Fran was still in her housecoat and the granddaughters in their pajamas watching TV. I got a very important phone call, and the doorbell rang. Fran was mortified. She had to go to the door... there stands a guy with a spray tank ready to go to work. It was her embarrassing moment of the day. I thought it was great!

My oncologist's office called today and said I needed to come and pick up a CD of my CT scans taken in the past few months. They evidently found a growth in one of my kidneys, and they recommend I get a biopsy. So it was a rush to get it to the Radiology Dept. of a Henderson hospital. This was unexpected. But it is a fact of life. I had to walk a long way to the radiology department to drop it off. Glad I had my 16-year-old granddaughter with me.

I had my wife and three teenage girls to deal with today. The plan was the girls wanted to go to the outlet malls which were kind of close to the hospital. I was outnumbered, so we went. This was one time my struggle with cancer helped. I told them I was really tired, and I was, so rather than shopping with four females, they let me go back to the car. Saved from shopping. The next thing planned was swimming at an aquatic center. I decided I could do that. It was a fun time. Then IHOP afterward and now home getting girls ready to fly home tomorrow. It was a good time.

August 31, 2012

All week long amid feeling good and having my granddaughters here, there have been some extremely hard, unexpected things happening in other parts of my family. Things that just make you want to cry out to God for their situations...

Sometimes the unexpected and circumstances beyond our control brings real discouragement. It is a good time to talk to ourselves like King David did in this Psalm:

Psalm 43:5 NLT

Why am I discouraged? Why is my heart so sad? I will put my hope in God! I will praise Him again—my Savior and my God!

Being able to sort out reality in the midst of hurt, confusion or chaos is so important. Speaking the word of God in faith into our spirit is so effective. It helps us not take ourselves so seriously. As an act of the will saying, "I will put my faith in my God, I will praise Him despite how I feel..." It really works...

September 1, 2012

The timing of the Lord is amazing.

I was relaxing this evening watching some news when Fran asked me if we could go driving somewhere. So I said, "Of course." We got in my pickup, and she wanted to go to Bootleg Canyon, which is very near to town. It has popular mountain bike trails, and there is a road to the top where you can see all of Las Vegas, Henderson and Boulder City. It is a rough road so I was in 4x4 low range so I could take it slow. It was almost dark, and we had our windows down. It is several miles to the top winding up the canyon with lots of steep drop-offs.

About a mile from the top I heard someone yelling about 100 yards down an embankment. I stopped the truck and got out to hear him better. He needed a ride to the top. He and friends drove to the top and left his jeep there and rode their bikes down to the bottom. They started riding back up, but it was getting dark. He said he would go back and get the jeep. He was told it would be about a five-minute hike. When he saw us, he had been hiking up the mountain on a bike trail for at least a half hour with no flashlight or water. He was so very grateful we came along... I told him if it hadn't been my wife wanting to go for a ride we would not have been there, and we were the only vehicle he had seen. He told us we had saved his life.

We finally got to the top, and there was his rental Jeep. He introduced himself and gave us his phone number. He is a doctor on a cardio team at the Beth Israel hospital in New York City. He said this was his first visit to Nevada and after this afternoon maybe his last. He gave us his phone number and invited us to New York City and promised a tour of the city. I hope we can take him up on it. By the way, Vegas was so beautiful from the top and the sunset so awesome.... it was so quiet and peaceful as we watched the doctor drive down the road to safety... perfect timing (just can't get away from those doctors).

———

I know why David wrote so many Psalms. There is power in speaking (or writing) your faith. David so often made the statements like, "I will trust," or "I will praise," or "You are the rock, You have healed me; rescued me." Through what he was facing or experiencing he was inspired by the Holy Spirit to claim and proclaim that God was his strength, hope, refuge, deliverer, Savior, and a dozen other declarations of faith.

I, too, am finding that is the only thing that brings sense to my life. Otherwise, all the things I am experiencing with cancer would make me lose heart. For example, I was so glad the doctor told me it would be OK to suspend my daily injections of Lovenox, a deterrent to blood clots, but last night I felt my left arm swelling and a pain in my neck where I had had a blood clot before... At midnight, I called an ER nurse about this and was given the advice to call my doctor this morning or if it became a greater concern to go into the ER. I have to admit that blood clots are very unnerving because they can be such a silent enemy to life and health. As Fran and I discussed it, she was crying and said, "It seems we cannot overcome this... we go ahead one step and then fall back two or three..."

This again was a time when we had to speak our faith...

Zechariah 4:6-7 (my version)

"It is not by might, not by power but by My Spirit says the LORD... this mountain that's before you will become a plain and you will know it is my grace that has done it."

I am believing that in worship and in the word preached today there will be healing in body, soul, and spirit.

September 2, 2012

I wrote these words Sunday morning:

"I am believing that in worship and the word preached today there will be healing in body, soul, and spirit."

I had told people I was going to be in Arizona on Sunday and the plans didn't work out. I got up at 5:00 A. M. struggling with the thought of a blood clot. I had a very bad headache... but as I was typing, I wrote those words. I decided we would visit a church in Vegas we had not been to for years. I told Fran where I wanted to go just an hour before service and we made it on time... Before we left, I was not feeling good but began to quote *Philippians 4:13 NKJV "I can do all things through Christ who strengthens me..."* and went out the door. On the way, I told Fran about quoting that scripture and also *Zechariah 4:6 NKJV 'Not by might nor by power, but by My Spirit,' says the Lord of hosts.'* I told her I was just trying to keep it all together and really needed a time of worship that would minister to me. We walked into this large church, and the pastor saw me, came to me, and talked to me about my struggle with cancer. He told me he was so sorry, as I told him a few things I had been through, but I said, "It cannot destroy my spirit."

The worship started, and the first song was about being able to do all things through Christ who strengthens me. As worship continued, each song was just what I needed. Then the pastor came to administer the communion service, and the worship team began singing *How Great is Our God*. Then into the *Revelation Song* and then to the song called *Healer*.

Then the pastor told the people about his pastor friend who was battling cancer, and the whole church prayed for me. I was prayed for two more times, and then the pastor in charge of the prayer ministry of the church came to me after the service and said they were praying weekly for me. What an awesome service that I believe was orchestrated just for Fran and me. We were weeping through most of the worship service, and I remembered what I had written that morning. I am convinced God is healing me...

We left there and went to a restaurant, and the people who had sat in the same row as we had in church were seated across the aisle from us. We struck up a conversation and before they left one of them came to our table and prayed for me. During the afternoon, I received calls from four different people from around the country who said they were praying for me. I am totally blessed. I know God is listening, but His timing is His timing, and His ways are above my ways, so I know I am in His hands...

It was such a good day. I went to bed hopeful, then got sick during the night, and it carried into the next day. It brought extreme weakness, abdominal pain, and nausea. I have blamed all that on chemo, but today it was different. I rarely vomit, but it led to that this evening. I was so tempted to scream, "This is not fair! I never even got to enjoy any retirement, and now this...!" But I know those feelings only lead to more negative and are not helpful at all.

So I again make a choice that even though the outward man is wasting away, my spirit does not have to succumb to human emotions. I choose to keep my faith in Jesus Christ no matter what comes...that is why I post this Psalm... note this is from a different chapter than I quoted a couple of days ago, but the words are the same:

Psalm 42:11 (NLT)

Why am I discouraged? Why is my heart so sad?
I will put my hope in God!
I will praise Him again— my Savior and my God!

September 4, 2012

Got up in the morning feeling so much better. Not sure what's going on. I was able to eat some Mexican food my wife made, and it was good. I had a much better day today but am not looking forward to my meeting with the oncologist tomorrow. Many friends have told me they would walk away from chemo, but they have never faced the possibility of death being the other option. I will let you know what I have decided tomorrow. I am praying so much to know the right thing to do.

I watched Michelle Obama speak tonight, and she was quite impressive. Tonight, Jena Lee Nardella, from Blood Water Mission prayed the benediction at the DNC. (I am republican but wanted to hear what the other party sounded like.) She thanked God for the saving grace of Jesus and prayed for Romney as well as Obama. Another part of her prayer was, "God, we thank you for the saving grace of Jesus..." and then concluded with a prayer of St. Francis of Assisi from the 1200's. I thought it was a good way to end the session and a good prayer to live by:

> *Lord, make me an instrument of your peace,*
> *Where there is hatred, let me sow love;*
> *Where there is injury, pardon; Where there is doubt, faith;*
> *Where there is despair, hope; Where there is darkness, light;*
> *Where there is sadness, joy;*
> *O Divine Master, grant that I may not so much seek to be consoled*
> *as to console; To be understood as to understand;*
> *To be loved as to love. For it is in giving that we receive;*
> *It is in pardoning that we are pardoned;*
> *And it is in dying that we are born to eternal life.*[15]

Most of the news networks ignored the prayer.... and personally, I thought it was the best part of the night.

I listened to some of the speakers at the DNC tonight, and one of them especially was using children as his emotional hook and talking about how we must help these kids who may someday be doctors, educators, etc. I then thought about the rhetoric on abortion rights and wondered how many doctors, educators, great leaders... never got a chance at life because a mother decided the baby was not worthy of life and made the choice to have the child killed. There have been so many words spoken for Pro-choice (death) and Pro-life that there is nothing I can say that hasn't been said, but like Paul the Apostle said:

> *2 Corinthians 4:3-5 (my paraphrase)*
> *The god of this world has veiled the minds*
> *of those who choose not to believe...*

September 6, 2012

Jeremiah 29:11, 12 NKJV

"For I know the thoughts that I think toward you," says the Lord,
"thoughts of peace and not of evil, to give you a future and a hope.
Then you will call upon Me and go and pray to Me, and I will listen
to you.

The decision has been made that I am off the brutal chemo and will take just the UCLA trial protocol which is protein based and should have minimal side effects. This still could be a placebo, but seems like there is an encouragement to do it for my sake, not the trial's sake.

We had prayed for direction, and I believe this is what God spoke to my heart. If it is a placebo, then my only hope is in Jesus Christ, not any medicine... matter of fact that is where my only hope is. However, my hemoglobin count was so low that they had to choose between a blood transfusion or an iron infusion. The doctor thought the iron infusion would be best. So, I had both infusions today... the anemia and the iron make me very tired, but it seemed a wise way to go.

I took the trial medicine through my port and just as it finished the insurance company agreed to more infusions. The iron always makes me feel wasted for a few hours. But today was a really good day even though I might be a quart low on blood. lol.

I was feeling good and wanted to get up and do things, but after cleaning up the kitchen, making the bed and pretending I was going to clean my garage, I knew I couldn't and decided to lie down and not feel guilty. I have another infusion tomorrow and then each week. I was able to eat normal today, and that was so wonderful...

Today was a good day for me physically. My appetite and some of my energy came back. As we pray tonight, we are confident again that Romans 8:28 is a truth to those who believe in God.

I was reading John 4 today about the woman that Jesus met in Samaria. Some of the translations say that Jesus "must go" to Samaria. Some people say He went there because that was the only road, but I sure look at it as Jesus was on a mission to meet a woman in her secret place and reveal her heart to her and then reveal who He was to her. If you haven't read it lately, grab it and read it.

Now most of us don't have a well that we go to when no one else is around, but there are secret places in our lives that Jesus is the only one that can get into it. Our secret thoughts, fears, dreams, desires, doubt, unbelief, hurts, anger, bitterness, revenge, and lust.

I have found it so amazing how Jesus can just show up, and without condemning or belittling us, He reveals what our secret is and then reveals who He is... The Living Water... where if we embrace His truth we find a refreshing that is better than any of our secret life. His truth sets us free from those strongholds that bind us to a life of turmoil.

The woman at the well was given a new beginning because she met Jesus. Each time I sense the light of Jesus invading my darkness, I find joy knowing that He knows all about me and loves me anyway and sets me free...

———

Psalm 33:11-13 NIV

But the plans of the Lord stand firm forever, the purposes of His heart through all generations. Blessed is the nation whose God is the Lord, the people He chose for His inheritance. From heaven the Lord looks down and sees all mankind...

I did listen to our President accept his party's nomination and appreciated the benediction when the minister prayed for both the President and Mitt Romney. I liked that because regardless of the party or political stand we are still all Americans. I pray that we can elect a President that all of America can be proud of because he is a defender of life and liberty and has a commitment to a moral law based on what Jesus Christ taught. Jesus taught us to love God with all we are and love our neighbor (fellow citizen) as ourselves. Can either candidate do that? I am sure praying for that. That may take a faith change in both men.

September 7, 2012

John 16:33 NKJV

These things I have spoken to you, that in Me you may have peace. In the world you will have tribulation; but be of good cheer, I have overcome the world. "

Today was another iron infusion. Before that, they did a blood test, and my hemoglobin had dropped lower. I had to take an iron infusion, but they told me to go to emergency tonight to get started on a blood transfusion. I gave more blood tonight, and it is back at 9:00 A. M. on Saturday to have the actual transfusion. Life is always full of challenges... but in all these things we are more than conquerors.

September 8, 2012

I'm in the Boulder City Hospital, on my second unit of blood. Just finished some hospital food, and it wasn't bad. Got about two hours to go. Noticed that I am getting color back into my fingers. This should give me more strength... Just read these scriptures:

Jude 1:20, 21 NIV

But you, dear friends, by building yourselves up in your most holy faith and praying in the Holy Spirit, keep yourselves in God's love as you wait for the mercy of our Lord Jesus Christ to bring you to eternal life.

———

I spent six hours in the Boulder City Hospital today receiving a transfusion of two units of blood. I had become very anemic for several reasons, and this will hopefully stabilize my body. I slept a lot of the evening, but late tonight I feel like the energized rabbit and Fran is having a hard time dealing with that as she was busy all day. Got to get a balance to our lives... being a caregiver is tough on her at times. I changed some words in Psalm 21 that I am posting here... you will see why and you could put your name in place of King:

Psalm 21:1-7 NKJV

The "pastor" (King) shall have joy in Your strength, O Lord; And in Your salvation how greatly shall he rejoice! You have given him his heart's desire, And have not withheld the request of his lips. (Selah)

For You meet him with the blessings of goodness; You set a crown of (life) pure gold upon his head. He asked life from You, and You gave it to him — Length of days forever and ever. His glory is great in Your salvation; Honor and majesty You have placed upon him. For You have made him most blessed forever; You have made him exceedingly glad with Your presence. For the pastor (King) trusts in the Lord, And through the mercy of the Most High he shall not be moved.

September 9, 2012

Today I felt new energy trying to convince my mostly inactive legs, arms, and body that I could do more than I have been doing and that felt good. Fran and I were invited to attend Bethany Baptist Church in Boulder City this morning to take part in an ordination service for Chaplain Bob, the one who came to my rescue so many times when I could not fulfill my duties. I was so thrilled when the Nevada State Veterans Home chose him to succeed me. We enjoyed worshiping with our friends there. Pastor Kurt brought a very good message from John 10 about Jesus being the Good Shepherd. The church provided a wonderful meal after the service in honor of the ordination. There were about a dozen residents from the veteran's home that attended. It was the first time I had seen them since I had to resign. They seem genuinely glad to see me. That indeed blessed me.

———

Matthew 9:35-38 NKJV

Then Jesus went about all the cities and villages, teaching in their synagogues, preaching the gospel of the kingdom, and healing every sickness and every disease among the people. But when He saw the multitudes, He was moved with compassion for them, because they were weary and scattered, like sheep having no shepherd. Then He said to His disciples, "The harvest truly is plentiful, but the laborers are few. Therefore pray the Lord of the harvest to send out laborers into His harvest. "

Listening to the sermon this morning about Jesus being the Good Shepherd, the Door, and the One who would lay down His life for His followers made me look at this scripture with interest. If you have ever been to a cancer center on a regular basis, you see the dozens of people who are in such need. I have been at the University Hospital ER in Las Vegas and have seen the incredible amount of suffering people that are seeking help. I have been in my office and had a half of a dozen people in just a few hours seeking for more help than we could give. You have seen the homeless and hurting of every community and if you care... if you care just a little, it is overwhelming. Read these verses, and it seems that Jesus came to the place that He realized He needed help to do what He came to do...

Compassion for the helpless was so strong He asked His disciples to pray for laborers to help touch the hurting of the world. Jesus came not to bring a utopia to the world, but to give every person the chance to know the God who could help them overcome the burden of a sin destroyed world... He had compassion...

As Fran and I prayed tonight for our family, BCA, friends with cancer, students with needs, and people in general, we were moved with compassion because there are so many who need to know the love of God and the peace of God that passes all understanding. We were asking God for another chance to minister to people who have never found the wonder of a personal relationship with Jesus Christ. We prayed for another chance to minister to people so they could find the joy of their salvation and could know the presence of God in their lives and live in the passion of the reality of our loving God. I would hope that some who read this will also open their hearts to God and hear God say, "As I sent Jesus, so send I you."

September 10, 2012

The second day after two units of blood and it has been a day of grace, not feeling sick... just a little weary, but all in all feeling good. I know that God still has a plan for my life as I am willing to seek it.

I spent some time watching TLC tonight as they aired some rarely seen pictures and videos of the terror of 9/11, 2001. It still stirs my emotions and my anger that such things can be done to humans by humans. And still this week there have been suicide murders by the dozens all over the Middle East. What tragedy that someone could love an ideology so much they are willing to kill themselves as they murder innocent people. One of the comments made by survivors of the twin towers was "Why me? Why am I alive...?" I think that would be good for all of us to answer... what is our purpose? Why am I surviving cancer today and feeling so good when thousands died today from cancer? Maybe the following scripture is an answer?

James 4:13-15 NKJV

Come now, you who say, "Today or tomorrow we will go to such and such a city, spend a year there, buy and sell, and make a profit"; whereas you do not know what will happen tomorrow. For what is your life? It is even a vapor that appears for a little time and then vanishes away. Instead you ought to say, "If the Lord wills, we shall live and do this or that."

So, my goal is that I will attempt to do what Paul says in

Romans 12:1-2 NKJV

I beseech you therefore, brethren, by the mercies of God, that you present your bodies a living sacrifice, holy, acceptable to God, which is your reasonable service. And do not be conformed to this world, but be transformed by the renewing of your mind, that you may prove what is that good and acceptable and perfect will of God.

Romans 1:16 KJV

For I am not ashamed of the gospel of Christ: for it is the power of God unto salvation to everyone that believeth; to the Jew first, and also to the Greek.

I love this scripture about power.

I attended an event held at the Nevada State Veterans Home honoring the new chaplain who succeeded me. It warmed my heart to see how Chaplain Bob has been so well received and accepted. I even got a chance to speak and give praise that God has raised this man up for such a time as this. The residents were so gracious to him (and even remembered me). It was a good time.

September 11, 2012

Isaiah 40:31 NKJV

But those who wait on the Lord shall renew their strength; They shall mount up with wings like eagles, they shall run and not be weary, They shall walk and not faint.

If you have been keeping up with my battle with cancer, I want to let you know that today was as normal as I have felt since last year. All your prayers have brought me to this place. Today I mowed the lawn without hardly any trouble, I cleaned the garage, did dishes, made the bed, did some laundry (even folded it), and took my car to get it smogged. It was rejected for a warning light, and I was told if I drove it at least 50 miles at one time it might clear the monitors that had failed. So, I drove 28 miles into Arizona and then back. It passed... So, except for some permanent nerve damage from the chemo, I am doing so well. I am so grateful. I do have to have a needle biopsy of one of my kidneys this week as the CT scan found a growth there. Oh well... should be a piece of cake.

Last night I prayed with great passion that God would send rain to stop the fires near where I once pastored in Idaho (Riggins). Today it rained here, more than it ever has on any September day in recorded history. Vegas had horrific flooding; some areas had more than two inches of rain in a very short period of time. I get the feeling that someone got the answer mixed up; I am sure I specified near Lucille, Idaho. I still am praying that the mountains of Idaho get some good steady rain.

September 12, 2012

Lamentations 3:22-25 NKJV

Through the Lord's mercies we are not consumed, because His compassions fail not. They are new every morning; great is Your faithfulness. The Lord is my portion, says my soul, Therefore I hope in Him! The Lord is good to those who wait for Him, to the soul who seeks Him.

Got to do two of my least fun things today. I went to the DMV and got an iron infusion at the cancer center. Actually, the DMV was fairly seamless and only waited about a half hour. Paying the money hurt. Did lab work at the doctors and my hemoglobin was up from 7. 5 to 10. 5 (should be around 13) but 10. 5 is the highest for months, thought maybe they wouldn't insist on the iron infusion, but they did, and after a well-deserved nap, I really am doing fine.

It was another exceptional day. Don't have time to tell of all the good things that happened today. One very precious answer to a prayer concerning a granddaughter. She is living in another state with her dad, and we have had only one little message from her since July. For the last couple of days, Fran and I prayed that she would let us know she still cared. I sent her another message, and she responded. She sent a message tonight telling us she loves us and misses us and can't wait to see us again... can't get much better than that...

September 13, 2012

Proverbs 3:5, 6 NKJV

Trust in the Lord with all your heart, and lean not on your own understanding; In all your ways acknowledge Him, And He shall direct your paths.

I am going to the hospital tomorrow to have a CT scan guided needle biopsy of my right kidney. I am praying that it is to prove it is not cancer. I guess I get to lay down for a few hours afterward to make sure there is no bleeding. I have felt so good today that I am having trouble to find reasons to relax in my big chair. It has been my habit for six months to be sick, so having trouble knowing what to do.

Washed my truck, got a haircut, and took my wife to lunch; went to Lowes; bought a lawn rake and a shovel; came home and raked up a trash can full of pine needles and cones. I haven't used my stomach muscles very much since surgery that I could feel them stretching as I raked and bent over. That is a good hurt. Not knowing what to do is when you need to start acknowledging God in your decision-making process. It is an act of faith that gives you confidence that the above scripture can really be true in your life.

September 14, 2012

Psalm 37:3-7

Trust in the Lord, and do good; Dwell in the land, and feed on His faithfulness. Delight yourself also in the Lord, And He shall give you the desires of your heart. Commit your way to the Lord, Trust also in Him, And He shall bring it to pass. He shall bring forth your righteousness as the light, and your justice as the noonday. Rest in the Lord, and wait patiently for Him;

There are so many promises to the believer in the Bible that it takes almost the whole book to list them.

I was so tense and nervous about the procedure which included going in and out of the CT scan at least a dozen times so they could position the needle correctly that would take the biopsy.

The tech showed me the needles that would go into my kidney, and that did not help my anxiety at all. They gave me at least three shots of localized lanacane. The first one was the only one that hurt a little. I was very glad when I heard the doctor say, only one more snip. After at least five different types of needles, the kidney biopsy was finished.

I had to spend about three hours in a recovery room to make sure of no bleeding then home to rest for as long as I could. (I am getting really good at that). It all took about six hours with recovery. I get the pathologist report on Wednesday.

Tomorrow Fran and I are going on a road trip to Sun Valley, Idaho to spend a few days away from the desert. We are leaving in a few hours. Hope to see family and go to Riggins and Kamiah to visit the cemeteries where our late spouses are buried. It will be a special time for us.

We look forward to cool nights and pleasant days.

One of the things I had really wanted to do when it looked like death would come before feeling good, was to visit the gravesite of where my first wife is buried... I never thought I would ever get to but the Lord willing I will be there next week. I have tried to delight myself in the Lord, and I believe He is giving me a desire of my heart.

We would cherish your prayers for Fran and me to have the strength and the refreshing we both need.

September 17, 2012

Psalm 34:2-6 NKJV

My soul shall make its boast in the Lord; The humble shall hear of it and be glad. Oh, magnify the Lord with me, and let us exalt His name together. I sought the Lord, and He heard me, and delivered me from all my fears. They looked to Him and were radiant, and their faces were not ashamed. This poor man cried out, and the Lord heard him, and saved him out of all his troubles.

In Ketchum, Idaho.... 46 degrees this morning... Enjoyed church at River Assembly yesterday. We had fresh Idaho corn on the cob, fried chicken, and watermelon for dinner last night prepared by my wife and sister-in-law. They are great cooks. I haven't had fried chicken for so long... Enjoying being in Idaho.

September 18, 2012

Psalm 37:23-25 NKJV

The steps of a good man are ordered by the Lord, And He delights in his way. Though he fall, he shall not be utterly cast down; For the Lord upholds him with His hand. I have been young, and now am old; Yet I have not seen the righteous forsaken, nor his descendants begging bread.

Fran and I are still in Ketchum with my brother Lyle and his wife, Lynn. Our sister Carol came down from Homedale today, and we celebrated Lyle and Lynn's 41st wedding anniversary. They celebrated today by riding bicycles to Hailey and back (22 miles). Lyle was having a rough time walking and sitting tonight when we went to dinner. I had to laugh at his discomfort, but at the same time, I was proud of his 41 years and 22 miles (at 6000 ft.). Fran and I walked to town and back (about a mile) and were satisfied with that.

My family joined me for our prayer time tonight and what a blessing.

September 19, 2012

Fran and I drove and rode over 450 miles today as we went from Ketchum to Kamiah and back to Riggins. We got a surprise of a lifetime when my sister Lewanna and her daughter Laura showed up in the lobby of our hotel here in Riggins. It was great!

So, I have three sisters, one brother, two of their spouses, and one niece here. There are nine of us staying in the Best Western on the Salmon River which is really nice except for the thick smoke from huge fires around the area. Fran and I had to check on cemetery plots in Riggins and Kamiah purchased when our first spouses died. This very unplanned reunion has been so fun.

September 20, 2012

Philippians 1:6, 12, 19-21 NKJV

"Being confident of this very thing, that He who has begun a good work in me will complete it until the day of Jesus Christ; But I want you to know, brethren, that the things which happened to me have actually turned out for the furtherance of the gospel, For I know that this will turn out for my deliverance through your prayer and the supply of the Spirit of Jesus Christ, according to my earnest expectation and hope that in nothing I shall be ashamed, but with all boldness, as always, so now also Christ will be magnified in my body, whether by life or by death. For to me, to live is Christ, and to die is gain.

These scriptures are meaningful to me since having been told I have terminal cancer.

We are back in Ketchum. We had such a wonderful time. I was able to get to see Pastor and Kathy Scheline and see the new parsonage that is so well done; saw the better half of Ed and Donna Jones; met the pastor of the community church, and stopped to see Lou and Noel Buchannan (Lou was gone to town, bummer) but Noel is one of my most favorite people...got some documents from city hall that showed I really was elected and served as a city council member in November of 1983. With all that and four of my siblings and family getting together and finding garnets by the Salmon River it was more than I could have imagined. Today was actually six months to the day since surgery, and I am sure my surgeon would be surprised that I drove over 700 miles in two days and am going strong... I give God the glory!

September 22, 2012

Isaiah 40:29-31 KJV

He giveth power to the faint; and to them that have no might He increaseth strength. Even the youths shall faint and be weary, and the young men shall utterly fall: But they that wait upon the Lord shall renew their strength; they shall mount up with wings as eagles; they shall run, and not be weary; and they shall walk, and not faint.

We are back home, 2100 miles later. Gas was so expensive, but I justified it as I thought (negatively) that this might be the last time I ever get to visit my first wife's burial site or with Fran to visit her husband's grave. We did both, and it was very moving for both of us. My brother Lyle and sisters, Lewanna, Carol and Patricia, Lyle's wife Lynn, Patricia's husband Dwight and Lewanna's daughter Laura all joined me in Riggins, Idaho where I pastored 30 years ago. We were all surprised how many people still recognized me or remembered me. Very gratifying. My strength and energy were like old times... and whatever I needed to do I did even at 6000 feet...

———

Lamentations 3:22, 23 NKJV

Through the Lords mercies we are not consumed, because His compassions fail not. They are new every morning; Great is Your faithfulness.

Back home last night at 10:30 P. M. - drove nearly the whole way... feeling good today... I am so blessed... Fran and I had such a great trip with so many memories of the past and those we made this week.

———

Galatians 2:20, 21 NKJV

... and the life which I now live in the flesh I live by faith in the Son of God, who loved me and gave Himself for me. I do not set aside the grace of God; for if righteousness comes through the law, then Christ died in vain.

For six months, I have been challenged by cancer, cancer treatment, surgery, feeding tubes, biopsies, CT-scans and hundreds of shots and IVs and this past week has been almost like BC (before cancer). I still have not heard the results of the kidney biopsy done a week ago, but hopefully, no news is good news. I will find out by Wednesday when I have blood tests and a couple of treatments. Suspension of the FOLFOX-6 chemo has allowed life to come back into my body. But I believe it is more than that. I believe that God has responded to the prayers of hundreds of people on my behalf. He has given me another chance to enjoy life. The life I live is because of the grace of God... if the chemo worked, it was because God answered our prayers that the medicine would do what the scientists and doctors hoped it would.

September 23, 2012

Saturday evening my son, Jon, invited me to join him, his wife and son (Caiden) at the water park. They were also taking care of two little girls, the oldest one is four. I knew her from when she came to church when I was pastoring BC Assembly. She saw me coming, and she was staring at me... I asked if she remembered me. She said yes, and so I asked if she remembered my name? She said, "You are Jesus." She called me that at church, and we all worked to get her to call me Pastor Duane, Pastor, or Pastor Jordan, and she finally did, but tonight I was Jesus to her again. In the swing she would say, "Jesus, swing me,"; when on the slide, "Jesus, watch me or help me;" "Jesus, let's play hide and seek..." At that park, there is a pipe fixed up to transmit voices from about 20 feet like a phone... When she said, "Come on Jesus, let's talk!" I thought wouldn't that be good to say to Jesus more often. What a fun night and then watching my 10-month old grandson taking some of his first steps was very joyous.

September 24, 2012

The past couple of nights we have had company and I just never got to the care page to write. Although I have had a new sense of energy, I have found that when I exert energy to do more than I have done for some time, I get tired quickly and my big chair calls for me. lol... I do not know if it is because I am so out of shape, or if I am getting anemic again or if it is still the residue of the chemo, but I sure get tired quickly.

Today I decided to go to a "pick-a-part wrecking yard" (a salvage yard) and try to find a part for an old Ford Bronco that my brother and I put a larger engine in. My son and I love to use it in the desert. It needs some things you can't buy in a parts store. I hadn't been to this yard for a year or so, and it was bizarre... everything was paved or concrete... no gravel or dirt, just row after row of hundreds of vehicles all on stands made from old wheels on concrete. It was so clean and organized... I think I walked a mile carrying a toolbox. I checked every Ford Bronco and Explorer there and could not find the part I needed. But wrecking yards used to be my favorite place to go, so it was a treat for me. It was kind of fun, but I had to make the trek back to my truck. By the time I got home, I needed my big chair.

Got home and all I could think of was resting... maybe it's because I am getting old? One of the reasons I stopped chemo was because the neuropathy was getting worse. I have numbness in my feet and ankles and in the ends of my fingers because of the chemo. Walking for a long distance is a challenge as at times my toes are so numb I lose my balance if I am not careful. But the good thing is that I can walk.

I have not heard anything about my biopsy, and honestly, I am not in a hurry. However, I am sure to find out tomorrow when I go in for blood tests, meet with the oncologist and then take an infusion of the trial medicine and iron. That all takes about three hours. Don't think there will be side effects (I hope).

It seems that the better I have felt, the less I have to say about trusting in God for my health. In my prior posts, all I could talk about was God being my hope and my strength. He was my only, only positive thing I had in those dark hours of being so sick. However, in the past few weeks, I have had new energy, strength, and no nausea and it's like I find myself not having to be so dependent upon my faith. I still know God is my eternal hope and my source of all I need, but not having a real crisis in front of me has somehow taken the edge off that desire for Him. Now that I am feeling better, I feel like I kind of have been lulled into a complacency in my prayer, my devotion and my focus of the One who is the author and finisher of my faith. I am glad that the reality of this has not gone unnoticed as it is so easy (for me) just to drift away from the apex (Jesus Christ) of my faith. I am glad I have recognized that and knowing that has made me try to shake off the complacency and to seek Him with new diligence. I don't want to be a fair/bad weather believer. I know I need Him no matter what is going on in my life. These scriptures have helped me just today:

Hebrews 11:1, 6 KJV

Now faith is the substance of things hoped for, the evidence of things not seen. But without faith it is impossible to please Him: for He that cometh to God must believe that He is, and that He is a rewarder of them that diligently seek Him.

Paul told us how to renew that faith...

Hebrews 12:1-2 NKJV

Therefore we also, since we are surrounded by so great a cloud of witnesses, let us lay aside every weight, and the sin which so easily ensnares us, and let us run with endurance the race that is set before us, looking unto Jesus, the author and finisher of our faith, who for the joy that was set before Him endured the cross, despising the shame, and has sat down at the right hand of the throne of God.

Romans 12:1-2 NKJV

I beseech you therefore, brethren, by the mercies of God, that you present your bodies a living sacrifice, holy, acceptable to God, which is your reasonable service. And do not be conformed to this world, but be transformed by the renewing of your mind, that you may prove what is that good and acceptable and perfect will of God.

For today, I choose to seek Him regardless of my circumstances... Today I choose to focus my faith on the One who has and will be my hope and my strength...

September 26, 2012

I am developing a complex... I think someone must really be mad at me... Lol... I just got the results of the kidney biopsy, and it says I have kidney cancer... three different cancers: prostate (eight years ago), stomach and now kidney cancer. Am I a cancer magnet? All treatment is suspended except iron infusion. UCLA dropped me immediately when they found out I had another cancer in my body at the same time. Since the stomach cancer is stable, there is no move to use chemo until the kidney thing is dealt with.

So here I go again. I am waiting for an appointment with a urologist to hear options that may be available. I don't like this at all but it is what it is, and I will not be sucked into fear or feeling sorry for myself. God was well aware of this announcement today. He is the same yesterday, today and forever... I can trust Him...

Please pray for Fran, she had to go back to work after the doctor broke the news and she said she broke down in tears in the car in the parking lot. It is harder on the one watching all this happen...

The following scripture is my strength tonight. I know that what I am going through is minute compared to what many people have faced and overcome. I refuse to let this disease dictate my faith or to destroy my peace or take away my hope. I am persuaded...

Romans 8:38, 39 NKJV

For I am persuaded that neither death nor life, nor angels nor principalities nor powers, nor things present nor things to come, nor height nor depth, nor any other created thing, shall be able to separate us from the love of God which is in Christ Jesus our Lord.

———

Psalm 37:23 KJV

The steps of a good man are ordered by the Lord:
and he delighteth in his way.

Psalm 37:24-28 KJV

Though he fall, he shall not be utterly cast down: for the Lord upholdeth him with His hand. I have been young, and now am old; yet have I not seen the righteous forsaken, nor his seed begging bread. He is ever merciful, and lendeth; and his seed is blessed. Depart from evil, and do good; and dwell for evermore. For the Lord loveth judgment, and forsaketh not His saints;

There are portions of the Bible that have just the right words for what we as humans go through. Psalm 37 is one such series of truths... Seems very simple and straightforward... walking in it is easier said than done.

September 27, 2012

When someone says, "This is the worst day of my life," they are clueless about what may still be ahead. After an amazing number of "worst days" of my life days, I decided those days should become stepping stones, learning sessions and times of looking for victory rather than defeat or succumbing to depression. The bottom line is there will be rough, tough and "worst days" for all of us.

Jesus said in John 16:33, "*In the world you will have tribulation...*" It is easy to agree with that part, but He went on and said, "*Be of good cheer.*" There must be a difference between cheer and good cheer... Good cheer must be the deep, unshakeable, solid joy that nothing can steal away. That comes from believing that Jesus really did mean He has overcome this world of sorrow and hurt and has given us the power and right to walk in triumph rather than anger, disappointment, despair, and defeat.

Yesterday had the potential of being a "worst day" finding out I now have two cancers to deal with, but I chose to practice what I preach... (At least for today... tomorrow could be another "worst day" that will force me to choose again how I respond). If all of that is too spiritual to handle, do as someone has said... "Eat a live toad the first thing in the morning, and for that day, things can't get much worse."

September 28, 2012

Someone told me I needed to read the lyrics to the Easter Hymn, "He Lives" ("I Serve A Risen Savior") so I did and decided to post them here... Maybe someone else will be blessed by it...

I serve a risen Savior, He's in the world today;
I know that He is living, Whatever men may say;
I see His hand of mercy, I hear His voice of cheer,
And just the time I need Him He's always near.

Chorus:

He lives, He lives, Christ Jesus lives today!
He walks with me and He talks with me
Along life's narrow way. He lives, He lives, salvation to impart!
You ask me how I know He lives: He lives within my heart.
In all the world around me I see His loving care,
And though my heart grows weary I never will despair;
I know that He is leading Thro' all the stormy blast,
The day of His appearing will come at last.

####

Rejoice, rejoice, O Christian, lift up your voice and sing
Eternal hallelujahs To Jesus Christ the King!
The hope of all who seek Him, the help of all who find,
None other is so loving, So good and kind.[16]

"HE LIVES"
Words and Music by Alfred Ackley
©1933 Word Music LLC (ASCAP)
All rights administered by WB Music Corp.

WB Music Corp. 100%
On behalf of Word Music LLC

September 29, 2012

Fran and I, along with son Rob, drove to Phoenix last night to see my daughter Suzi's family and celebrate our oldest grandson's birthday. After the party, we took Rob to the airport to fly back to Portland, Fran and I drove to Tucson to see our good friend Lance who is recovering from treatment for cancer.

It was a good visit, and he insisted we not get a hotel room but stay at his house. So here we are in Tucson, AZ, believing that God can use us to encourage our friend and to be encouraged. I believe that regardless of prayers answered or not, when we have exhausted all of our resources to beat cancer or any other life-threatening situation, there is only one place where we can find hope, peace, and courage. I have posted this verse many times, but for me, I need to cherish the truth of these simple words:

Proverbs 3:5-8 NKJV

Trust in the Lord with all your heart, and lean not on your own understanding; In all your ways acknowledge Him, And He shall direct your paths. Do not be wise in your own eyes; Fear the Lord and depart from evil. It will be health to your flesh, and strength to your bones.

Today at my grandson's birthday party, I got to meet Jill Leebrick, one of my daughter's friends who has posted a few times on my CarePage. She and others like her always lift my spirits when I read what they post. The scripture below reminds me of those who are encouragers:

2 Corinthians 1:3, 4 NKJV

Blessed be the God and Father of our Lord Jesus Christ, the Father of mercies and God of all comfort, who comforts us in all our tribulation that we may be able to comfort those who are in any trouble, with the comfort with which we ourselves are comforted by God.

September 30, 2012

Jude 20-21 NKJV

But you, beloved, building yourselves up on your most holy faith, praying in the Holy Spirit, keep yourselves in the love of God, looking for the mercy of our Lord Jesus Christ unto eternal life.

This morning Fran and I spent our worship time being with and helping our friend in the hospital. He had a car in the parking garage and needed it taken to his home away from home in Tucson. It was pretty funny with us looking for his car at that huge hospital. He told us the floor it was on and we looked and looked and looked and finally realized we were in the wrong garage... We found it and got it home.

Understandably, our friend is discouraged... he has been so sick for so long that it is hard to believe that God really is there or if He is there that he really cares... Most of us have a belief that there is a Higher Power than us... we have to, or else we cannot wrap our mind around all the unknowns in life. However, that also complicates things because when bad things happen to us, and there seems to be no change no matter how hard we pray or believe it seems to knock faith right out of our being. I think we all have been at that point: questioning our faith and our beliefs. I know I have. I have looked at circumstances that have no answer and have seen this become a tool in the hands Satan to attempt to pry faith from me. You probably know what I mean.

The New Testament says, "We walk by faith, not by sight" ... that faith is the substance (the only tangible thing that we can grasp when walking in the unknown) of things hoped for, and it is the evidence of things not seen... When despair invades our lives, we can retreat into depression and anger at God and play the blame game, or we can begin to strengthen ourselves in the Lord and let faith begin to do its work in our spirit. When we read the Word, speak the Word, pray the Word, sing the Word, and listen to the Word, there is a power that springs within us that can overcome the greatest power of despair, and of course, that is faith. When you cannot read, sing your faith... when you cannot sing, listen to someone else sing their faith... Worship builds faith... build your faith...

———

Home again... Nothing like driving from Boulder City to Phoenix, to Tucson to Phoenix and back to Boulder City and all we did in 48 hours. It was a great time. On the one hand, celebrating my grandson's birthday and on the other spending time with a friend who is valiantly fighting cancer in a Tucson hospital. It was hard to leave my friend as he is alone without family until tomorrow. Please pray for Lance: for healing and hope. I have several friends who are in a life and death struggle with cancer... Personally, I have found this scripture to be such an incredible source of strength and hope... it embodies my belief in this life and in life after life...

Psalm 23 NKJV

The Lord is my shepherd; I shall not want. He makes me to lie down in green pastures; He leads me beside the still waters. He restores my soul; He leads me in the paths of righteousness For His name's sake. Yea, though I walk through the valley of the shadow of death, I will fear no evil; For You are with me; Your rod and Your staff, they comfort me. You prepare a table before me in the presence of my enemies; You anoint my head with oil; My cup runs over. Surely goodness and mercy shall follow me all the days of my life; And I will dwell in the house of the Lord Forever.

October 2, 2012

Today I got up with the energy to mow the lawn, trim, use the blower on the driveway and sidewalk and sweep all the debris. I took the trash out, cleaned up the dishes and the kitchen and took clothes out of the dryer and hung and put them away. This was while Fran was sick in bed with perhaps the flu or a really bad cold.

A Christian neighbor stopped by and we talked about faith and dealing with things we cannot change. She told me about a sermon series online about faith (which I listened to one). Then she asked me what I am going to do with my time...That question, without her knowing it, was so loaded that it began to eat at me all day long.

I retired from pastoring 10 months ago and have been sick almost eight months out of that time. I turned 67 while I was the sickest. In the past few weeks, I began to feel like I was getting my life back. But now I find I have another cancer to deal with, and I have to tell you, today I began to get discouraged. I began to rationalize with myself that I have very little future that will mean anything. I thought about getting a job or maybe looking for a smaller church that could use a seasoned pastor and then I thought about what my resume would look like... A 67-year-old man who is fighting stomach and kidney cancer is looking to put his skills to use. There were some other things, but they affected me enough that I didn't want to pray tonight...but I did anyway and began to confess my weaknesses and God's strength. As I did this, prayer was easier, and something began to stir in my spirit.

I remembered these words that Jesus spoke:

John 6:63 NKJV

It is the Spirit who gives life; the flesh profits nothing. The words that I speak to you are spirit, and they are life.

And the words of that verse began to do something in me that I couldn't. Life began to chip away at the discouragement... Then I remembered this verse:

Jude 20 NLT

But you, dear friends, must build yourself up in your most holy faith, pray in the power of the Holy Spirit...

"Pray in the power of the Holy Spirit...?" I heard in my spirit, not just my mind that there is a power of the Holy Spirit that does give life and I needed that to overcome the discouragement... And although nothing has changed in my circumstances, once again God has come to reinforce my faith and give me hope.

Here are some other verses I began to meditate on:

Acts 1:8 NKJV

But you will receive power when the Holy Spirit comes upon you. And you will be my witnesses, telling people about Me everywhere— in Jerusalem, throughout Judea, in Samaria, and to the ends of the earth.

Ephesians 6:18 NKJV

Praying always with all prayer and supplication in the Spirit, being watchful to this end with all perseverance and supplication for all the saints...

Romans 8:26-27 NKJV

Likewise the Spirit also helps in our weaknesses. For we do not know what we should pray for as we ought, but the Spirit Himself makes intercession for us with groanings which cannot be uttered.

1 Corinthians 2:4-5 NKJV

And my speech and my preaching were not with persuasive words of human wisdom, but in demonstration of the Spirit and of power, that your faith should not be in the wisdom of men but in the power of God.

1 Corinthians 14:15 NKJV

What is the conclusion then? I will pray with the Spirit, and I will also pray with the understanding. I will sing with the Spirit, and I will also sing with the understanding.

The Spirit helps us when we cannot help ourselves, and I am so blessed for that.

October 5, 2012

Posting to these pages has seemed harder lately for several reasons, but I know that by typing out words that are my feelings seems to always help.

Some of the pre-chemo symptoms are recurring as well as some new health issues. Having a second cancer working in my body is stressful.

Years ago, we were in a building project at the first church I pastored. It was an exciting time and yet stressful as it was the first time I had ever done anything like this. It was before YouTube, mp3 players and streaming live sermons so I was in a tape club in which I received three tapes each month (unless I failed to send them back). Being so busy I hadn't listened to the last tape of the set and put them aside for a couple of months. On a day when I was discouraged over some trying circumstances, I had opened my Bible that morning to Zechariah 4:6-7 and read some very familiar verses... and during the day I kept remembering them:

Zechariah 4:6-7 NKJV

So he answered and said to me: "This is the word of the Lord to Zerubbabel: 'Not by might nor by power, but by My Spirit, 'Says the Lord of hosts. 'Who are you, O great mountain? Before Zerubbabel you shall become a plain! And he shall bring forth the capstone with shouts of "Grace, grace to it!"

That night I decided as I went to bed to put the last tape in and listen with earphones while my wife was sleeping. I pushed the play button, and it was Jack Hayford who said... "I want to talk to you today from Zechariah 4:6-7..." I sat up in bed and was totally alert. God knew I needed that sermon on that day. Pastor Hayford touched every issue I was facing in my soul that night. I listened and prayed... it was a life-changing moment as this man spoke that by God's grace we would make it through this building program with the grace of God. To a young pastor, it was an awesome reminder that God knows what we are going through and makes all things work together for good for believers. We finished the building...

—

2 Thessalonians 3:16 NKJV

Now may the Lord of peace Himself give you peace always in every way. The Lord be with you all.

A couple of nights ago, I was feeling very down, and my son, Jon, and Re brought our 11-month old grandson to see us. Caiden is so full of energy and generally so happy that he truly cheered me up. I know that the joy of the Lord is my strength, and this little guy helped me look beyond my own problems and enjoy the moment.

October 6, 2012

Fran and I had such a busy weekend. Friday, we were blessed by a delayed 25th-anniversary gift from our kids that was a helicopter flight up the Colorado River a bunch of miles into the west end of the Grand Canyon. What an incredible treat.

After we got back, we were asked to take our granddaughter to a softball scrimmage because her parents were unable to. Then again last night to her first game and then we agreed to keep our 11-month old grandson overnight.

That was all great, but there was a longing in our heart to go to church because it is such an important part in the lives of Christians. Having pastored for 35 years, it has been such a change to no longer be involved in leading a service. Many times I have heard that you don't really appreciate some things as you should until they are no longer available to you. In this case that seems very true.

One thing I have also noticed is that any of us can become numb and insensitive to worship and the presence of God. When that happens, we become dull in our passion and can easily miss what God desires to bless us with.

The thing is that when the privilege of being in a worship service is taken away, or we withdraw because something wasn't quite the way we liked it, we may discover how much we have missed being in the presence of God in a worship service.

I found this Psalm that David wrote:

Psalm 143:4-8 NLT

I am losing all hope; I am paralyzed with fear. I remember the days of old. I ponder all your great works And think about what you have done. I lift my hands to you in prayer. I thirst for you as parched land thirsts for rain. Come quickly, Lord, and answer me, for my depression deepens. Don't turn away from me, or I will die. Let me hear of your unfailing love each morning, For I am trusting you. Show me where to walk, for I give myself to you.

Psalm 84:1-2 NLT

How lovely is your dwelling place, O Lord of Heaven's Armies. I long, yes, I faint with longing to enter the courts of the Lord. With my whole being, body and soul, I will shout joyfully to the living God.

Psalm 84:4-5 NLT

What joy for those who can live in Your house, always singing Your praises. What joy for those whose strength comes from the Lord,

Nehemiah 8:10 NLT

*"... Don't be dejected and sad,
for the joy of the Lord is your strength!"*

If it has been a long time since you enjoyed worship or have not been in a worship service, ask God to restore to you the joy of your salvation. Find a church, worship in spirit and in truth... it is not about the song or the leader, the pastor, or even about you, it is about you coming into the presence of the Lord and being strengthened by Him.

October 7, 2012

What a blessing to be in church today and worship with old and new friends. I loved singing songs of worship that stirred my soul. I truly enjoyed singing and meditating on the chorus, "Glorious Day." The words were some I needed today. The pastor's sermon was good for all of us to hear out of the book of Joshua...

Psalm 84:10 NLT
A single day in your courts is better than a thousand anywhere else!

October 8, 2012

Psalm 23:6 (my version)
Surely goodness and mercy have followed me all the days of my life and someday I shall dwell in the house of the Lord forever.

Fran and I drove to our appointment with a new doctor for us, a urologist 45 miles on the Northwest end of Vegas.

We prayed for wisdom last night to be able to determine the best course of treatment for this second cancer. The doctor looked at my records and CT scans and then tried to give us his best plan of action. He saw that I have some small lesions in my lungs and thought the stomach cancer had spread there. I tried to assure him those had been there for years from valley dust (pulmonary doctor's words) ... not sure if he believed me.

He then said the kidney cancer is a very slow growing cancer and it would be best to concentrate on the cancer that was incurable (stomach) and wait until the next CT scan to see which cancer was the more serious. He said surgery would probably be more harmful to my body at this point than the kidney cancer is. He was trying to say in a diplomatic way that the stomach cancer is going to take your life so why worry about the kidney... So back to the oncologist on Wednesday.

What I have decided is that I want to cherish every day that I have...

This is my scripture of the week... I have read it over and over... read it to Fran tonight and she began to weep and said we should print it out and put it on our bedroom mirror. We talked and agreed that anxiety is detrimental to peace... and as we pray, God's word here promises a peace that surpasses all of our understanding of our circumstances. I am so grateful that we have access to this peace... it is not gritting of our teeth or pulling ourselves up by our bootstraps, but it is a powerful anointing of the Holy Spirit to those who choose to pray and believe over being anxious and fearful.

Philippians 4:6-7 NKJV

Be anxious for nothing, but in everything by prayer and supplication, with thanksgiving, let your requests be made known to God; and the peace of God, which surpasses all understanding, will guard your hearts and minds through Christ Jesus.

I am printing this scripture and putting it on the mirror in our bedroom... Such a powerful reminder that anxiety never changes anything...

October 9, 2012

Wednesday morning is another doctor's appointment. This time the oncologist. Each time I go they draw blood for a lab test so the doctor can see quickly if there is anything that is not right. Not sure what I am going to do in dealing with the cancer issues. Chemo and radiation are the two of the few things that oncologists use to fight the cancer. He will most likely advise more chemo to fight the stomach cancer and watch the kidney cancer. After a busy day running around with my youngest son, I certainly don't want to think about being sick day after day... but I must make a decision for not just my sake but for my family's too. It has been wonderful to be off the chemo and to get my life back, but there are new problems surfacing that when I described them to the urologist yesterday, he just said, "It is most likely the stomach (gastric) cancer that is causing those symptoms." He may be right... That is where fear begins pounding on the door of my life trying to bring panic and anxiety.

Just a note of advice: Until you face choices of life and death, be careful to be slow to speak about what you would do. Jesus showed us that in the life and death struggle in the garden that He cried out for that cup to pass from him... He wanted another way, another day, an easier way. His disciples did not understand the severity of Jesus' battle and fell asleep while He made Himself ready for the last battle. My battle right now is in my face. Is more chemo a good thing to have a longer life? Is not taking chemo a step of faith and the nobler thing to do? We prayed tonight for wisdom and peace... this scripture just kind of popped out at me. I have posted it several times, but it is still free. I truly need to understand and know wisdom:

Isaiah 40:28-31 NKJV

Have you not known? Have you not heard? The everlasting God, the Lord, The Creator of the ends of the earth, neither faints nor is weary. His understanding is unsearchable. He gives power to the weak, and to those who have no might He increases strength. Even the youths shall faint and be weary, and the young men shall utterly fall, but those who wait on the Lord Shall renew their strength; They shall mount up with wings like eagles, they shall run and not be weary, they shall walk and not faint.

October 10, 2012

Sitting in the cancer center-getting an iron infusion. I have an access port in the upper left area of my chest. They pierce the port with a needle to pump chemo or iron into my body rather than an IV in my hand or arm. Before they inject any medicines, the nurses must be able to suction blood from the port. For some reason, I am the only one of the many patients here that they have trouble each time getting that to happen. Today was no exception... They had to lean me back in a chair till I was almost upside down; that didn't work, and the nurse tried several other tricks, and I finally told her I was going to pray... almost immediately she got blood flow... I told her I am going to have to remember to pray before the next time. I tend to always forget to pray first about things in life (except eating).

My hemoglobin blood test showed my blood is healthier than it has been for a long time. I had been to a low of 7.5, and now before the iron treatment, it is 12.1. The doctor was impressed. No treatment has been advised until after a CT scan next week. Hoping no sign of kidney cancer or stomach cancer.

It was a busy day... after the infusion, I took one of my daughters to a very intense interview in downtown Vegas that took quite a while... she needed the moral support, and she did very well.

I, on the other hand, got nauseated after I got home and felt like I was back on chemo. The iron has sometimes done that to me for several hours. Hope it goes away soon.

Have you noticed that for a Christian, hope is not a delusional fantasy but is from an inner anticipation based on faith?

Consider these scriptures:

Romans 15:13 NKJV

Now may the God of hope fill you with all joy and peace in believing, that you may abound in hope by the power of the Holy Spirit.

Hebrews 11:1 KJV

Now faith is the substance of things hoped for, the evidence of things not seen.

October 11, 2012

Psalm 107:27-30 NLT

...and were at their wits' end. "Lord, help!" they cried in their trouble, and He saved them from their distress. He calmed the storm to a whisper and stilled the waves. What a blessing was that stillness (love this picture) as He brought them safely into harbor!

What a beautiful day in the southern Nevada desert. The lightning, thunder, and rain were so welcomed (by me). I was struggling with nausea and abdominal pain (I think from the iron infusion) through the night and into the morning, and it was so nice to be able to lay back down at about 8:00 A. M. and hear the rain and enjoy the darkness so I could get some needed rest. About noon I began to feel much better which was nice... It feels good to feel good...

When the nausea and pain subsided, it reminded me of Psalms 107 and Mark 6 which have similar storylines with men being in boats that are tossed by the sea and then God brings a calm. Just reading those two scriptures tonight reminded me of how God gives to us His peace, forgiveness, and healing and calms the storms of our lives...

Mark 6:47-51 NKJV

Now when evening came, the boat was in the middle of the sea; and He was alone on the land. Then He saw them straining at rowing, for the wind was against them. Now about the fourth watch of the night He came to them, walking on the sea, and would have passed them by. And when they saw Him walking on the sea, they supposed it was a ghost, and cried out; for they all saw Him and were troubled. But immediately He talked with them and said to them, "Be of good cheer! It is I; do not be afraid. " Then He went up into the boat to them, and the wind ceased.

Jesus saw them toiling and straining with little progress and came to them. In other places, Jesus calls us to Him and promises rest when we come, but here He came to them... I am so grateful when in the midst of all my ineffective toiling Jesus comes and calms the storm of my life... I sense that right now...

October 12, 2012

Proverbs 3:5, 6 NKJV

Trust in the Lord with all your heart, and lean not on your own understanding; In all your ways acknowledge Him, And He shall direct your paths.

Fran and I are in Florence, Montana. We flew to Seattle then to Missoula. I had one of those divine appointments on the flight to Seattle and was able to share my faith with a businessman (a pastor's son but has not been to church in years) who has gone through cancer and chemo... it was an encounter that would not have happened if I had not also experienced cancer. So I again know that God can cause all things to work for good as we love Him and follow His calling. I shared with him this scripture (and a lot more) as I assured him he could have a lasting peace regardless of circumstances.

October 13, 2012

Proverbs 3:21-26 NKJV

My son...Keep sound wisdom and discretion; So they will be life to your soul and grace to your neck. Then you will walk safely in your way, and your foot will not stumble. When you lie down, you will not be afraid; yes, you will lie down and your sleep will be sweet. Do not be afraid of sudden terror, nor of trouble from the wicked when it comes; For the Lord will be your confidence, and will keep your foot from being caught.

Woke up in Montana to deer in the yard and my niece telling me (through Fran) to get my lazybones (something like that) out of bed. Dan and Dawn had bacon, eggs, waffles, and coffee waiting for me. It was so nice to be pampered for a little bit. We drove around Missoula (love this area) and then I actually worked a few hours with Dan building stair treads for his deck... It was good to do some manual labor... lol

Many are concerned about the future and who will be our president. I read [these] scriptures that talk about wisdom. If you have time, think and meditate on them.

James 1:5 NKJV

If any of you lacks wisdom, let him ask of God, who gives to all liberally and without reproach, and it will be given to him.

We are headed for church in the morning at Christian Life Center in Missoula, Montana. One of our friends, Pastor Jim Hicks, is on staff there. Look forward to worshipping with them... Hope some of you will find a good church in the morning if you can and look for an encounter with God.

October 15, 2012

Romans 12:9-15, 18 NKJV

Let love be without hypocrisy. Abhor what is evil. Cling to what is good. Be kindly affectionate to one another with brotherly love, in honor giving preference to one another; not lagging in diligence, fervent in spirit, serving the Lord; rejoicing in hope, patient in tribulation, continuing steadfastly in prayer; distributing to the needs of the saints, given to hospitality. Bless those who persecute you; bless and do not curse. Rejoice with those who rejoice, and weep with those who weep. If it is possible, as much as depends on you, live peaceably with all men.

Fran and I are flying from Missoula via Seattle back home. We are at about 37,000 ft. and over 500 miles per hour. What a great way to travel. Thanks, Rob Jordan. We had a wonderful time with Dan and Dawn... they were awesome hosts. Just read the above scriptures, and they affect us where we live. They are one-line principals to live by...

October 16, 2012

I haven't posted here on CarePages for two nights because I felt shaken by some events that were very close to me. Sunday night, after visiting some pastor friends in Missoula, Fran and I drove back to her brother Dan's home where we were staying. Dan was up, and we both started watching some mindless movie that neither of us was into and I decided to check my Facebook. There I learned that two of my friends that I have been talking with and praying for, one in Moscow, Idaho, and the other in Dallas, Texas both died because of cancer that day. Both within hours of each other. I tried to talk about it but could only begin weeping.

Sue Davis, the one in Texas had worked with us in our church in Boulder City, and her family was active in our church before moving to

Texas. Just last week I talked to her and her husband on the phone. I could tell the end was near.

Sonia Todd lived in Idaho. She and her husband had two young sons. Our lives had parallels with the most recent being cancer. About six weeks ago, the doctors told her she had just weeks to live. She celebrated her birthday with a huge party and seemed to never quite get over the exertion.

Both ladies were totally at peace with what seemed to be the inevitable. Sonia and I communicated weekly through Facebook telling each other our adventures with chemo and treatment. We both encouraged each other as we went through our battles.

Sue's funeral is Friday evening, and Sonia's is Saturday morning. But Sunday night, all I could do was cry. Not because I didn't believe that they were with the Lord, but because I felt such a void in my world. I cried for Brian Todd and for James Davis and their families knowing that there were such hard adjustments coming. I have prayed for their peace.

I didn't write because I have been having some acute pains in my stomach and kidney areas and begin to think more about death than life.

With the lives of these two awesome women of God being ended on Earth, I began to feel that I could very well be next. I was sad because knowing Fran and my family will have to handle the void I will leave when I die. On the other hand, I was kind of envious of Sue and Sonia because their battle is over. No more doctors, no more treatment, no more surgeries, no more awful medicines, no more pain, sickness, sorrow and no more concern of the unknown.

So, in many ways, I was dealing with anxiety and not knowing how to deal with what certainly could be a reality. Having dealt with hundreds of people who were dying, I have a wealth of knowledge of what can be said, read and done when one is dying, so I know how to deal with death, even my own, but it is dealing with what I will leave behind that is the unnerving part. Notice this scripture:

John 16:33 NKJV

These things I have spoken to you, that in Me you may have peace. In the world you will have tribulation; but be of good cheer, I have overcome the world.

Jesus said, "I have spoken these things that in Him we could have peace..."
I paraphrase: There is no doubt that in this life, (world) you will have
tribulation, struggles, shortages, needs, sorrow, pain, and tears... no getting
around it. It will happen... I like the big BUT here... But be of good cheer
(I wrote of this before). This cheer is more than just being cheerful... this
is an inner work of the Holy Spirit bringing joy as we believe... the thing
we can be cheerful about is that there is nothing in this world or life that
can win over what Jesus Christ has done and will do in us. I can look up.
I can have hope. I can believe that life is much fuller than just a few days
of sorrow that loss brings... I can trust that Jesus will take care of what I
cannot do... He asks me to trust in Him with all my heart and not to lean
on my own understanding of the situation... I can close my eyes in sleep
on this earth and know that everything will work out for good, or I can
close my eyes in death and know "it is well with my soul."

———

Matthew 6:19-21 NKJV

*"Do not lay up for yourselves treasures on earth, where moth and rust
destroy and where thieves break in and steal; but lay up for yourselves
treasures in heaven, where neither moth nor rust destroys and where
thieves do not break in and steal. For where your treasure is, there
your heart will be also."*

When I talked about being more concerned over what I leave behind than
about facing my own death that is true. In humor, I say, that I am not sure
the world can get along without me, but in reality, I know it will. When
trying to imagine me not being here anymore is difficult. As I look at
what is going on right now as I deal with health issues, I see a type of fear
in Fran's eyes when she sees me wince in pain and when I cannot swallow
my food very well... she doesn't try to show it, but it is there. My kids are
not with me every day, so they don't quite know what I am going through,
and I hate to cry wolf or sound like I am giving up, but they too will find
it hard to deal with if the disease is really beginning to progress. My heart
goes out to my wife, my kids, and grandkids that all seem to love me very
much and I know it will be hard on them when my time comes.

Ecclesiastes 3:2 NKJV

A time to be born, and a time to die;
A time to plant, and a time to pluck what is planted;

I have lived my life believing that God would always take care of me and mine (and He has) but now as I consider me not being here, it is hard because of what I will not leave. I have never made very much money being a pastor in small towns and coming to Boulder City, we spent much of our savings in the early years of planting the church. There were times we did not have enough income to survive had we not used our savings and retirement. We did splurge a few times like traveling to Europe and Japan using our savings, and I have no regrets being with our families there and experiencing what we did.

However, choices like that have left very little inheritance to pass on. We made some unfortunate financial decisions that have consequences now, but there is nothing we can do about that. I have sadness that Fran will not have the comfort of a good retirement from me. I know my kids and grandkids will inherit very little from me as I can leave them little more than memories.

My hope is that the wealth of knowing Jesus will be worth more than houses or lands. I am at peace knowing my life has meant something to a lot of people because of pastoring nearly 40 years. The inheritance I leave is bound up in the Word of God. I hope what I lived and believed is a cherished inheritance they can build their lives on.

As I have struggled with my thoughts concerning lack of retirement and savings, I remembered these verses:

Philippians 3:20-21 NKJV

For our citizenship is in heaven, from which we also eagerly wait for the Savior, the Lord Jesus Christ, who will transform our lowly body that it may be conformed to His glorious body, according to the working by which He is able even to subdue all things to Himself.

Philippians 3:13-14 NKJV

*Brethren, I do not count myself to have apprehended; but one thing I
do, forgetting those things which are behind and reaching forward to
those things which are ahead, I press toward the goal for the prize of
the upward call of God in Christ Jesus.*

For tonight, I will let go of my anxieties and believe the Word.

October 17, 2012

Tomorrow morning I will attempt to drink two containers of berry
flavored barium in preparation for the CT scan with which the doctors
will look for any changes in the stomach and kidney cancers. The doctor
mentioned an endoscopy to see what is going on inside the stomach and
esophagus. Not sure when that will be. I am having continuing symptoms
in my digestive system that makes me aware that things are not normal.
Today there has been pain of several descriptions in my stomach and
bowels. As I said, those things tend to try to make me anxious... and the
scriptures I have posted several times come back to me:

Philippians 4:6-7 NKJV

*Be anxious for nothing, but in everything by prayer and supplication,
with thanksgiving, let your requests be made known to God; and
the peace of God, which surpasses all understanding, will guard your
hearts and minds through Christ Jesus.*

Each night, as I write, there is something supernatural that happens in my
spirit as I describe my problems and then turn to the word of God. Peace
and hope appear from unseen sources. Peace that surpasses understanding
and hope that never leaves one ashamed or embarrassed. I know God had
and has a purpose with my nightly attempt to express myself. I noticed
tonight that there have been 10,070 times people have opened this
CarePage to look and read what I have typed. For that, I am amazed and
humbled. I read the following scriptures in the Message Bible which of
course is a paraphrase, but I happened to like the way this scripture is

expressed: It made me stop and think about who I am and so maybe it will bless you too:

Galatians 6:1-5 MSG

Live creatively, friends. If someone falls into sin, forgivingly restore him, saving your critical comments for yourself. You might be needing forgiveness before the day's out. Stoop down and reach out to those who are oppressed. Share their burdens, and so complete Christ's law. If you think you are too good for that, you are badly deceived. Make a careful exploration of who you are and the work you have been given, and then sink yourself into that. Don't be impressed with yourself. Don't compare yourself with others. Each of you must take responsibility for doing the creative best you can with your own life.

October 18, 2012

Psalm 23:1-6 NKJV

The Lord is my shepherd; I shall not want. He makes me to lie down in green pastures; He leads me beside the still waters. He restores my soul; He leads me in the paths of righteousness for His name's sake. Yea, though I walk through the valley of the shadow of death, I will fear no evil; For You are with me; Your rod and Your staff, they comfort me. You prepare a table before me in the presence of my enemies; You anoint my head with oil; My cup runs over. **Surely goodness and mercy shall follow me All the days of my life; And I will dwell in the house of the Lord Forever.**

I love this scripture... focus on verse six (in bold).

I drank the barium (well most of it... it started to refuse to stay down, so I quit) ... last time I used a clamp to hold my nose shut... didn't have to this time. I had the CT scan and am waiting probably till Wednesday for the results... His grace is sufficient.

Going to take another trip tomorrow to meet my son, Rob, in Seattle; fly to Redmond, Oregon; drive to Silverton to see two of my awesome granddaughters (and their wonderful mom) and then the next day fly to Spokane, Washington to try to get to Moscow, Idaho for the funeral of a person I never met in this life, but am confident I will in heaven (she was only 38). We were kind of a cancer support group, and I got to hear her heart as she wrote about her battle with cancer and her struggle with leaving her family. God gave her so much peace in this walk through the valley of the shadow of death... God gave me words that her husband said were a great inspiration to her. I hope I can make it. Two friends died last Sunday, and their funerals are on the same day... I could only make it to Idaho.

October 19, 2012

1 John 4:10-11 KJV

Herein is love, not that we loved God, but that He loved us, and sent His Son to be the propitiation for our sins. Beloved, if God so loved us, we ought also to love one another.

I flew to Seattle, met my son, Rob, then we flew to Redmond, Oregon and were surprised by Sheila who once attended the church I pastored in Prineville, Oregon. Rob and I then drove over Santiam Pass to Silverton. Rob had wanted me to see the beauty of the Oregon foliage. It was pretty, but the rainy season decided to start today. Rain all the way. Rob has two daughters who love me for no other reason but that I am Grandpa. Both teenagers were so excited to see me, as I was to see them. My daughter-in-law, Jenny built a fire in their fireplace stove, and I enjoyed the warmth so much, as well as her cooking. Family love is as close as it gets to God's love.

October 21, 2012

Saturday, Rob and I got up at 4:00 A. M. and drove to the Portland Airport and flew to Spokane, Washington. (Rob works for an airline so we can fly free if there are seats available). Rob rented a beautiful Buick LaCross that felt like a rocket and got to Moscow just minutes before the funeral of my friend, Sonia Todd. Sonia wrote her own obituary, and last night we know that at least 200 newspapers picked it up and so it has gone viral (check it out: Google "Sonia Todd obituary"). I went to this funeral because Sonia was introduced to me by a mutual friend and thought we could help each other in our fight with cancer. So, by messaging on Facebook, we shared our struggles with the disease, the agony of our treatments, our faith, our hopes, and fears. I never met her but felt like God had given me another daughter... Below is an example of what she wrote to me just weeks before her death:

"Don't tell anyone, but even though I am sad, sometimes I get excited about going to heaven. It is like when you are five years old and you know Christmas is just days away, and you know there is a really special present for you. You don't know what it is, but you know it is waiting for you, and you are so excited you are about to burst. Sometimes when I am sad about dying, that is what I think about. Then I make a list of all the things I don't have to do once I go to heaven--like no diets, no taxes, no pills, no injections, no IVs and transfusions, no more infections, no more vomiting. And, best of all, I think they will still have chocolate."

Here is her obituary:

Sonia Elaine Todd, 38, of Moscow,
died on Sunday, Oct. 14, 2012.

My Obituary

My name is Sonia Todd, and I died of cancer at the age of 38. I decided to write my own obituary because they are usually written in a couple of different ways that I just don't care for. Either, family or friends gather together and list every minor accomplishment from the cradle to the grave in a timeline format, or they try and create one poetic last stanza about someone's life that is so glowing one would think the deceased had been the living embodiment of a deity.

I don't like the timeline format because, let's face it, I never really accomplished anything of note. Other than giving birth to my two wonderful, lovable, witty and amazing sons (James and Jason), marrying my gracious, understanding and precious husband (Brian), and accepting the Lord Jesus Christ as my personal savior—I have done very little. None of which requires obit space that I have to shell out money for.

I also didn't want a bunch of my friends sitting around writing a glowing report of me which we all know would be filled with fish tales, half-truths, impossible scenarios, and out-right-honest-to-goodness-lies. I just don't like to put people in that kind of situation.

The truth, or my version of it, is this: I just tried to do the best I could. Sometimes I succeeded, most of the time I failed, but I tried. For all of my crazy comments, jokes, and complaints, I really did love people. The only thing that separates me from anyone else is the type of sin each of us participated in. I didn't always do the right thing or say the right thing, and when you come to the end of your life, those are the things you really regret, the small, simple things that hurt other people.

My life was not perfect, and I encountered many, many bumps in the road. I would totally scrap the years of my life from age 16 to 20 . . . Ok, maybe 14 to 22. I think that would eradicate most of my fashion disasters and hair missteps from the 80's. But mostly, I enjoyed life. Some parts of it were harder than others, but I learned something from every bad situation, and I couldn't do any more than that.

Besides there are some benefits to dying youngish, for example, I still owe on my student loans and the jokes on them cuz I'm not paying them. Plus, I am no longer afraid of serial killers, telemarketers, or the IRS. I don't have to worry about wrinkles or the ozone layer and/or hide from the news during election season.

Some folks told me that writing my own obituary was morbid, but I think it is great because I get a chance to say thank you to all the people who helped me along the way. Those that loved me, assisted me, cared for me, laughed with me, and taught me things so that I could have a wonderful, happy life. I was blessed beyond measure by knowing all of you. That is what made my life worthwhile.

If you think of me, and would like to do something in honor of my memory do this:

-Volunteer at a school, church, or library
-Write a letter to someone and tell them how they have had a positive impact on your life
-If you smoke - quit
-If you drink and drive—stop
-Turn off the electronics and take a kid out for ice cream and talk to them about their hopes and dreams
-Forgive someone who doesn't deserve it
-Stop at all lemonade stands run by kids and brag about their product
-Make someone smile today if it is in your power to do so[17]

What a precious service for this wonderful 38-year-old mother and wife. I so hurt for her husband and young sons. There were several hundred there to honor her life. She wrote most of the funeral message and emphasized what the Gospel is and who Jesus is... I am sure many were impacted by the message and songs. Rob and I met old friends, Phil and Julie Good, from Riggins, Idaho who now pastor in New Meadows, Idaho. Julie played piano and led us all singing, *"I'll Fly Away"* at the close of the service. This is one scripture that was used.

John 11:25, 26 NKJV

Jesus said to her, I am the resurrection and the life. He who believes in Me, though he may die, he shall live. And whoever lives and believes in Me shall never die.

Do you believe this...?

Rob and I were moved by the service but had to leave quickly to get back to Spokane to fly back to Rob's home. We decided to drive through Coeur d'Alene, Idaho as it had been years since we had been there... we felt bad driving through so quickly because we have family there, but we had a tight schedule to get back to the airport. Northern Idaho and the Spokane area are breathtaking in beauty... We got home at about 9:00 P.M.

Paul the Apostle said, *"For me to live is Christ, but to die is gain. "*

Paul had had visions of heaven and knew something we can only receive by faith. If you read 2 Corinthians 5 and 2 Timothy 4 you can see more of Paul's relationship with eternity.

October 25, 2012

Psalm 56:3-4 KJV

What time I am afraid, I will trust in thee. In God I will praise His word, in God I have put my trust; I will not fear what flesh can do unto me.

Today was the day that I went to see the oncologist again to get the readings on the latest CT scan. The cancer in the kidney has not changed, so that is good, my hemoglobin is the highest it has been for almost a year or more, that is good, the gastric cancer (stomach) was unnoticeable where it was before, so that is good, but they found ascites (fluid-filled nodules) on a membrane (omentum) that connects the stomach with other organs across the middle of my stomach. I have had increased pain in that area in the past couple of weeks as well as pain in my sides and lower intestines... very uncomfortable and the doctor said that was probably caused by the cancer. We discussed treatment. One treatment would cause me to lose my hair and require a pump for four days every three weeks. After eight rounds of brutal chemo, I needed a while to think over all my options so no treatment today.

October 26, 2012

> *James 1:2-4 NLT*
>
> *Dear brothers and sisters, when troubles come your way, consider it an opportunity for great joy. For you know that when your faith is tested, your endurance has a chance to grow. So let it grow, for when your endurance is fully developed, you will be perfect and complete, needing nothing.*

Today I got up feeling somewhat rejuvenated. I am becoming such a domesticated housekeeper. I made breakfast, did the dishes, made the bed and washed, dried, and folded or put away four loads of laundry. Then put my bike in my pickup and drove to a storage shed we need to empty and saw tons of books that I once had in my office library. Sorted through a few boxes and noticed I was not enjoying that very much. I closed the storage unit and drove to a bike park above our little city. It is where you can park and ride on a bike path that makes a 35-mile loop around Boulder City and Henderson and along Lake Mead. No one was there, so I got to try my bike out with no one watching. I have not ridden my bike more than a couple of blocks for about eight months. What a joy to get on it and have the breeze blow in my face as I began riding with a goal to go just to the top of a small hill not more than a quarter of a mile. It was gear one and one before I got to the top and I was breathing hard. Going back down was so fun. I knew I had to take it easy, so I rode around on the mostly level areas for about another mile. I came home and collapsed in my big chair.

Then this evening went to watch my granddaughter, Kaia, play fastpitch softball. Those girls are amazing. Then back to the chair. I probably did more than I should have... my pain is much more noticeable tonight... not looking forward to bed... I will have to have something to kill the pain...

My doctors have offered little hope for my future reminding me this week there is no cure for my cancer. Most cancer patients rejoice in the good days and try to tolerate the other days. Today was a tough day with lots of pain and discomfort. When I mentioned my problems to a doctor, he said it was most likely caused by the cancer. People have offered me many miracle cures and some I tried, but I couldn't swallow or tolerate... So, if one is between a rock and a hard place, where does hope come from? Without hope, depression comes in very strongly. I have decided I must look outside of me... Reading Psalm 91 was good for me today... maybe for you too?

October 28, 2012

John 3:16-17 NKJV

For God so loved the world that He gave His only begotten Son, that whoever believes in Him should not perish but have everlasting life. For God did not send His Son into the world to condemn the world, but that the world through Him might be saved.

Too late to say anything that makes a difference, but here is a scripture that we can all deal with... I put my name in this verse, and you can put your name in it... it is powerful when you read it... For God so loved Duane... that if Duane... you get it, right?

I had such a good seat at the Patriot's game, and then at the World Series... it was my huge recliner...felt so rough today all I could do was sit... but at least I could watch when I was awake... I was dwelling in the secret place of the Most High... I am praying for those on the east coast...

Isaiah 43:2 NKJV

When you pass through the waters, I will be with you; And through the rivers, they shall not overflow you. When you walk through the fire, you shall not be burned, nor shall the flame scorch you.

What can I say? Not too much... had a very rough day but thank God for the comfort of the arms of my easy chair... and His presence and that the Joy of the Lord is my strength. Heard someone say today that God is serious about joy...

"Consider it pure joy," James says, "when you go through various trials..." considering that right now...

October 30, 2012

When we quote the scripture or sing the song, "This is the Day that Lord Has Made," and believe it, it truly is a statement of faith.

Today, this 24-hour gift of time is an opportunity to experience life from a unique position. We have the power to accept the events of the day as negative or as a positive adventure of life.

Last night through a series of unusual events, I ended up in the emergency room (I was actually in the emergency hallway as no beds available) where my youngest daughter is an RN. (Fortunately, she can't treat me). I had an opportunity to drink a contrast for a CT scan, and my stomach did not welcome it at all and there in the hallway a whole lot of people got to share my experience... probably kind of gross for them... lol. They found some disconcerting clues for my condition, and it all came back to cancer and fluid buildup in my abdomen and am seeing my oncologist today about it being drained by needles... I am sure this is a positive adventure of life. This is the day the Lord has made!!!

October 31, 2012

Philippians 4:6, 7 NIV

Do not be anxious about anything, but in every situation, by prayer and petition, with thanksgiving, present your requests to God. And the peace of God, which transcends all understanding, will guard your hearts and your minds in Christ Jesus.

I am up way too late, but sleep is elusive tonight. My son, Jon, Fran, and I met with my oncologist about what happened at ER the night before. The doctor had all the files from ER and had already examined the CT scan report and immediately began to tell me what he believed was going on.

The scan showed that the ascites (fluid) between the omentum and inner layer of skin had increased because of the cancer and this increase was causing pressure on the intestines and was distending my stomach. This was the reason for my pain and the digestive and elimination problems. The fluid was also seeding the whole abdomen with cancer and the only way to slow it was with chemo. As he had said before, this might increase my quantity of life but would rapidly diminish the quality of my life. He said we were not talking years of life (more like months). He said it was time to consider palliative care now (comfort rather than cure) and then hospice. I am having the fluid drained tomorrow which might relieve some of the pain.

So again, Fran and I are facing news that we wanted to live without. Tonight, we talked about the peace and joy of God being our strength. This is not just in words, but I believe it is truly implanted by the Holy Spirit into our hearts and minds.

I thought we had dealt with my mortality before, but now reality and truth were in my face. It was not easy talking about my death but know unless God gives a miracle... I cannot speak for Fran or the rest of my family, but I am at peace... These last 10 months of training have brought me to that place that I have peace.

What I wrote about my latest prognosis that says I need to realize my life is not about years but months is not saying that I am going to roll over and die before I am dead. I am choosing to live life and not worry about death. Thinking about death and pain, and terror is just not a good mindset. Maybe that is why I really do not like Halloween. However, I am so outnumbered in my opinion that I usually don't say anything about it. Being a pastor, I always tried to make this holiday be more of a focus on life rather than death, on joy and fun rather than fear and suffering. I have conducted hundreds of funerals and had hands-on experience with the sorrow side of death and vividly remember trying to comfort the sorrowing family of a murdered child, a father who accidentally shot his son while hunting and the stories go on and on. I do not like celebrating death. I do love the little children coming to my door as they did tonight (at least 50 little kids and dozens of teens) so excited about ringing my doorbell and getting candy... I love making children smile, laugh, and love life. Just wish we didn't have to mix evil and gross with innocent fun. Here is my goal for my life:

Psalm 118:17 NIV

"I will not die (before my time) but live,
and will proclaim what the Lord has done."

I choose to make the most of every day that I have. This is the day that The Lord has made... I will rejoice and be glad in it...

November 1, 2012

Hebrews 12:1-2 NKJV

Therefore we also, since we are surrounded by so great a cloud of witnesses, let us lay aside every weight, and the sin which so easily ensnares us, and let us run with endurance the race that is set before us, looking unto Jesus, the author and finisher of our faith, who for the joy that was set before Him endured the cross, despising the shame, and has sat down at the right hand of the throne of God.

Fran and I are sitting in a hospital waiting room again. Our dates may not be exotic, but at least they are eventful. I am waiting to have a paracentesis done to remove the ascites from my omentum. Interpreted: removing fluid from the membrane around my stomach with a long needle and ultrasound. This is palliative care to relieve consequences of cancer. They think this has been causing lots of my pain...

I just returned from the procedure which involved a bunch of needles, and they suctioned 5.1 liters from the lining around my stomach. I lost 10 pounds in 45 minutes. I cannot describe how much better I feel.

Fran and I walked out... she went to get lunch, and I went home for a nap... what a great date. Hope Fran's lunch was as good as my nap.

It is interesting that this fluid built up without me knowing it was happening. And little by little it began to cause my life to be in so much pain.

I have noticed that when we become inattentive to important areas of our lives, the same thing can happen. Our weight, habits that are detrimental to our lives, our relationship with the ones we love, and our relationship with God. We can let things go so far that without a miracle there is no way back. God used a miracle to position me to have this fluid drained. (Too long to go into, but it was a series of God-ordained events that got my doctor's attention).

Sin in our lives can also become too easy to ignore until it begins to ruin our lives. It encourages us not to remain how we have always been but to get rid of destructive things in our lives.

———

When I got home, I began to experience pain from the weeks of pressure on the inner part of my body. I experienced something I knew this evening as I was just vegetating on the couch watching Texas Car Wars. I like the mindless show when I am not able to do much, so I was familiar with the characters. One of the shop owners called his workers together and told them the reason his wife had been away was because they just found out she had Stage III breast cancer... I started tearing up... wiping my eyes hoping Fran wouldn't see, but later in the show, a whole bunch of people raised money for her treatment, and I couldn't keep my tears from my wife.

It moves me so much to know someone else has their lives so messed up by this disease. As they shaved her head on TV, I was reminded of all the feelings that rush over us when faced with our own mortality. I think that is why I cried. Facing an unknown is scary, and it shatters all your plans, hopes, and future. It takes time to grab hold of hope... but thank God we can find a hope that endures through the pain, the fear, and helps us face the finality of our lives, but also will go with us into eternity. My hope is built on nothing less... than on Jesus...

November 3, 2012

Jude 24-25 NKJV

Now to Him who is able to keep you from falling (stumbling), and to present you faultless before the presence of His glory with exceeding joy, to God our Savior, who alone is wise, be glory and majesty, dominion and power, both now and forever. Amen!

I love this doxology of Jude: It is such a perfect ending to so much of what we say.

I woke up yesterday morning vomiting (not sure what the best word is) and went through the day trying not to go to ER. My daughter Suzi and her daughter Abbey arrived in the late afternoon. So good see them.

Towards evening I finally had to take some pain pills and went to sleep but at 1:00 A. M. I again started almost dry heaves. I had had that buildup of fluid on my stomach and intestines for weeks, and it began to compact my bowls, and much of the pain was from that. Fran and I decided ER was the only way, but God intervened, and I slept and planned on going today, but by the grace of God I have not had to. It is funny what we take for granted can become so important.

I was able to eat a little for the first time in days. I have discovered, if you stop eating you can lose weight... I am where I wanted to be last year, but not in this way. lol I am not in as much pain tonight, so may get some sleep.

November 4, 2012

So enjoyed being in church this morning at BCA. Good worship, ministry, and sermon. Encouraging to have wonderful friends still loving and praying for us. Thanks, Pastor Blayne

Here are part of the lyrics of a chorus I love:

"I Will Rise"

There's a peace I've come to know
though my heart and flesh may fail.
There's an anchor for my soul I can say, "It is well"
Jesus has overcome and the grave is overwhelmed.
The victory is won He is risen from the dead

[Chorus:]

And I will rise when He calls my name
no more sorrow, no more pain
I will rise on eagles' wings before my God
fall on my knees
And rise. I will rise[18]

November 5, 2012

Since I have no job or anything exciting going on in my life I tend to talk about that which is getting most of my attention. Unfortunately, it is cancer. Actually, that is not totally true as Suzi, my daughter, and her girl, Abbey, are here, and granddaughter Kaia, and Jen, my daughter, and Jon, son, his wife, Re, and their little man Caiden (almost one-year-old) have all been here too.

Caiden walked with me, barefooted, out to the mailbox today and then the two of us sat on our patio swing for the longest time. He never once asked me how I was. We just sat there, his hand on my leg and we just swung. I think he knew I needed just some question-free-time. It was precious. His mom took a video of our time... I hope someday he gets to see it and is thankful for time with Grandpa.

Without the aid of any sleep aide or pain medicines, I have been sleeping so much more. Not sure that is a good sign but when I am awake I am in so much discomfort in my abdomen. Tonight, the pain is intensifying, and I probably will have to take some kind of pain pill. However, I can say with an assurance that I am alive today and it is well with my soul. These words resonate in my spirit this evening.

Psalm 32:7 NIV

You are my hiding place; You will protect me from trouble and surround me with songs of deliverance.

(Tonight, I played many songs of deliverance as we worshiped in our house).

Psalm 33:2-5 NIV

Praise the Lord with the harp; make music to Him on the ten-stringed lyre. Sing to Him a new song; play skillfully, and shout for joy. For the word of the Lord is right and true; (He doesn't make a mistake). He is faithful in all He does. The Lord loves righteousness and justice; the earth is full of His unfailing love.

Tomorrow is my oldest son's birthday. Robert Duane Jordan. I was so blessed that on November 6, 1969, I was handed this little guy that was my first son. I was young enough that we kind of grew up together (at least he grew up). We did so many things together that cannot be measured by how much they cost but what they were worth. He is a man of God that is not ashamed of the Gospel of Jesus Christ. He is probably his company's best employee and hardest worker. He has an awesome wife and two precious daughters that love Grandpa... so Happy Birthday Rob Jordan. I love you so much!

Regardless of the outcome of our election today, I believe God will cause good to come to every believer and to our nation as we love God and live according to our calling in Christ Jesus. I choose to pray for and support as best I can the man who will be elected as The President of the United States of America. If President Obama is defeated, I am praying for an inner peace, and a mature statesmanship that will help him and his family exit the White House gracefully.

If Governor Mitt Romney loses that he too will exhibit the character of a statesman and will graciously concede in a timely manner. Then I pray that all the media (even ones I agree with) will go cover stories in the Sahara Desert or Siberia and not be heard from for months so we can see if our nation can be managed without them.

Matthew 5:9, 13, 14, 43-48 NIV

Blessed are the peacemakers, for they will be called children of God. "You are the salt of the earth. But if the salt loses its saltiness, how can it be made salty again? It is no longer good for anything, except to be thrown out and trampled underfoot." "You are the light of the world. A town built on a hill cannot be hidden." "You have heard that it was said, 'Love your neighbor and hate your enemy.' But I tell you, love your enemies and pray for those who persecute you, that you may be children of your Father in heaven. He causes His sun to rise on the evil and the good, and sends rain on the righteous and the unrighteous. If you love those who love you, what reward will you get? Are not even the tax collectors doing that? And if you greet only your own people, what are you doing more than others? Do not even pagans do that? Be perfect, therefore, as your heavenly Father is perfect."

November 6, 2012

On these pages, I have shared a lot of my latest feelings, faith, fears, and news since March of this year. Because of the latest, at months not years of life, Fran has wanted to find a way to spend more time with me. Unfortunately, she has used all her family leave and sick pay so to have income and insurance she needed to keep working. There is a way that fellow employees who have massive leave time built up can donate their leave to people like her in emergencies. She has wanted to do this, but I asked her to call my oncologist for his opinion on timing.

He told her that he had bad news. He said the fluid was analyzed and it was cancerous and that he would help with paperwork to help her get time off. He said he hoped family could get together and try to have a good Thanksgiving. He said we need to look at Hospice services.

My poor wife had such a hard day... She had to let the kids know. So, what do I do? One of my kids wants me to go get treatment in a more sophisticated cancer center, friends want me to take a thousand different natural treatments, some want me to rebuke the demon of cancer, renounce the work of the enemy in my body and claim and proclaim God's Word and power. Some have told me not to admit to being sick or having cancer. Honestly, friends, I believe I have gone and have done all I know how to do and can do but guess what, "I still have cancer."

What I know I hear more than anything in my spirit is; "Be still and know God." And that is what I plan to do. My God is my resurrection and life.... even though I may die I will live... In Jesus Christ, I am experiencing a peace that surpasses all understanding. (I even have a peace after this election today). It is well with my soul. Even though we are not prepared as well as we should have been for Fran to be on her own, yet I have a peace our Father will take care of her till it is her time to go home. I know pain will hurt and I will be sedated more and more, but His presence will be with me. Some don't want me to talk of death, but "Oh death where is your victory, where is the sting?" My death will be gain for me... I am numbering my days and am going to plan my funeral. And if you live close, I hope you will come to comfort my family and honor my life and faith.

I have many things I really want to finish... I want to finish a number of short stories for children that I have told my grandkids through the years, called Sidney and the Cat. Someone used that title years ago, but never told the stories I have... lol. I also want to compile some of my favorite sermons on CDs or at least digital storage, and I surely would like to compile these pages into a story form. So, I have to get busy. Please pray for me for strength to do what I think I can. Please pray for Fran and my family. They will miss me.

God is still my Healer, but is never obligated to anything but His word and His will. I ask and rest in His will. I am beyond negotiating and am content in knowing that I will live if I don't die and if I die I will live anyway. Fran and family need your prayer and support. I sure do not want to leave family, but if we have the same hope, it is only temporary. I will try to post daily updates and words of hope from a man going through the valley of the shadow of death. Maybe I will get a glimpse of heaven...?

November 7, 2012

Romans 13:1-7 NIV

Let everyone be subject to the governing authorities, for there is no authority except that which God has established. The authorities that exist have been established by God. Consequently, whoever rebels against the authority is rebelling against what God has instituted, and those who do so will bring judgment on themselves. For rulers hold no terror for those who do right, but for those who do wrong. Do you want to be free from fear of the one in authority? Then do what is right and you will be commended. For the one in authority is God's servant for your good. But if you do wrong, be afraid, for rulers do not bear the sword for no reason. They are God's servants, agents of wrath to bring punishment on the wrongdoer. Therefore, it is necessary to submit to the authorities, not only because of possible punishment but also as a matter of conscience. This is also why you pay taxes, for the authorities are God's servants, who give their full time to governing. Give to everyone what you owe them: If you owe taxes, pay taxes; if revenue, then revenue; if respect, then respect; if honor, then honor.

I CERTAINLY DO NOT KNOW WHAT THE NEXT four years will hold, but this Word has survived 2000 years and still seems to be a rule of heart for Christians. You can argue who it was meant for, but a good place to start with is the examination of your own heart.

———

I know I am being prayed for every day. Today I have felt like a life preserver being put around me and lifting me up into a new reality of peace. Tonight, I have taken a pain pill and am feeling more than good... hard to believe that there is anything wrong with me compared to yesterday. I am not giving up hope... I know that doctors can say a few days or weeks or months, but it is God who says what will truly happen.

Psalm 90:10 NLT

"Seventy years are given to us! Some even live to eighty. But even the best years are filled with pain and trouble; soon they disappear, and we fly away. "

I can feel the fluid building up again, but what shall I say to these things... if God be for us who can be against us... I have been made more than a conqueror... I have decided that I will look far beyond Thanksgiving... I will have a funeral ready and my house in order, but I am looking towards what God says the extent of my life can be and not a random timeline given by circumstances of fluid and cancer cells... Each day can be a new surprise... I will write more tomorrow the Lord willing...

November 8, 2012

Still alive. Today I met with the doctor who discovered I have cancer. He is helping give the palliative care I am going to need concerning my colon and intestines which have been very painful when I had the fluid buildup. If the following is TMI for you skip this part, but he showed me on a life-size diagram where stool can harden because the fluids are being diverted by the cancer. I asked how best to remove the stool... I used the word stool, but the doctor said the "poop" can be removed digitally. I asked what kind of a tool that was... he held up his first finger... his digital tool. He wanted to know if I wanted him to do it now? I chose to wait. I think he was relieved too. But I was thankful he was willing to discuss all methods that could be used to bring relief. When we are in pain or great need we might be willing to do anything to find relief. Jesus was willing to endure the unthinkable that we could have life. Consider Philippians 2:5-11. Jesus did not think it robbery to leave heaven to take our sins on him...

November 9, 2012

I see where some friends are in Italy in a little fishing village and tomorrow in Rome... I am so happy for them, but I just read these verses talking about my next trip:

2 Corinthians 5:1-7 NIV

For we know that if the earthly tent we live in is destroyed, we have a building from God, an eternal house in heaven, not built by human hands. Meanwhile we groan, longing to be clothed instead with our heavenly dwelling, because when we are clothed, we will not be found naked. For while we are in this tent, we groan and are burdened, because we do not wish to be unclothed but to be clothed instead with our heavenly dwelling, so that what is mortal may be swallowed up by life. Now the one who has fashioned us for this very purpose is God, who has given us the Spirit as a deposit, guaranteeing what is to come. Therefore we are always confident and know that as long as we are at home in the body we are away from the Lord. For we live by faith, not by sight.

November 10, 2012

What a busy day. The very first youth pastor I hired, 20 some years ago, came and spent the night with us. Steve Slater is a missionary who is on lend to Vanguard University in Costa Mesa. What a blessing to have him.

At 12:30 A. M. my oldest son Rob and wife, Jenny, and daughters arrived from Portland. Of course, we stayed up way too late.

Surprise phone calls and then a visit from friends Nancy and Albert from Kingman followed by more family visiting and coming to spend the night.

We have 11 people in our house tonight. I spent several hours in bed just trying to ease my various pains, so I wasn't very good company.

It has been wonderful to have my family here over the weekend, but it has been hard as I have been in so much discomfort. Right now, it has come to the place I need a pain pill to make it through the night.

Thought of this old song, third verse as a comfort tonight:

> *Are we weak and heavy laden, cumbered with a load of care?*
> *Precious Savior, still our refuge; take it to the Lord in prayer.*
> *Do thy friends despise, forsake thee?*
> *Take it to the Lord in prayer!*
> *In his arms he'll take and shield thee;*
> *thou wilt find a solace there.*[19]

Regardless of the challenges, there is an overcoming spirit in the lives of Believers. We will not be overcome by things present or things to come... Jesus said,

> *"...in this world there will be tribulations but be of good cheer; I*
> *have overcome this (the) world..."*

> *– John 16:33 NIV/KJV*

Resting in the "overcoming" and the "good cheer"!

November 11, 2012

Not feeling like writing tonight... long day ... pain has been often, now nausea... hope I can sleep without pills tonight... We had 17 in the home today, down to eight right now. My kids are gone in the early morning, brother Lyle and wife Lynn arrived at 1:30 A. M.

On November 11th, we celebrate my youngest son's birthday. Not only are we proud of him as a good man, husband, and father, but very proud that he is a Marine veteran, who served his country bravely, along with many generations of veterans so we could have a country where freedom still reigns, and we still have our Bill of Rights. It may seem like those are eroding away, but as long as there are men like my son who are willing to put their lives on the line for our country those rights will endure. God bless the USA! Happy Birthday Jonathan and Happy Veteran's Day.

———

What a beautiful service at church today. The worship was anointed, and the guest minister was so effective as he used the word of God and life's stories to bring us all to an altar of surrender.

As the pastor was closing in prayer, a member came and shared that a former deacon, Lance Kirol had just died from cancer a few moments before. What a sobering announcement as he was so loved by all. Hard to shake the loss I feel from losing such a good friend...These scriptures help.

Romans 8:35-39 NKJV

Who shall separate us from the love of Christ? Shall tribulation, or distress, or persecution, or famine, or nakedness, or peril, or sword? As it is written: For Your sake we are killed all day long; We are accounted as sheep for the slaughter. Yet in all these things we are more than conquerors through Him who loved us. For I am persuaded that neither death nor life, nor angels nor principalities nor powers, nor things present nor things to come, nor height nor depth, nor any other created thing, shall be able to separate us from the love of God which is in Christ Jesus our Lord.

November 12, 2012

John 14:1-6 NKJV

Let not your heart be troubled; you believe in God, believe also in Me. In My Father's house are many mansions; if it were not so, I would have told you. I go to prepare a place for you. And if I go and prepare a place for you, I will come again and receive you to Myself; that where I am, there you may be also. And where I go you know, and the way you know. " Thomas said to Him, "Lord, we do not know where You are going, and how can we know the way?" Jesus said to him, "I am the Way, the Truth, and the Life. No one comes to the Father except through Me.

Today was a first for me. I broke down and cried for me because I recognized that without a miracle, I am not going to get better and that I am going to soon lose this battle with cancer. I was home alone, and the sobbing just rolled over me for some time as I cried out to God to heal me or give me strength to face the future. Then I just began to worship God, and a peace flooded my soul and spirit, and the grieving was done, and I began to look at what God was doing already. A little later Fran came home and told me that Hospice had called me and wanted an interview with me on Tuesday. Had this happened earlier before the peace came, I think I might not have been able to compose myself. As it is I am OK. Will write more as I can...

We had so much family here this weekend, and it was so kind of them to make the effort to come see me at this time of my life. My brother, Lyle, and wife Lynne are here, and their son Dan flew in this afternoon from Portland. Before he left, all who were there gathered around my bed and prayed for a miracle. I am believing that at some point God will heal me, but if not I know that He will give my family and me the strength to find joy in each day, living in hope of eternity.

November 14, 2012

I love these scriptures:

Hebrews 10:35-38 NKJV

Therefore do not cast away your confidence, which has great reward. For you have need of endurance, so that after you have done the will of God, you may receive the promise: For yet a little while, And He who is coming will come and will not tarry. Now the just shall live by faith;

2 Corinthians 5:6, 7 NKJV

So we are always confident, knowing that while we are at home in the body we are absent from the Lord. For we walk by faith, not by sight.

Today I mustered my strength and went to Lowes with my family. Lyle, Lynne, and Fran stopped to get lunch, and I couldn't eat, but it was good to be out. On the way home, we talked with Jon. He and Re wanted to go to the ghost town of Nelson, Nevada about 25 miles from Boulder City. A beautiful day for a drive so Lyle drove us there and we met up with Jon and Re at the Eldorado Store which is an incredible place with antiques of every kind. There was a wrecked airplane from an old movie where Jon wanted to take pictures of Caiden for his first birthday. I sat in old pickups like I had when I was a teenager... They got a great picture of Caiden and me in a 1949 Dodge pickup. We then drove five miles down to Lake Mohave (Colorado River), and I actually threw some rocks into the water and managed to skip a stone or two.

Got back home and slept about four hours... Very exhausting, but worth the effort. I have to have my abdomen drained again tomorrow and meet with hospice on Thursday. Hard to face such things but glad I still am able to help make decisions.

November 15, 2012

Psalm 42:11 NIV

Why, my soul, are you downcast? Why so disturbed within me? Put your hope in God, for I will yet praise Him, my Savior and my God.

———

Psalm 107:28-31, 43 NIV

Then they cried out to the Lord in their trouble, and He brought them out of their distress. He stilled the storm to a whisper; the waves of the sea were hushed. They were glad when it grew calm, and He guided them to their desired haven. Let them give thanks to the Lord for His unfailing love and His wonderful deeds for mankind. Let the one who is wise heed these things and ponder the loving deeds of the Lord.

Went to St. Rose Hospital today and had fluid drained. They only got two liters, but that has been enough to cause pressure that shuts down my digestive system. I slept most of the afternoon. I have to do a colonoscopy prep in the morning... I can barely drink a bottle of water so I hope I can do this liter of sad tasting stuff. I have been telling myself, "I can do all things through Christ who gives me strength. " Early this morning I felt a need to read the Word and listen to praise music. Fran woke up, and I read many scriptures, and she fell asleep, and I lay there with earbuds listening to worship. I know it gave me the strength to go through the drain which for some reason really hurt badly this time.

——

Today was a new step of faith in this walk with cancer. I am now the proud member of Nathan Adelson Hospice program. This means that I will stay at home and receive comfort care as I battle cancer. It does not mean I am dying soon, but there is an understanding that (without a miracle) I will not survive this disease. I did this by doctor's orders because they believe there is no more treatment that can heal me. I know my God can still heal me and I prayed with great faith that this will happen as I believe many hundreds more are. But if He does not heal me, I refuse to play the blame game or let bitterness destroy my peace and my faith. I know there will be battles in my mind and spirit, but no one or nothing can separate me from the love of God I have in Christ Jesus.

Fran wept a bunch of tears today knowing that without a miracle I will not be with her and the family as long as she would hope. For Fran, this was a very hard day. It is as though it is an admission that I will not be with her and the family for as long as they hoped. Having gone through so many medical procedures, it seemed to me as just another step in the process of trying to do the best thing. I did not ever think I would have to call on hospice, but here it is. But in prayer tonight we both felt the burden of fear lift, and we are going forward with faith in our lives.

[Nathan Adelson Hospice] are awesome, caring people who will do their best to help me have the best days I can for the rest of my life. I hope I am not leaving soon, but I believe there are people in the generations following me who will listen to the heart of God and give themselves to the Kingdom of God and will fight the good fight and finish their course with no excuses: From the Message Bible...

2 Timothy 4:6 MSG

You take over. I'm about to die, my life an offering on God's altar. This is the only race worth running. I've run hard right to the finish, believed all the way. All that's left now is the shouting—God's applause! Depend on it, He's an honest judge. He'll do right not only by me, but by everyone eager for His coming.

November 16, 2012

Ecclesiastes 3:1-3 NKJV

To everything there is a season, A time for every purpose under heaven: A time to be born, and a time to die; ...And a time to heal;

A friend from Springfield, Missouri who works with Convoy of Hope has called me four times in the last two days wanting to pray for me. Each time I had company or was unable to take the call. This afternoon he called, and I was at my grandson's birthday party that took all my energy to go, and Jeff called again. I went into the bathroom to get away from the noise, and that room became the Throne Room as he prayed for me. Nothing different than hundreds of other prayers, but in the chaos of a birthday party I felt the presence of the Lord. I came home and went to sleep almost immediately. I woke up hungry, which has not happened for days. I got up and fixed myself an unusual dish of sliced boiled eggs, a slice of cheese, and a slice of tomato. I ate three helpings of that. Then Fran heated up a burrito that my brother had made before leaving. Everyone loved them, but I could not even taste one... but tonight I ate nearly a whole one. I drank more fluids than I have for days and felt more refreshed. Later I even had a small bowl of vanilla ice cream with a little chocolate syrup. That was all a miracle for me.

Then I began to read messages people sent to me and not sure whose it was, but a thought penetrated my heart and mind.

This is the beginning of the Christmas season. The Hallmark Channel calls it a season for miracles... In Ecclesiastes 3:1 it says there is a time and a season for everything... A time to be born and a time to die... and lists a lot of other things... but it was like the Holy Spirit reminded me that it also talks of a time to mend... I felt I was supposed to take that this is a season of healing and mending... So, I hope you will pray with me that this season will be a season of healing. I am not afraid of dying, but I would sure like it to be the right season of life not out of season as it feels. Regardless, tonight I feel better than I have for a long time.

———

Pastor Blayne Corzine, pastor of Boulder City Assembly of God Church, has asked me to preach this Sunday morning. I have preached at least 3,600 sermons in my lifetime... but none in the last 10 months. I am excited to get this opportunity as I am not sure I will get many more chances or to be able to. Would you please pray for me for physical strength and spiritual anointing? This verse is what I hope will happen.

Luke 4:18, 19 NIV

"The Spirit of the Lord is on me, because he has anointed me to proclaim good news to the poor. He has sent me to proclaim freedom for the prisoners and recovery of sight for the blind, to set the oppressed free, to proclaim the year of the Lord's favor. "

———

I know where I was one year ago today... I was celebrating the birth of my youngest grandson who for the past year has been one of the great joys of my life. There never has been a boy that has had such an infectious smile as this little guy has. He is one year old today and has a God-given gift of melting the hardest heart with his wonderful smile. I was called Smiley a lot in my life, and maybe Caiden will be like his grandpa in that way. Bless you, Re and Jon Jordan for giving us such a wonderful grandson. We are blessed!

This is the day that The Lord has made... I will rejoice and be glad in it...

November 18, 2012

Pastor Blayne Corzine invited me to preach today at the church my family, and I started in Boulder City 17 years ago. The church was packed (as full as I have ever seen it) and the BCA worship team was amazing. They have a multi-generation group that was so good. I was so moved by that time.

When I was given the opportunity to preach, I was already pretty tired, but as I saw this wonderful crowd of people, I felt an energy invade my body. Fran had just whispered to me asking if I was OK. I told her my body isn't, but my spirit is. God energized me until the service was over.

I brought a very simple message that I hope people will always remember me by. I used Psalm 37:25 (KJV) just the first part: *I have been young, but now I am old, YET I have never seen the righteous forsaken.* I told that the writer never mentioned how tough life had been but how faithful God was to anyone who would desire to be in right standing (righteous) with God.

I used my own history to show why I believed this scripture was true. Even with a life-threatening disease, I have never felt forsaken. I explained what not being forsaken means in simple terms and then told them the reason I believed I have never felt forsaken is that from the time I was 16, at a youth camp in the mountains of Idaho and used many examples of different times in my life when I had prayed, "Lord, I will go wherever you lead me, and I will do whatever you ask me to do." I have meant that at each change of life including being told I have terminal cancer.

Then my daughter Suzi and I led the old hymn, *"Great is Thy Faithfulness."* Looking around I saw very few dry eyes in the place as people recalled God's faithfulness. The worship team led a closing song I love called, *"I Will Rise."* After the pastor dismissed in prayer, all my energy was gone too, and I couldn't wait to get home and lay down and rest. It was a great day.

I was going to use the following quote (do not know where I found it) to close out my message yesterday but ran out of time:

Life is short,
Grudges are a waste of perfect happiness.
Laugh when you can. Apologize when you should.
Let go of what you cannot change.
Love deeply and forgive quickly.
Take chances. Give everything and have no regrets.

> *Life is too short to be unhappy,*
> *You have to take the good with the bad.*
> *Smile when you are sad as well as when you are happy.*
> *Love what you have and always remember what you had.*
> *Always forgive, never forget.*
> *Learn from your mistakes....*
> *People change. Things go wrong but always remember:*
> *Life goes on.*
> *Dance like no one is watching. Sing like no one is listening.*
> *Love like you have never been hurt. Live like forever begins now...*

> —*Author Unknown*

Not bad advice.

November 20, 2012

> *Philippians 4:4-7 NIV*

> *Rejoice in the Lord always. I will say it again: Rejoice! Let your gentleness be evident to all. The Lord is near. Do not be anxious about anything, but in every situation, by prayer and petition, with thanksgiving, present your requests to God. And the peace of God, which transcends all understanding, will guard your hearts and your minds in Christ Jesus.*

I know I have used these verses a lot lately, but they are so true.

Yesterday was one of those days that got lost in the haze of what I called the inevitable. The morning started so amazingly as my good friend Father Kasio from Kenya called me and when we prayed together, it was such an incredible revelation that although we were some 10,000 miles apart, together, in the spirit, were in the Throne Room of God. As we prayed there was not one pain in my body, and I drifted off to sleep praising the Lord.

Later Pastor John and Kittie stopped by and delivered some incredible apricot bread and then prayed with me.

Then my next two visitors were from hospice, and they were wonderful, but after they left, that haze engulfed my spirit like a fog as I realized their goal is to make me comfortable till I die.

I laid down and was ready to give in to the inevitable. For several hours, I was wanting nothing but being alone. I had nothing positive to say to anyone... I finally asked my son Jon to come and talk with me, more listen to me and laid out my feelings and then I began to tell him about Father Kasio, and the tears flowed, and my hope and my peace came back because I remembered the Throne Room. I told him I am not going to let my disease dictate my hope and told him I was going to do some spontaneous things.

So today, I got up early this morning and took the trash out, it was so warm and beautiful that I got in my truck, bought a breakfast and drove to Arizona about seven miles then back to town. That was too lame and drove to the dry lake about 10 miles the other way, and I was by myself on the smooth part and made several passes (each at least one mile) across it going faster each time till I was familiar with the surface. My goal was to go 100 miles an hour... I got to about 80 or 90 and decided that was fast enough... the highway running parallel has a speed limit of 75, so it wasn't that big of a thing, but the dust rooster tail was amazing and for some reason I felt I was at Bonneville. It was a thrill, and then I drove the 4x4 across the desert on my way home and hit some hills only bikes had used. I felt alive... I washed the dust off the truck and then drove Fran to a doctor's appointment in Vegas and have been just enjoying a day not thinking about anything but life.

November 21, 2012

Psalm 92:1-2 NKJV

It is good to give thanks to the Lord, and to sing praises to Your name, O Most High; To declare Your loving kindness in the morning, and Your faithfulness every night... Those of us who are older need to always remember to rejoice, give thanks, be thankful, and remember the faithfulness of God as well as family and friends... Being thankful increases the opportunities for the following:

Psalm 92:12-15 NKJV

The righteous shall flourish like a palm tree, he shall grow like a cedar in Lebanon. Those who are planted in the house of the Lord shall flourish in the courts of our God. They shall still bear fruit in old age; They shall be fresh and flourishing, to declare that the Lord is upright; He is my rock, and there is no unrighteousness in Him.

Rob, Jenny, and girls came in from Portland last night, and we all woke up to a beautiful day here. They were experiencing flooding in the Salem/Portland area with rain so heavy it is almost unbelievable.

I was the first one up in our house, so I decided to go on a walk and was going to try to duplicate yesterday in the way I felt... I made it about two blocks and could feel my strength going. Unfortunately, I had walked downhill first, so I had to come uphill to get home.

What a difference a day makes... I was not the only one having struggles today as Fran is fighting pain in her lower back and hip. Thankfully Rob was here, and he drove us to see an orthopedic surgeon. Poor Fran had to wait over an hour in the examination room before the doctor came in and found little relief, but we are believing God is going to give her strength. Rob drove us home, and I was back to bed...

I have great one-day-spurts of feeling good... ha.

I am determined to be fully rested for the day of Thanksgiving when all my immediate family and maybe some others are here to celebrate together. I do have so many things to be thankful for... today it was family and friends as well as a bed that gave me lots of comfort...

Have a great Thanksgiving!

———

James 1:17 NKJV

Every good gift and every perfect gift is from above, and comes down from the Father of lights, with whom there is no variation or shadow of turning.

My oldest sister Clara and her husband Lorin came to see us from Yuma, Arizona. So good to see them again. We talked Clara into making her famous coconut cream pie for us before she left. She makes pies like my mom used to, so this is a sacred blessing. We remembered when she made a meringue pie at our house when my mom was 89... I got the idea of putting 89 candles on the pie. We managed to light them all before the firestorm started. Nearly burned the kitchen down... By the time we got the inferno out the heat had crystalized the top of the pie. Not a smart thing to do, but makes good stories to talk about now. It is a good day...

I mentioned that Father Kasio called me from Kenya, but never mentioned that Emanuel called from Kenya the day before and then that same day his mother Naomi called us. Then to get to see Barnabas and Fenice at church was like a family reunion. We have such an amazing past together.

I have much to be thankful for. Fran and I realized that choice we made years ago, to come to Boulder City allowed us to be part of great relationships like these. I love this verse:

Romans 8:28 NASB

And we know that God causes all things to work together for good to those who love God, to those who are called according to His purpose.

Looking back over life shows us we have every reason to be thankful as we look forward in life.

November 22, 2012

As good as the days were before, today was bad. We can tell the lining around my stomach is filling back up again with liquid and today of all days, I was able to only sip a little water and could eat only small bites of turkey and all the fixings. I enjoyed watching everyone else eat. We had around 28 people in our house at one time.

My family surprised me by presenting me with a booklet that they had collected from friends and family of memories they had of me through the years. It was precious. I have not yet read through everything, but what I have read choked me up so much I couldn't read them out loud, so Fran had to. Even though I could not enjoy the food, I cherished the love and memories. There is so much food and dessert here I hope my kids stay long enough to eat it all... lol.

The following verses may not fit with what I have written above, but I believe it is what I needed today:

James 3:17, 18 NKJV

But the wisdom that is from above is first pure, then peaceable, gentle, willing to yield, full of mercy and good fruits, without partiality and without hypocrisy. Now the fruit of righteousness is sown in peace by those who make peace.

November 23, 2012

None of us are ever exempt from problems in life. What may be my mountain, to another may be just a speed bump. How we face and handle adversity either molds our character or reduces us to the base human emotions of anger, hatred, revenge, bitterness, fear, and many more which are self-destructive. I love these verses out of Romans 5 that tells us what our troubles can produce. I plan on meditating on these:

Romans 5:1-5 NKJV

Therefore, having been justified by faith, we have peace with God through our Lord Jesus Christ, through whom also we have access by faith into this grace in which we stand, and rejoice in hope of the glory of God. And not only that, but we also glory in tribulations, knowing that tribulation produces perseverance; and perseverance, character; and character, hope. Now hope does not disappoint, because the love of God has been poured out in our hearts by the Holy Spirit who was given to us.

November 24, 2012

Psalm 27:4, 5 NKJV

One thing I have desired of the Lord, that will I seek: That I may dwell in the house of the Lord All the days of my life, To behold the beauty of the Lord, and to inquire in His temple. For in the time of trouble He shall hide me in His pavilion; In the secret place of His tabernacle He shall hide me; He shall set me high upon a rock.

I love this Psalm.

I was so blessed to have my four children, Suzi and Ed, Rob and Jenny, Jenny and Mike, and Jonathan and Rebekah, and my grandkids, Erika, Mary, Kalani, Amy, Kaia, Abbey and Caiden all at my house for Thanksgiving.

They certainly made my day. Hate to see them all go back home... it will be quiet here. I am also so blessed that my awesome wife is doing all she can to take care of me during this battle with cancer which is such a hard thing for her but she has always been there for her family.

———

Just got back from taking Rob and family to the airport. Kalani came and told me goodbye at about 6:00 A. M. on her way to the airport to return to her dad's in San Antonio; so sorry to see her go. Suzi and Ed are back home in Phoenix, so it is quiet at home. Driving is still a function I can do well and enjoy very much. But my family is so trying to protect me from getting too tired. I pretty much know when I have had enough, but I humor them... lol.

The hospice nurse suggested I check myself into their facility to have the fluids drained from my stomach lining, but I am trying to hold out till Monday as they can then insert a drain and valve for home use. It is very miserable at times, but think I am going to make it.

I have tried to avoid anger and self-pity during this struggle, but I felt it coming on last night... think about it, seeing all the good leftovers and pie without being able to eat it... lol. But in reality, just the constant reminder that according to the medical field I don't have much of a future... try that thought process on sometime especially since there are so many things

I would still love to do. But, there always is a way that hope and peace overcome my anger or self-pity.

When I try to attain anything enduring through human means, I always lose. But with God's help I will actually do valiantly in the face of crisis or chaos and the enemies of my life:

Psalm 60:11, 12 NKJV

Give us help from trouble, For the help of man is useless. Through God we will do valiantly, for it is He who shall tread down our enemies.

November 25, 2012

I am listening to one of my favorite Christmas songs, *When the Christmas Baby Cried*, by the Annie Moses Band. The music is so beautiful and full of peace that I can listen to it over and over, and the words are almost inconsequential. But one night I heard some of the words and began to realize the incredible miracle of the Son of God being born to a woman and when that little baby cried for the first time, and the breath of life filled his lungs for the first time, it was the fulfillment of many prophecies and the beginning of so many more. I meditated on the times that as an adult the New Testament tells us He cried.

His cry at birth was to announce the coming of a Savior, then as an adult in John 11 he wept at the tomb of a friend, and I believe it was because he saw the incredible pain that death brought to hearts of His creation. He knew that in a short time he was going to face death that would bring an eternal hope for all who would believe.

Later, on His way to Jerusalem, He looked over the city knowing that many of them would choose not to believe, call for His crucifixion and would miss an eternal opportunity of life and hope. They would do that, yet He would in love die for them too.

Then from the Cross Jesus cried, "It is finished!" That cry was the last time this God-man would cry. In just a few days He would rise as the first fruits of the resurrection for His creation. He would be our Savior, Redeemer and all we would ever need. I am so glad that the sound of the

Christmas Baby was the sound that heralded hope for the world. Merry Christmas...

November 26, 2012

I am listening to Fran play worship songs on the piano. Such a blessing after prayer to hear those great old songs of faith. "We are standing on Holy Ground," reminded me of Ronnie who used to love that song... he would stand no matter where he was whenever he heard that song, even in the church van. He was in ICU and two other guys, and I started to sing it and the next thing you know, he was standing there with all his tubes and in an open gown trying to sing about Holy Ground. The nurses came running as the alarms went off but he told them why he was standing... it became an easy way to talk about the Lord.

I struggled since last Wednesday because of fluid buildup in my abdomen, but yesterday after a great message on healing, several people prayed for me... I have been able to eat and drink more than I have for a while. I am also asking God to heal me. The following scriptures meant so much to me today:

Psalm 103:1-5 NKJV

Bless the Lord, O my soul; And all that is within me, bless His holy name! Bless the Lord, O my soul, and forget not all His benefits: Who forgives all your iniquities, Who heals all your diseases, Who redeems your life from destruction, Who crowns you with loving-kindness and tender mercies, Who satisfies your mouth with good things, so that your youth is renewed like the eagle's.

Made it through the whole day without getting caught up in Cyber Monday. I think it is because I am broke or maybe old? No... guess it's both.

One of my favorite songs: *YOUR GRACE IS ENOUGH*.[20]

Great is Your faithfulness oh God.
You wrestle with the sinner's heart.
You lead us by still waters and to mercy
and nothing can keep us apart.
So remember Your people. Remember Your children.
Remember Your promise Oh God.
Your grace is enough. Your grace is enough.
Your grace is enough for me.
Your Grace is Enough

November 27, 2012

Isaiah 40:31 NKJV

But those who wait on the Lord shall renew their strength; They shall mount up with wings like eagles, they shall run and not be weary, They shall walk and not faint.

I had a visit from the hospice nurse again today, and for whatever reason, I still have not been able to have the fluid drained from my abdomen. May have to go to ER if there is no answer tomorrow as this causes so much discomfort. The good thing is that I believe I have had divine help to make it this long. Tonight I just need another touch.

Fran and I went to a Christmas party for senior pastors of the Assembly of God in this area. They were kind enough to invite me even though I am not pastoring now. Beautiful setting, festive decorations, and the food was excellent (at least the small amounts I tried). We had to go home early as I was exhausted. The bed felt so good.

I got a wonderful gift from one of my nieces and her dad when they made a recording of an old hymn singing just for me. Fran and I both wiped the tears as they sang and we heard the truth that God walks with us and talks with us and tells us that we are his own... (recognize the song?). I felt revived after hearing it... God has a way of doing that, doesn't he?

November 28, 2012

Today was kind of a miracle day for me. Still no drain, but God somehow has caused a reduction in the fluid enough to eat and... well.

I drove Fran to a doctor's appointment for her (only places we go anymore), and afterward, we decided to eat at IHOP. I have not eaten at a restaurant for quite a while. I got the smallest breakfast I could and ate about 3/4, and it was good. Can't eat bacon anymore... strange the changes... it is amazing the power of the brain as it thinks of the wonderful things of the past, like 32 oz. of Pepsi or coke with ice on a hot day, a bowl of ice cream with chocolate syrup and now none of that does anything to me except in my memories of how much I loved those things.

Reminds me of the stories of the Old Testament how the people got to thinking about how some of the things in slavery in Egypt weren't that bad and made them want to go back. It is easy to let the past paint a picture of perfection even when we know it isn't, and we know if we went back to those things it would cause great chaos... Here's some good advice:

Hebrews 12:1-2 NKJV

Therefore we also, since we are surrounded by so great a cloud of witnesses, let us lay aside every weight, and the sin which so easily ensnares us, and let us run with endurance the race that is set before us, looking unto Jesus, the author and finisher of our faith, who for the joy that was set before Him endured the cross, despising the shame, and has sat down at the right hand of the throne of God.

November 29, 2012

Romans 8:28 NLT

And we know that God causes everything to work together for the good of those who love God and are called according to His purpose for them.

Romans 15:13 NKJV

Now may the God of hope fill you with all joy and peace in believing, that you may abound in hope by the power of the Holy Spirit.

I cannot explain to anyone the "why" of my life, but I met the "Who" of life who is so able to make sense of the senseless, to give peace that surpasses our human understanding, who gives hope when there is no obvious reason for hope...The "who" is Jesus, the Son of God.

7:00 A. M., my hospice nurse, was at my door waiting to draw blood for a lab test for the drain on Friday. After she left, Fran and I got into our car and headed for Phoenix for an appointment with Bank of America Loan Modification specialists. We got here at 2:00 P. M. and now it is 6:20 P. M. and still have one more specialist to see. I wanted to do all I could for Fran's sake to get some things in order in case cancer takes my life sooner than later.

My son Rob heard about us needing to drive home tonight, so he flew from Portland down to Phoenix to drive us home... and then he will fly back to Portland tomorrow. That was an unexpected gift. To make things more exciting, our daughter in Phoenix ended up in a hospital with kidney problems. She was dismissed today while we were in meetings and Rob took her home in a Camaro convertible he had rented (with the top down of course). Her daughters loved it too. We missed the convertible but picked Rob up at the rental place... I was so glad to see my driver. He was a lifesaver to me. We saw Suzi and family, and then Rob drove us home getting here at about 12:45 A. M.

Got to be up in five hours for minor surgery...

November 30, 2012

John 10:10 NKJV

The thief does not come except to steal, and to kill, and to destroy. I have come that they may have life, and that they may have it more abundantly. (Jesus)

We were at Desert Radiology at 7:00 A. M. to have my abdomen drained and a permanent drain put in. Yesterday I kept telling Fran I really was hoping I would not have to have that happen. I was in my surgical robe, they had put all the monitor tabs on me, and the nurse was ready to give me an IV when the Physician Assistant stopped her. He had overheard me saying I thought the fluid buildup had gone down and wanted to do an ultrasound to see how much fluid there was. He found that there were only small pockets of the fluid and said to put the valve in would be very painful with that little bit of fluid and that it didn't need to be drained. I asked him where the fluid had gone... he said maybe the liver started catching up. He said he had no answer... His doctor came in and concurred and told me to go home. I am kind of suspicious that someone has been praying for me. For today it is an answer to my prayers... We didn't obey the doctor, we had some breakfast and went to a Harbor Freight store.

December 2, 2012

Psalm 37:3 - 5;7,23-26 NLT

Trust in the Lord and do good. Then you will live safely in the land and prosper. Take delight in the Lord, and He will give you your heart's desires. Commit everything you do to the Lord. Trust Him, and He will help you. Be still in the presence of the Lord, and wait patiently for Him to act. The Lord directs the steps of the godly. He delights in every detail of their lives. Though they stumble, they will never fall, for the Lord holds them by the hand. Once I was young, and now I am old. Yet I have never seen the godly abandoned or their children begging for bread. The godly always give generous loans to others, and their children are a blessing.

These verses were a strength for me today.

Today has been a difficult day in some ways but exciting in others. I was asked to bring the eulogy (message) and lead two songs at my good friend, Lance Kirol's memorial service. Lance passed away on November 11 because of cancer. I was able to do what was asked of me, and it was for me, a very good service and a good way to honor a friend and say goodbye. I will ever be thankful that I came to Boulder City, so I was able to meet friends like him. He was a very good man... we had lots of good times together in and out of church.

After the service and going to lunch with other friends, I was so exhausted I slept for several hours and got up to try to talk with our company from Oregon (Mike Peck and his two sons and his mother, Karlene) Then more family came and as I talked all the energy washed away and Fran said I slept for four more hours. Catching up I guess for all the busyness I have had this last week?

———

It was good to be in church today. It is a good thing to give thanks to The Lord.

I used a term recently and called it "seasons of healings." And I think I have had some kind of healing. I rejoice that God truly answered my prayer for not having a drain installed. It appears the fluid is being handled again by the body for some reason, and I am very happy for that.

Unfortunately, there are so many other things that are making life hard right now. Eating is so difficult, and drinking is limited to sips... I was driving with Fran in town this afternoon and thought back to the times we would have pulled into DQ for a cone or somewhere for a little treat. Can't do that now. I am trying to negotiate with God about having a season of enjoying comfort foods again... I told him I wouldn't be a glutton. So far, no change. Comfort foods probably caused me to weigh 220 pounds a year ago, and without them 170. You'd think a little would be O. K. lol Maybe some of you have a little more pull with Him in that area and could ask for me, especially at Christmas time.

Even as sick as I feel to my stomach, there is something I can taste that I never tire of or get too much of. Read these scriptures and see if you agree:

Psalm 119:103,105 NKJV

How sweet are Your words to my taste, Sweeter than honey to my mouth! ... Your word is a lamp to my feet and a light to my path.

Psalm 34:8 NKJV

Oh, taste and see that the Lord is good;
Blessed is the man who trusts in Him!

1 Peter 2:1-3 KJV

Wherefore laying aside all malice, and all guile, and hypocrisies, and envies, and all evil speakings, as newborn babes, desire the sincere milk of the word, that ye may grow thereby: If so be ye have tasted that the Lord is gracious.

December 3, 2012

Romans 10:17 NKJV
Now [So] then faith comes by hearing,
and hearing by the word of God.

As long as I don't eat, I feel pretty good, but tonight after eating a few bites of some good tasting potatoes and gravy and a few green beans, I doubled up with pain with no control over it stopping. Fran came and prayed for me, and I looked at my beautiful wife and could only hug her, and we both broke down and cried.

My tears were for her that she has to go through this and hers were probably for me because she couldn't help me. The tears stopped, and we both have a faith that goes beyond the obvious situations or beyond the temporal part of our lives. We are believing for my healing and are encouraged by the fluid drainage that cannot be explained, but we still want to see a complete miracle. Faith comes by hearing and hearing by the word of God. We are listening for that command that says; "Now. " And then we will pray the will of the Father and have a confidence that if we pray anything according to His will, He hears us...

1 John 5:14 NKJV
…if we ask anything according to His will, He hears us.

December 4, 2012

Got up early and took the trash out to the street and was feeling pretty good; got Fran to go to Costco but stopped by the bank on the way... I took a drink of water and while driving in the next few blocks told Fran I have a problem, and she knew I was about to throw up. I hurriedly found a side street, began throwing up... stopped long enough for Fran and me to change places.

Back home and as timing would have it, my hospice nurse showed up, and a half hour later a hospice doctor showed up. They could not find any good reason for my nausea but are having me try some new meds. They still don't understand the fluid on my abdomen being gone... I told them I was praising God for this. They are happy for me as I am. Today again I am holding to:

Romans 8:28 NLT

And we know that God causes everything to work together for the good of those who love God and are called according to His purpose for them.

December 5, 2012

Much better day today. I was able to drive Fran to shop at Costco. There was a truck full of Christmas Trees outside the entrance, and it smelled like being in the mountains of Oregon... by the time we did our shopping, no room for a tree. Reminds me of Psalm 121.

Psalm 121:1-3 NIV

I lift up my eyes to the mountains—where does my help come from? My help comes from the Lord, the Maker of heaven and earth. He will not let my foot slip—He who watches over me will not slumber;

I have done much better today compared to days ago. An old song I used to sing had lyrics like this:

"I don't know about tomorrow, I just live from day to day ... many things about tomorrow I don't seem to understand, but I know who holds tomorrow and I know who holds my hand."[21]

I believe Jesus is my healer, but if I am not healed in this life, I don't want a foggy message about Jesus... or Christmas... I want to know a Savior was born and if I believe in Him, I will not perish but have everlasting life. It's not about stockings hung with care, but is it well with your soul...? Has the Christ of Christmas become your Savior? How does a sleigh filled with toys mix with the reason for this season? My hope is built on nothing less than Jesus Christ and Righteousness. That's my soapbox sermon for Christmas.

———

If it weren't for doctor appointments maybe Fran and I would have time to enjoy some quality time together, but then in the last 10 months we have kind of forgot what we think that means. I am beginning to feel every moment with her has a quality and a quantity that heaven is giving us. It is getting harder and harder to share that time with too many others. Fran is the one who has put up with me for 25 years. There is not another person on the planet who has been so dedicated to me and who has been there through so many things as her. She was truly a gift from God to me and my family and hers, as well as to every church we pastored. There is no one like her. Mary, my first wife who died of cancer 27 years ago, told me I could not survive without a wife... I think she must have prayed I would meet the right woman, and I did. These are private thoughts that I want everyone to know because I am struggling physically with a lot tonight. But I am persuaded...

Romans 8:37-39 NKJV

Yet in all these things we are more than conquerors through Him who loved us. For I am persuaded that neither death nor life, nor angels nor principalities nor powers, nor things present nor things to come, nor height nor depth, nor any other created thing, shall be able to separate us from the love of God which is in Christ Jesus our Lord.

December 6, 2012

James 5:16 NKJV

Confess your trespasses to one another, and pray for one another, that you may be healed. The effective, fervent prayer of a righteous man avails much.

So, I suspect God is listening to someone's prayers. I woke up at 1:00 A.M. and was hungry. I got up and fixed myself a cup of soup and a toasted bagel with peanut butter and fell back to sleep listening to a sermon (about time I did what others have done when I preached). Woke up at 9:00 A. M. and fixed breakfast for the first time in weeks. Ham and eggs on a bagel (we must have lots of bagels?). Later I went to our storage unit where I had built a shelf that was about 10 x 10 (kind of like a second floor). Cleared it off and then dismantled it board by board (2x6x10) plus particle board. I had built this so I could store Jon's Karmann Ghia (which is now in Oregon) in there plus all the rest of the treasures we could not live without... lol. Fran brought me a Taco Bell Gordita, and I ate the whole thing... Loaded all the material in my pickup and backed it in my garage... I sat down in my chair and woke up an hour later. A friend had been helping Fran clean while Fran went to a meeting. When I woke up the house was dark, I had no idea our friend left. I got up and unloaded the pickup. Most productive and hardest I have worked for months. Thanks for praying...

2 Chronicles 6:19 NIV

Yet, Lord my God, give attention to your servant's prayer and his plea for mercy. Hear the cry and the prayer that your servant is praying in your presence.

December 7, 2012

Isaiah 55:8-9, 11 NKJV

For My thoughts are not your thoughts, nor are your ways My ways,"
says the Lord. "For as the heavens are higher than the earth, so are My
ways higher than your ways, and My thoughts than your thoughts...
So shall My word be that goes forth from My mouth; it shall not
return to Me void, but it shall accomplish what I please, and it shall
prosper in the thing for which I sent it.

These scriptures may help you understand why we can face the unknown.

Can you believe I am snacking on Fruity Cheerios? Never heard of them before tonight, but they actually taste pretty good. Must still be feeling better. It has been a good day.

Fran and I agreed to watch our one-year-old grandson while his parents went to a company Christmas dinner. He is a handful for young folks, so imagine what it is like for old folks like us. Caiden has been walking for over a month now and is good at running into walls and tables etc., but seldom gets hurt. He is just tall enough to open doors with lever type handles which all our doors have (except the front). We have French Doors out to our patio, and he headed towards that during my turn to watch him, and I decide to see what he would do if I just let him go outside (still warm here). He opened the door, stood there and waved goodbye to someone outside and then stepped across the threshold onto the deck. He walked a couple of steps and then looked at the darkness and scurried back to me and grabbed both my legs and held on for a second and then back to the door again then back to my legs...I decided to go out with him and pushed him with my leg, but he would not budge nor let go of my leg. So, I stepped out in front, and he grabbed my hand and headed out with me. We headed towards his favorite swing on the deck and then he froze. I could not pull him forward as he looked into the darkness at a pile of leaves that had never been there before and in the dark, must have looked very ominous. He wanted up...he almost jumped into my arms...and then he was OK wherever I went. He was quite ready to go back inside.

His actions reminded me of me in the days as I have battled with this cancer and the unknown is out there. I think I have about got my fear of the unknown conquered till it gets a little darker and I have to run to the

Father…at some point if there is no miracle I will face that pile of leaves and have to leap into the Father's arms. I hope when I do that it feels as good to God as Caiden's arms around my neck felt to me…

December 8, 2012

Isaiah 53:4, 5 NKJV

Surely He has borne our griefs and carried our sorrows; Yet we esteemed Him stricken, Smitten by God, and afflicted. But He was wounded for our transgressions, He was bruised for our iniquities; The chastisement for our peace was upon Him, And by His stripes we are healed.

It was another good day. I think I am gaining weight not from fluid buildup but from increased food intake. These scriptures came to life today as I was reminded that it is not about what we do, but about what Jesus has already done that makes the difference…

People come and go in our lives, but some people remain true friends no matter how seldom you see each other. True friendship does not depend on the frequency of visits or even the amount of communications, but just the fact that they are friends. Two such people came into our home this afternoon: Bill and Maureen Williamson. Bill was one of the men who dedicated himself to helping me get Boulder City Assembly started. He, in fact, became my much-needed administrator of business as we went through the maze of all the government's requirements for a new corporation. He and I have had much in common, and Maureen added so much to our friendship. We will be in church together tomorrow at BCA. I hope you saw the pictures of my grandson and me raking leaves. What I wrote last night may have more meaning as you see his size.

December 10, 2012

Philippians 3:13-14 NKJV

... but one thing I do, forgetting those things which are behind and reaching forward to those things which are ahead, I press toward the goal for the prize of the upward call of God in Christ Jesus.

We went to church this morning and one nice thing is all the friends there, but it was also nice being with Bill and Maureen, friends from Arizona. A great time of worship and a guest missionary speaker who had a very compelling message for sharing our faith. Something he said stirred my mind concerning my health.

After church, I invited my wife to lunch so she would not have to prepare anything. On the way to Henderson, I told her that since I have been feeling so good, how would I deal with not being sick since that has been my way of life now for 10 months? It sounded exciting. However, I think that being sick can be addictive. It has been all I have known for months, and being sick does get a lot of attention. It is kind of a sick mentality. Can I function without that attention? I had to deal with that this afternoon, especially since I got very ill trying to eat lunch (not the food's fault) it just wouldn't go down. I could chew but not swallow... lol I have decided fully, that I would choose health and no attention over being sick and getting attention.

I have dreams of what I will do if and when I am well enough to do them. The Bible says that God will pour out his spirit on all flesh, young men will have visions and old men will dream dreams. Guess you know where I am in that mix?

I have a dream that would involve moving to another area and starting a church that would be unlike any other that I have seen. I have visited a dozen churches recently and have seen some real needs not being addressed, especially in the larger churches... I would name the church BB Worship Center, and you will have to privately ask me what that means and what I am talking about. (Not a city or bad boy) ... lol

Even though the past has great memories, I want to move beyond the past and reach for the future whatever that may be: In the scripture above, Paul the Apostle did not forget about the past, he just put it in its proper perspective so it would not rule what God was doing in his life. He did not forget about what Jesus Christ did or his living, vital relationship with

Jesus Christ, but he was willing to forget the things that would keep him from fulfilling the goals he knew Jesus had given him.

For me, I do not forget my past and how I became a believer and a worshiper, but I don't let it keep me from the present or my future. On the other hand, I will not let the trendy, the contemporary, the techno things, or the cutting edge take me away from those things that brought me to where I am today. Paul said he wanted to know nothing but Jesus Christ and Him crucified. That is one thing we must never forget... There is a focus we need and as Christians that always must be Jesus Christ.

December 11, 2012

Today I broke and cried. Partly because of a dear friend who is also struggling with setbacks with cancer. Her cancer is more acute than mine. But I saw on Facebook people telling her to fight on, that she is a superhero, and many other ways telling her she is going to be healed or should be healed and knowing the pressure that puts you under.

Just yesterday I was talking about what I would do when I am well, and today was so miserable... my car even stalled and would not start and Jonathan, my son, had to come to my rescue. Not only am I having struggles, so is Fran with vertigo and something in her back and hip... all this cascaded around me and so Fran wouldn't know I let the tears come in my bathroom. But she happened to go by the door and knew something was wrong. We both decided it was time to pray and to find the rest God promises to our soul.

The following scriptures invaded my mind and spirit tonight. Paul, an apostle of Jesus Christ, was in prison for his faith and had been given the death sentence. His words evoked peace in my spirit as I realized, he knew he no longer had to fight for his life or keep the faith... he had already done that. He was resting from the fight and resting in his faith. My life has been one step forward and three backward since yesterday. Friends and family want to hear good news about my health, but today there is none that I know. There is pressure from myself and so many to claim my healing, to fight on, to take a cancer cure, but today I am tired, and I hear the words of Jesus:

Matthew 11:28 NIV

"Come to me all who are weary… and I will give you rest. "

And so, like Paul, I am saying,

2 Timothy 4:7, 8 NKJV

I have fought the good fight and kept the faith… Now I will rest in God's will, and I will fear no evil… tomorrow I may fight again, but tonight I rest… I have fought the good fight, I have finished the race, I have kept the faith…

Finally, there is laid up for me the crown of righteousness, which the Lord, the righteous Judge, will give to me on that Day, and not to me only but also to all who have loved His appearing.

———

Have you ever noticed that traditions seem to be more powerful than truth especially at Christmas time? We have woven our Christian Christmas beliefs in with the world's view of Christmas to the point that godly worshipers will have a reindeer, elves, and Santa near the nativity scenes and if we ever had to explain our Christmas trees and decorations to people unfamiliar with Christmas the explanations would be lost in the snowmen, snowflakes, Santas and all those traditions. All the magical stories that we like certainly distract from the baby born to a virgin girl in a stable in Bethlehem, and the message; "For unto you a Savior is born…"

Just something to mess with your minds as you listen to Christian radio and hear, *Here Comes Santa Claus…* back to back with *O Holy Night.*

Wednesday, December 12, 2012

I listened again today to a song; *Live Like That,* by a group called Sidewalk Prophets and the words and music were powerful. The words made me think about how I still want to live the life I have… Here are the verses:

Sometimes I think, what will people say of me
When I'm only just a memory
When I'm home where my soul belongs
Was I love when no one else would show up
Was I Jesus to the least of those
Was my worship more than just a song
Am I proof That You are who you say You are
That grace can really change a heart
Do I live like Your love is true?
People pass and even if they don't know my name
Is there evidence that I've been changed
When they see me, do they see You

Chorus:
I want to live like that and give it all I have
So that everything I say and do
Points to You
If love is who I am then this is where I'll stand
Recklessly abandoned never holding back
I want to live like that
I want to live like that[22]

Regardless of how long I may live, I want to live like that... Enjoy 12/12/12.

———

Today Fran and I were blessed to have two of our pastor-friends visit with us, and for over an hour we just talked about the Lord. One of them asked me if there was something significant that I had learned, discovered, or realized during this battle with cancer. I told them that the most important thing that I realized is that none of us will get out of this world alive. We will all die at some point regardless of who we are or what we have or don't have. All our theology will be boiled down to one verse: John 3:16. If we believe in God's only begotten Son, will we have everlasting life? I told them, if this part is not true, then we have wasted all our lives preaching a Gospel that is not true. But if it is true, then the instant my spirit leaves my body, I will be forever in the presence of the Lord enjoying the beginning of everlasting life. Cancer and disease will have no power at that second... sin will be powerless, death will be defeated, and I will dwell in the house of the Lord forever and ever and ever... I told them, another thing is that as we live through the adversities of life, we don't walk by theory, but by the knowledge that what we have believed is true. I don't have to theorize that God's love and mercy and power is real, I know it is because I have experienced it.

December 13, 2012

My wife, Fran, received a call tonight from Kenya, Africa from Naomi, a very precious friend. She spoke to Fran and through Fran to me to tell us that at this time in our lives it is so needful that we stay close to Jesus. Both Fran and I felt like the Holy Spirit orchestrated that call to remind us of a very real truth. As Fran was taking the call, I was being sick in the bathroom... but coming out Fran relayed that message to me, and we both realized we have let our frustrations and our situations steal, kill, and rob the most important. Prayer time was later but a real blessing. Look at this scripture I have used many times... tonight there was fresh meaning to it:

John 10:10 NKJV

The thief (enemy) does not come except to steal, and to kill, and to destroy. I have come that they may have life, and that they may have it more abundantly.

We let Satan steal the joy of our salvation, but we got it back... Here is another pointed scripture:

Habakkuk 3:17-19 NKJV

Though the fig tree may not blossom, nor fruit be on the vines; Though the labor of the olive may fail, And the fields yield no food; Though the flock may be cut off from the fold, and there be no herd in the stalls Yet I will rejoice in the Lord, I will joy in the God of my salvation. The Lord God is my strength; He will make my feet like deer's feet, And He will make me walk on my high mountains...

2 Timothy 1:12 NKJV

For this reason I also suffer these things; nevertheless I am not ashamed, for I know whom I have believed and am persuaded that He is able to keep what I have committed to Him until that Day.

Our will is to stay close to Jesus... His will is to keep us there.

December 14, 2012

Fran and I had decided that since I was feeling better, we would try to make a quick trip to Portland with the first priority to see Fran's Aunt Louise from Denver who is staying with her daughter in Portland. We had our itinerary settled and were anticipating going. My mind was ready to go, but my body just got so tired that I could not imagine being able to walk the long distances across the airport here or in Portland. I was so disappointed that I was too weak to go. My spirit was willing but my flesh was weak. For some reason, my emotions are so close to the surface that I could not keep the tears back. I had never canceled travel plans because I was too weak... I always found a way to gather my strength and go... but I just couldn't this time, and it just overwhelmed me... and of course if my emotions get out of control, it makes Fran afraid. I really am fighting for life, and that makes me feel bad for her, but it makes me man up and stops the tears.

You have heard the old saying, "that when it rains, it pours?"... (It has rained over a half an inch today here on the desert). I went out to the garage (before it started raining) to get luggage and saw water on the floor... our water heater had started leaking. I had to move a bunch of things that could be affected by the water and mop up the water. I got it done but had to lie down because I was exhausted. Maybe good came from the leak because it alerted me to just how weak I have become. For all my adult life, I have enjoyed believing I had the strength to accomplish anything that needed to be done. If I wasn't strong enough, I could always figure a way out to get almost anything done. But not today... that is devastating to a guy's pride...

While going through chemo I experienced weakness, but this is different... then my strength would come back after the chemo wore off... but now it just doesn't come back. I am now at the same weight I was when I was 21. 165 lbs. I am not bragging nor complaining, just stating some facts that I wish were different.

The weakness of one's body does not have to diminish the strength of one's spirit. Tonight, it is very wet outside, but inside it is dry and warm, that is kind of like my life. My body is weak, but I still feel strong in my spirit and in my faith. I am not bragging, just stating what I believe is true. When God inspired men to write the Bible, it seems there are little nuggets of truth embedded in the contents that have an answer for almost anything in life. For example:

2 Corinthians 12:9-10 KJV

And He (Jesus) said unto me, "My grace is sufficient for thee: for My strength is made perfect in weakness." Most gladly therefore will I rather glory in my infirmities, that the power of Christ may rest upon me. Therefore I take pleasure in infirmities, in reproaches, in necessities, in persecutions, in distresses for Christ's sake: for when I am weak, then am I strong.

As I have said before, I am not sure I take pleasure in my infirmities but yet I do know that my problems certainly make me depend more on the Lord than before.

By the way, I am going to see if my home warranty will cover my water heater replacement. This could be another test of my faith... lol

———

I have heard preachers and others through the years when talking about a Christian who had died say that we should not grieve for the one who died because death is not punishment, but it is a promotion; or a Christian publication reporting on a person's death would write, "Brother So-n-So was promoted to glory". Promoted or promotion were terms used instead of saying passed away or died.

Last night, Fran and I on the way back from a doctor's appointment decided to go to Panda Express so Fran would not have to prepare a meal (which is hard because I can't eat very much). Making a long story longer, I did eat some of the food, which tasted good, just hard to swallow. Then I noticed my fortune cookie and broke it open and my fortune said, "You are next in line for promotion. " Maybe I am morbid, but I had to laugh because immediately I remembered how the word promotion had been used. I don't know when I will be promoted, but as the Psalmist said:

Psalm 90:12 KJV

So teach us to number our days,
that we may apply our hearts unto wisdom.

Another great Psalm:

Psalm 91:14-16 KJV

Because he hath set his love upon me, therefore will I deliver him:
I will set him on high, because he hath known My name. He shall
call upon Me, and I will answer him: I will be with him in trouble;
I will deliver him, and honor him. With long life will I satisfy him,
and show him My salvation.

December 15, 2012

The following verse is kind of a strange verse, but in light of the events of today, there is a message for us.

Ecclesiastes 9:4 DJV (Duane Jordan Version)

As long as there is breath, there is hope: it has been said,
that a live dog is better than a dead lion.

In the writer's time, a dog was of little value whereas a lion was revered as a mighty creature. Even a dead lion was respected more than a live dog. But the writer is reminding us that to be alive, to have breath, is a reason for hope. To be a live, barking dog is better than a lion that has no life in it.

The tragedies of today in Newtown, Connecticut at the Sandy Hook Elementary School should make all of us realize that nothing we are going through is worse than what happened to the victims of that senseless violence.

If you are reading this, no matter what your circumstances of life are, you are alive. We are alive, even if we can't pay our bills, we have terminal disease, can't find a direction in life, maybe rich with no purpose in life, a student without a major, a tired and weary mother or a discouraged father; no matter how bad we may think life is, we are alive…There can still be a purpose for being and still having breath. Listen,

James 5:16 NIV

"The prayers of a righteous person are powerful and effective."

I think most of my nearly 600 friends are believers in Jesus Christ and each of you can make a difference in your world. Here is something every one of us can do!

The law says we cannot pray in the public schools, but there is no law that says we cannot pray for the schools; the students, the teachers, the staff, and administrators.

I would encourage each of you to pick a school close to your home and daily pray that our God of mercy and grace will keep evil from harming any of the precious students or staff in the schools. There are four schools within blocks of my home…I am going to invade each of them with prayer every day, and I believe my prayers are effective and powerful.

If you can, walk around them, drive around them while you are praying…I may have to find someone to push me in a wheelchair or drive me around the schools, but while I have breath, I am going to partner with God to keep our schools safe in my town.

If you don't know what to pray, pray the Lord's Prayer

(Matthew 6:9-13) KJV "…deliver us from evil…"

Let's start a movement of prayer! Adopt a school. I believe God will keep evil from harming the innocents…

Matthew 18:10 NLT

Beware that you don't look down on any of these little ones. For I tell you that in heaven their angels are always in the presence of my heavenly Father.

A few years ago, several men joined me three days a week at 4:30 A. M. to walk around the schools of Boulder City, the churches and places of government to pray. As far as I know, during that time, there were no acts of violence in the schools, there was a greater unity among the churches, and our church found favor with city government. Unfortunately, we became weary in well doing and after a year or so, we stopped. But I believe it time to revive prayer that is effective...

Psalm 34:17-19 NLT

The LORD hears His people when they call to Him for help. He rescues them from all their troubles. The LORD is close to the brokenhearted; He rescues those whose spirits are crushed. The righteous person faces many troubles, but the LORD comes to the rescue each time.

December 16, 2012

Fran and I were guests at a church in Las Vegas today. We were so blessed by our hosts and the good service. I appreciate the people so much who give themselves to be worship leaders, singers and musicians in every church I have had the pleasure to attend and today was no exception. The preaching of the Word was great as the pastor talked about no limitations with God. We went to lunch afterward with our friends at Chili's, and I actually ate most of my lunch. Coming home was a good thing, however, as I need my beauty sleep in the afternoon (not doing much good yet, but I have my hopes).

I have talked of seasons of healings before and the last couple of days have been very pleasant compared to those in the past. I don't know what is happening, but I have actually gained a few pounds. I love this time of the year as we are reminded of what the angels said to the shepherds:

Luke 2:10-14 NKJV

Then the angel said to them, "Do not be afraid, for behold, I bring you good tidings of great joy which will be to all people. For there is born to you this day in the city of David a Savior, who is Christ the Lord. And this will be the sign to you: You will find a Babe wrapped in swaddling cloths, lying in a manger. " And suddenly there was with the angel a multitude of the heavenly host praising God and saying: "Glory to God in the highest, And on earth peace, goodwill toward men!"

I love those words to the shepherds, "... For there is born to you a Savior, this day..." It was personal, and it was immediate. It was well defined... and the baby is the Messiah/Christ the Lord... They were told where to find the baby and then the great news, God wants peace on earth and goodwill toward men... a new covenant through this baby was going to be ours... Through my lifetime, I have experienced that peace and goodwill God wanted me to have. I cherish my faith and my hope in Jesus Christ. It is truly the greatest gift ever given...

———

Today was a good day in comparison with some in the recent past. I had much more energy than a few days ago. We have had an interesting couple of days. The battery in our fairly new car failed (out of warranty), and it took going to three places to find one. Then our hot water tank began to leak, and we felt OK about that because of the home warranty. The technician who came today said the tank was covered but not the labor and parts to bring it up to code... It is a 12- year-old tank. The extra cost was $700. 00. We got him down to $450. 00 with us doing some things ourselves like pulling our own permit which will save $180. 00. However, that cannot happen till Monday so it will leak until then.

It is impossible to be upset in comparison to what the parents of the first graders in Connecticut are going through today, so we grin and bear it... knowing:

Romans 8:28 NASB

...that God causes all things to work together for good to those who love God, to those who are called according to His purpose.

So, we look for the good in all circumstances.

The following scripture from the Message Bible shows the heart of God towards children... those who hurt and harm children will not get away with their deeds even if they commit suicide... they will have to answer to a just God who loves children:

Mark 10:13 MSG

The people brought children to Jesus, hoping He might touch them. The disciples shooed them off. But Jesus was irate and let them know it: "Don't push these children away. Don't ever get between them and me. These children are at the very center of life in the kingdom. Mark this: Unless you accept God's kingdom in the simplicity of a child, you'll never get in." Then, gathering the children up in His arms, He laid His hands of blessing on them.

In another place, the Word says it would be better never to have been born than to hurt one of these little ones...

As school starts again for most kids tomorrow, please be in prayer for the schools near you and the ones your kids and grandkids attend. If you can drive or walk around the schools and pray the Lord's Prayer and whatever you want to pray. Remember in the Lord's prayer, Jesus taught us that we have to pray to see an answer, (and I believe) and action... the last part of the prayer is *"and deliver us from evil"* (some versions say "the evil one," but regardless it is a prayer Jesus taught us to pray). Jesus emphasized it so we should too... deliver us from the evil that could come to the schools...

1 John 5:14-15 NKJV

Now this is the confidence that we have in Him, that if we ask anything according to His will, He hears us. And if we know that He hears us, whatever we ask, we know that we have the petitions that we have asked of Him.

If we pray what He told us to pray, then it must be his will...

December 17, 2012

Today, except for the gaunt look on my face you might not realize that I have been fighting cancer for almost 11 months. I had an extraordinary day like few I have had since February of this year. I cannot explain it, and I have no idea what tomorrow may bring, but today was phenomenal.

I got up and headed for the city hall to pull a building permit to replace my leaking water heater. Since the repairmen were going to charge us over $400 beyond the price of the water heater and they would not fix the soaked drywall or repair water damage, I called our warranty company, and they will pay for the water heater so I decided I could replace it as it needed to be done right away. So, for the entire day, I have been working with my son Jon to get it replaced. I rebuilt the stand, replaced drywall, and Jon and I replaced the water heater, installed the earthquake straps, put on sweat fittings and fired the thing up. We were very proud of ourselves until we noticed a dripping on a valve. We have water, but waiting until tomorrow to fix the problem.

The good news is I spent the whole day working as though I were well and that was awesome. I was blown away by my stamina and strength to do what I did today; the first kind of day like this since February. Not sure what is going on, but it was refreshing to get tired and not just feel weak... There is a truth to the seasons of healings that it seems God gives to me. I am tired, but I sat in my big chair only a short time and worked a 10-hour day. For me that is unbelievable. I still cannot eat normally, but I ate enough to have the strength to make it through the day.

Job went through a lot of questioning about his life. I think he really wanted to die because he was suffering so much. I love what I read in the Message Bible when he was struggling with a seemingly incurable disease and the strength issue. His friends told him what he ought to be thinking, saying and doing. This is part of his reply:

Job 6:11-13

"Where's the strength to keep my hopes up? What future do I have to keep me going? Do you think I have nerves of steel? Do you think I'm made of iron? Do you think I can pull myself up by my bootstraps? Why, I don't even have any boots!"

That's the way we feel sometimes. That there is no strength, no hope, no nerves, no sense that things will ever change... but David gives a little different twist. He had a different take on strength or help. Again, from the Message Bible:

Philippians 4:13 MSG

Whatever I have, wherever I am, I can make it through anything in the One who makes me who I am.

Psalm 121:1-2
I look up to the mountains; does my strength come from mountains?
No, my strength comes from God, who made heaven, and earth, and
mountains. Our strength comes from the Giver of life and the hope
of our lives.

December 18, 2012

This is the second day of wonder for me. Again, I had the energy to do what I needed to get done. I was out in the garage by 9:00 A. M. and was able to fix the problem in just a short time and then the rest of the morning and afternoon was spent trying to return the garage to its intended use (parking a car in it). With the garage door open, and the pickup backed in so we can throw away junk and with rain falling all morning we were able to get it almost back to normal.

I was moving some boxes and found some old yearbooks of Fran's going all the way back to junior high. I opened one of her college yearbooks, and there she was beautiful and young with hair nearly a foot high (was that the poof style?). I showed it to her, and she found where her late husband, Stan, had written a whole page to her (the year before they married). I told Fran to go read it where it was warm, and she never came back to the garage. Must have been a good message from Stan... As soon as I could, I came in, took a hot shower and went to bed for a couple of hours.

Fran and I both lost our former spouses to death. They died within three weeks of each other, and both of us have allowed the other to hold memories of our former spouses as precious. Our love for each other allows us to never deny the love we had in our first marriage. We both agree we have a great marriage.

The love we share is founded in the love we have found in our relationship with Jesus Christ. The things the New Testament teaches about love can be lived out daily.

The love Jesus taught was radical:

Matthew 5:43-44 NKJV

"You have heard that it was said, 'You shall love your neighbor and hate your enemy.' But I say to you, love your enemies, bless those who curse you, do good to those who hate you, and pray for those who spitefully use you and persecute you,"

That does not fit in normal human interaction, does it?

Matthew 22:37-40 NKJV

Jesus said to him, "You shall love the Lord your God with all your heart, with all your soul, and with all your mind.' This is the first and great commandment. And the second is like it: 'You shall love your neighbor as yourself.' On these two commandments hang all the Law and the Prophets. "

John 15:13 NKJV

Greater love has no one than this, than to lay down one's life for his friends.

Ephesians 5:25 NKJV

Husbands, love your wives, just as Christ also loved the church and gave Himself for her,

1 John 4:7-8 NKJV

Beloved, let us love one another, for love is of God; and everyone who loves is born of God and knows God. He who does not love does not know God, for God is love.

All the scriptures above talk about how we should love, but the ultimate example of love is how God loved us...

John 3:16 NKJV

For God so loved the world that He gave His only begotten Son, that whoever believes in Him should not perish but have everlasting life.

Christmas is about Love... Love came into this world as a helpless baby but grew to the place that He willingly became the supreme sacrifice for God's workmanship: us.

December 20, 2012

Luke 2:10, 11 NKJV

Then the angel said to them, "Do not be afraid, for behold, I bring you good tidings of great joy which will be to all people. For there is born to you this day in the city of David a Savior, who is Christ the Lord."

Today is day three of stellar energy. I had a 9:00 A. M. meeting with a Veteran's Rep about VA benefits. His office is where I used to be a Chaplain at the Southern Nevada Veterans Home. The meeting was good and was over just as Chapel was starting. The new Chaplain invited me to speak to the congregation, and they all clapped as I greeted them. They remembered me. I was blessed. They were so kind. The Chaplain said I was the best Christmas gift he could have received. It was good to have the energy to be able to be there.

I have been busy all day. I even cooked supper tonight. It has been months since I tried to eat steak. I barbecued one tonight and fixed baked potatoes and was able to eat all my portions.

I kept busy up till 8:00 P. M. then drove to the airport to pick up Rob and Jenny and girls from Portland. They do not have In-and-Out in Oregon, so that was their first stop on the way home. I asked the girls to listen again to one of my favorite Christmas songs, *"When the Christmas Baby Cries,"* by the Annie Moses Band. As I said before, the music is so beautiful and full of peace that I can listen to it over and over, and the words are almost inconsequential. However, one night I heard some of the words and began to realize the incredible miracle of the Son of God being born to a woman and when that little baby cried for the first time, and the breath of life filled his lungs for the first time, it was the fulfillment of many prophecies and the beginning of so many more. His cry at birth was to announce His life and that the Savior had arrived. I am so glad that the sound of the Christmas Baby was the sound that heralded hope for the world.

Merry Christmas...

December 21, 2012

Another wonderful day! Fran and I went to a Boulder City Christian Minister's Christmas breakfast this morning that Christian Center hosted. It was a great time seeing my old friends that I have not seen in months. At the close of the breakfast the pastor of the Seventh Day Advent Church asked our leader if we could have an anointing service to pray for me. It was such a precious time, but we prayed for her too as she has MS. Then two other pastor's wives were prayed for. I was president of this group several times and what a precious Christian fellowship we have.

Again today I have been able to eat more than I have for months. I take this as a season of healing and am enjoying my family who are here...

———

For no good reason, I am still up. Just found out that at 3:11 A. M. [locally] it is 12:11 A. M. on Saturday, December 22 in Nuku'alofa, Tonga which with all the time zone variation is exactly 24 hours ahead of us, so I can safely report that the world did not end on Friday, December 21, 2012.

Matthew 24:36 NKJV

But of that day and hour no one knows, not even the angels of heaven, but My Father only.

My heart still aches for the 20 children and their teachers whose world ended for them last Friday. I pray for the parents of those innocent little children who must be suffering so deeply with the loss of their children.

I am glad that Jesus told us that He has prepared a place for us when we come to the end of our lives on this planet. These are just some of the many scriptures that make us believe there is life after life...and not an end of everything as the Mayan calendar was interpreted to say:

John 14:1-6 NKJV

Let not your heart be troubled; you believe in God, believe also in Me. In My Father's house are many mansions; if it were not so, I would have told you. I go to prepare a place for you. And if I go and

*prepare a place for you, I will come again and receive you to Myself;
that where I am, there you may be also. And where I go you know,
and the way you know. " Thomas said to Him, "Lord, we do not
know where You are going, and how can we know the way?" Jesus
said to him, "I am the way, the truth, and the life. No one comes to
the Father except through Me.*

Psalms 23:4-6 NKJV

*Yea, though I walk through the valley of the shadow of death, I
will fear no evil; for You are with me; Your rod and Your staff, they
comfort me. Surely goodness and mercy shall follow me all the days of
my life; and I will dwell in the house of the Lord Forever.*

———

I went to the dentist yesterday, and I am not sure they knew how to deal
with a person who Hospice thinks has less than six months to live. I had
a broken crown on a bridge, and the dentist told me it would cause me
no pain so did I want it replaced. It is a warranty replacement as the lab
evidently did not do something right. I told him of course I do. If I live
it makes me look better, and if I die I will look better in the casket. He
pretty much didn't know what to say.

By the way, my water heater passed city inspection so Rob and I took
the old one to the dump, took a pickup full of giveaways to Goodwill and
then realized my brakes were not working right on my pick up so took it
to George's Auto Repair here in BC and left it for him to fix. I was a little
tired, so my family left me home alone and Chuck, from George's, called
and told me it was ready. I decided to ride my bike up there (notice the
word up?). It is about a mile (felt like 10), but I made it. Was sure glad
Tyler helped me load the bike... got home but I was noticeably winded.
But it was a good feeling. I am going to try a ride as often as possible. I am
so blessed to have this second chance at life... God is giving me strength
and the will to live. I love these scriptures:

Psalm 103:1-5 NKJV

Bless the Lord, O my soul; Bless the Lord, O my soul, and forget not all His benefits: Who forgives all your iniquities, Who heals all your diseases, Who redeems your life from destruction, Who crowns you with loving-kindness and tender mercies, Who satisfies your mouth with good things, So that your youth is renewed like the eagle's.

Isaiah 40:31 NKJV

But those who wait on the Lord Shall renew their strength; they shall mount up with wings like eagles, they shall run and not be weary, they shall walk and not faint.

December 22, 2012

Another great day! All our family went sledding at Mt. Charleston today which is about an hour and a half from our house. All 17 of us. Mt. Charleston is about 9000 ft., and there actually was about a foot of snow up where we were sledding. We had an area all to ourselves. We had a blast. Fran and I even attempted to come down the hill... we were like a couple of beached whales when we got to the bottom. What a great memory day! All my kids and grandkids were here (except Kalani and Jay). God gave Fran and me the chance to make some awesome memories.

Just a short distance from our desert dwelling is this incredible island of Douglas Fir, high mountains, ski lifts, and snow. It is amazing. It is a lot like leaving the desert of our lives that is composed of rushing, working, worrying, hopelessness and trouble and finding the presence of the Holy Spirit (God) and being refreshed by Him. There is an old song that says,

> *"There is a quiet place, far from the rapid pace where God can soothe my troubled mind... Sheltered by tree and flower, there in my quiet hour with Him my cares are left behind... Whether a garden small or on a mountain tall, new strength and courage there I find... then from this quiet place, I go prepared to face a new day with love for all mankind..."*

—There is a Quiet Place[23]

The following verses were given to Israel centuries ago, but I believe they are promises for the individual today.

Isaiah 32:17, 18 NKJV

The work of righteousness will be peace, and the effect of righteousness, quietness and assurance forever. My people will dwell in a peaceful habitation, in secure dwellings, and in quiet resting places,

We are home and ready to eat chili and enchilada soup with hot chocolate. From the desert to the snow and from the snow back to the desert. What a great memory day!

December 24, 2012

Matthew 1:20-23 NKJV

But while he thought about these things, behold, an angel of the Lord appeared to him in a dream, saying, "Joseph, son of David, do not be afraid to take to you Mary your wife, for that which is conceived in her is of the Holy Spirit. And she will bring forth a Son, and you shall call His name Jesus, for He will save His people from their sins." So all this was done that it might be fulfilled which was spoken by the Lord through the prophet, saying: Behold, the virgin shall be with child, and bear a Son, and they shall call His name Immanuel, which is translated, God with us.

Luke 2:9-11 NKJV

And behold, an angel of the Lord stood before them, and the glory of the Lord shone around them, and they were greatly afraid. Then the angel said to them, "Do not be afraid, for behold, I bring you good tidings of great joy which will be to all people. For there is born to you this day in the city of David a Savior, who is Christ the Lord."

Galatians 4:4-7

But when the fullness of the time had come, God sent forth His Son, born of a woman, born under the law, to redeem those who were under the law, that we might receive the adoption as sons. And because you are sons, God has sent forth the Spirit of His Son into your hearts, crying out, "Abba, Father!" Therefore you are no longer a slave but a son, and if a son, then an heir of God through Christ.

MERRY CHRISTMAS TO ALL, AND TO ALL A BLESSED NEW YEAR!

December 25, 2012

John 14:1-6 NKJV

"Let not your heart be troubled; you believe in God, believe also in Me. In My Father's house are many mansions; if it were not so, I would have told you. I go to prepare a place for you. And if I go and prepare a place for you, I will come again and receive you to Myself; that where I am, there you may be also. And where I go you know, and the way you know." Thomas said to Him, "Lord, we do not know where You are going, and how can we know the way?" Jesus said to him, "I am the way, the truth, and the life. No one comes to the Father except through Me."

Everyone was gone, just Fran and I at home and before getting out of bed I asked Fran if she had any cinnamon rolls she could fix. I was remembering back to the years before when we would get up and around the tree with the kids; eat some kind of sweet rolls and have a hot cup of coffee. Fran said she had a mix and I fell back to sleep and woke up as she brought me a hot cinnamon roll and a cup of coffee. The memory of the taste of the roll and the coffee made me get up to enjoy it around the tree.

Reminiscing Christmas past. So many memories of when a child. One special memory was when I was five or six, my father had died, and things were probably very tough on my mom as she had 11 children. Mom had a sister married to a wonderful farmer who had a big farm and a big Buick. He promised to come and get us for Christmas... I remember watching every car that came down our street, thinking he would never come.

He finally did and took us to his home where I remember the biggest Christmas tree I had ever seen. I do not remember the gifts, if any, but I remember my uncle kept his promise. I never heard a word about Santa, but I sure did about Jesus. This story reminds me of the reason Jesus came. He came to make a way we could come to the Father's House.

Jesus will keep his promise!

I actually ate two rolls and drank a cup of coffee, and it tasted so good, but about an hour later everything changed to nausea and stomach pains as something began not to work right in me. The neuropathy seemed to amplify and from that point on it has been a very hard day physically. Even chicken soup did nothing to dispel the sickness. I have had such a wonderful week until today and now to feel so bad is very discouraging.

Did you ever notice when you don't feel good is when you can get discouraged very quickly? I think I relived every unwise decision I had ever made in my life and those times where I did not ask for wisdom and failed to trust God. That just dug a hole deeper in my day. In my despair, I thought of what the angel said to the shepherds.

"For unto you is born this day... a Savior..." and I know I heard the Holy Spirit say to me, "If you were perfect, you would not need a Savior, you wouldn't need me. " Oh, how I need a Savior, how I need a healer, how I need a friend that will not abandon me when I am in despair. I believe I was led to listen to Lincoln Brewster and his little boy do the song, *"Everlasting God." "Strength will rise as we wait upon the Lord..."*[24] and those scriptures I have quoted many times here began to lift my spirit. Physically I do not feel better, but spiritually I feel renewed. Let me post the scriptures I am speaking of:

Isaiah 40:28-31 NKJV

Have you not known? Have you not heard? The everlasting God, the Lord, The Creator of the ends of the earth, neither faints nor is weary. His understanding is unsearchable. He gives power to the weak, and to those who have no might He increases strength. Even the youths shall faint and be weary, and the young men shall utterly fall, but those who wait on the Lord Shall renew their strength; they shall mount up with wings like eagles, they shall run and not be weary, they shall walk and not faint.

I pray you will find strength and hope in this tonight. Merry Christmas.

———

Remember I replaced our water heater? The day we finished it, it was raining hard. I remember looking at the ceiling where the gas vent pipe went out, and it was leaking. It was raining so hard that I could not do anything about it but mentioned it to my sons. They chose this afternoon in the middle of a windstorm to see what was wrong. Turns out the pipe had separated in the attic, and I had to get up on the roof three times. We got it fixed, and it looks great, repaired the ceiling, and I think it is as good as new. They prevented a potential hazard by fixing it, so I am praising God for that.

But it has been another good day for me even if I am not as strong as I would like. Eating is still a challenge although I have been hungry all day long. I even ate two original Mexican chicken tacos and enjoyed them very much. Another season of healing. I drove Rob, Jenny, and girls to the airport tonight and when we got home, Fran made chicken soup for our daughter Jen who has a bad cold. We were both ready to sit down and relax. We plan on a very low-keyed day tomorrow, but will see. Here is my hope for you tomorrow and into the New Year:

Romans 15:13 NKJV

Now may the God of hope fill you with all joy and peace in believing, that you may abound in hope by the power of the Holy Spirit.

December 27, 2012

I am very suspicious that God is listening to someone's prayer again... The nausea started leaving, and I decided that even if I wasn't feeling strong, it was time to take the outside Christmas decorations down. That was kind of sad in a way. My two neighbors and ours blended into a beautiful scene as people came around our corner, but I knew I had just a window of opportunity to get them down. So, Fran and I were able to get the decorations put in the garage in about an hour. Fran knew this morning I wasn't feeling good (slept till 10:30 A. M.) she rolled our garbage to the curb, but it wasn't garbage day, it was recycling day and so nothing was picked up. lol... So, I made two runs to the dump today as well.

I was still feeling rough, but was feeling so much better. I could feel hope coming back into my being. Fran wanted me to go to Henderson with her, and so I drove her and ended up at Target and Wal-Mart... Then she asked to go to Arby's for a sandwich. We were going to go in to wash and order but were going to take out. The waitress for some reason said, "Why not eat here?" No reason to but I decided to. We were being set up by God for a very special moment: As I asked God to bless our food (I was going to try to eat), I heard a song begin to play in the store speakers. It was Whitney Houston singing *"I Will Always Love You."* I looked across the table at the wonderful person who has loved me for over 25 years and there in Arby's we had one of the most romantic moments of our recent past.

Both of us had tears in our eyes as was sang to each other pledging that we would always love each other. It was a special moment that God gave us in the middle of all the struggles we have gone through this year.

There is nothing more powerful than love. Nothing more precious than loving and being loved. Do you know, all my nausea began to leave…and I began to feel alive again? Thank you, Father, for that moment in Arby's.

I know what the Bible says about me loving my wife, and maybe someone needs to hear this tonight. From the Message Bible:

Ephesians 5:25-28

Husbands, go all out in your love for your wives, exactly as Christ did for the church —a love marked by giving, not getting. Christ's love makes the church whole. His words evoke her beauty. Everything he does and says is designed to bring the best out of her, dressing her in dazzling white silk, radiant with holiness. And that is how husbands ought to love their wives. They're really doing themselves a favor — since they're already "one" in marriage.

December 28, 2012

I had an eye exam this morning which as I filled out the paperwork and they wanted to know my medications, all I could put down was Hospice. They are always trying to make me comfortable while living through this six months' prognosis. I told the eye doctor my problems and all he could do was look at me and say he was sorry. My eyes are good with my present prescription, so I told him I want to write a book so I need to be at my computer a lot, so I am getting prescription computer glasses. I told him what I told the dentist about looking good if I live or looking good in the casket if I die... he did get a good laugh from that.

I have enjoyed the day... got a bunch of work done including taking our tree down and taking it to the dump. Had dinner with some old friends and got to pray with a dear friend in Washington who is struggling for her life. We saw each other on Facetime. I quoted John 14:1-6 to her and I know it helped. After a day of being anxious on Tuesday, today was a day of faith and hope: Please read and meditate on the following verses:

Philippians 4:6, 7 NIV

Do not be anxious about anything, but in every situation, by prayer and petition, with thanksgiving, present your requests to God. And the peace of God, which transcends all understanding, will guard your hearts and your minds in Christ Jesus.

I have this posted on my mirror in my bathroom... helps me remember.

December 29, 2012

Today I decided I was going to start another project in my garage. This project today was to take things out of my garage attic that had been there for years and to make a place to store our Christmas decorations. I was up and down a ladder dozens of times. I managed to drop an antique guitar and break it in a bunch of pieces... that was sure disappointing. I found one box that had stuff left by a friend from Africa who had to have me store it because his luggage was overweight for the airlines. It had been there for years, and we had totally forgotten about it. Fortunately, one of his sons lives in Vegas and is picking it up tomorrow.

Tonight, we had dinner with Fran's late husband's brother and sister-in-law as they are on their way to snowbird in Phoenix from Oregon. How blessed I am that they and their family have accepted me as family. Before they left, they got on their knees by me and prayed for my healing, comfort, and care for Fran, committing us to God's keeping.

One of the hard things is knowing that I am not getting stronger, I am just using the strength I have and as I put Christmas things away realizing that unless there is a miracle, I will not be here next Christmas to unpack those decorations. *(Please refer to photo section in the back of the book.)* As my family knelt around me and we realized we may not see each other again, it kind of reminded me of the storyline in Acts 20 as Paul is getting ready to leave Greece for Jerusalem:

Acts 20:24; 36-38 NKJV

"… But none of these things move me; nor do I count my life dear to myself, so that I may finish my race with joy, and the ministry which I received from the Lord Jesus, to testify to the gospel of the grace of God. And when he had said these things, he knelt down and prayed with them all. Then they all wept freely, and fell on Paul's neck and kissed him, sorrowing most of all for the words which he spoke, that they would see his face no more…"

The awesome thing is that Paul finished his race….

2 Timothy 4:7-8 NKJV

I have fought the good fight, I have finished the race, I have kept the faith. Finally, there is laid up for me the crown of righteousness.

Whether soon or later, this is my desire to finish the race, keep the faith and then receive the crown of righteousness… You make your choice, but I hope it is similar…

December 30, 2012

We enjoyed being in church this morning and sensing the presence of the Lord there. Then coming home and seeing our one-year-old grandson driving to our house in his new car… you have to see the picture on Rebekah Jordan's FB.

I was saddened for my friend Ron, whose mother passed away this morning from her battle with cancer. I had the joy of leading her to Jesus years ago, and then being able to pray with her a few days ago, was a gift.

I am thankful that for her this was not a random event but what the Bible calls a time and a season and that in God's timing he makes all things beautiful. We now have a sister and hero waiting in heaven for us. He will comfort the family through this time.

I am not one to deny reality because having lost five good Christian friends to cancer this year I know that the battle that I am having is encroaching on my life. In the last two days, there have been some new struggles that I am experiencing. I am having a very difficult time swallowing anything, and even small sips of liquids can cause me to be sick. I am losing weight... not too much pain, but it sure is uncomfortable trying to eat. I climbed a ladder several times yesterday and have not really recovered my strength from that time. I feel so sad that my dear wife has to watch this process, but we did make our vows for better for worse, in sickness or in health... I know she is thankful that she is with me... we are not giving in or up, just watching...

By faith, I am daily asking God to preserve my life, but I know it is in his hands. I am praying that I will have the opportunity to finish the book on my journey-caused-faith-to-triumph-over- fear. I hear words from the Gospel that will help my family and me through these times: This is from the Message Bible... a unique paraphrase of an age-old invitation to come to Jesus...

Matthew 11:28-30

Are you tired? Worn out? ... Come to me. Get away with Me and you'll recover your life. I'll show you how to take a real rest. Walk with Me and work with Me — watch how I do it. Learn the unforced rhythms of grace. I won't lay anything heavy or ill-fitting on you. Keep company with Me and you'll learn to live freely and lightly.

Daily I am trying to keep learning from Him.

Two wonderful friends happened to stop by at about the same time, and my gracious wife fixed lunch for them (and me). It was an enjoyable time. Barnabas from Vegas (via Kenya) and Lee and his grandson from Lewiston, Idaho. I had been pastor to both men at different times in their lives. Barnabas came to pick up the box left at my house years ago by his father, and Lee (who is a preacher/teacher/exhorter) came to share the Word. You have to know Lee to appreciate his passion for the Word. As he speaks his voice gets louder and louder, and you can't help but listen.

lol. He also prayed for my healing. He wasn't as loud when he prayed, but I believe God heard him on my behalf. I was grateful for the words he spoke and prayed.

This morning in my meditations, I found these scriptures and notice I changed two words. I put my name in the scripture, but I am holding on to these words for my life:

Psalm 21:1-4 NLT

How Duane rejoices in your strength, O Lord! He shouts with joy because You give him victory. For You have given him his heart's desire; You have withheld nothing he requested. You welcomed him back with success and prosperity. You placed a crown of life on his head. He asked You to preserve his life, and You granted his request. The days of his life stretch on forever.

Hezekiah asked God to extend his life, and it was answered. I am asking that daily and thank you for agreeing with me in this request.

January 2, 2013

The following is not a New Year's Resolution, but I am resolved to make it my goal for every day. My year has been kind of rough so far because of new challenges, but nonetheless, I must have a goal:

Philippians 4:6-8 NIV

Do not be anxious about anything, but in every situation, by prayer and petition, with thanksgiving, present your requests to God. And the peace of God, which transcends all understanding, will guard your hearts and your minds in Christ Jesus. Finally, brothers and sisters, whatever is true, whatever is noble, whatever is right, whatever is pure, whatever is lovely, whatever is admirable—if anything is excellent or praiseworthy—think about such things.

January 3, 2013

For two days, I have felt closer to death than life. It has been easier to sit on the side of my bed, neither getting up nor laying down. For two days, I have eaten virtually nothing because the food or liquids will not go down. Six months ago, I weighed nearly 220 pounds but today I am under 160, and that is not from a weight loss program...lol. With that much body mass gone you know my energy level is low. I would have fully given up yesterday, but some circumstances beyond my control would not allow me to do that and by the time I got up today there has been a new sense of life in me, and I have eaten some food.

I am on my way to see about an endoscopy and hopefully a procedure that can expand my esophagus where the tumor may be so I can swallow nutrients. It might give me a little time to get stronger for what may be next.

Do you know how many hamburgers I saw being consumed on TV yesterday? Lol. I was getting so jealous of those who can eat... ha... I would cherish your prayers today.

There is one food more important than hamburgers:

Matthew 4:4 NIV

Jesus answered, "It is written: 'Man shall not live on bread alone, but on every word that comes from the mouth of God."

John 6:35 NIV

Then Jesus declared, "I am the bread of life. Whoever comes to Me will never go hungry, and whoever believes in Me will never be thirsty.

1 Peter 2:2, 3 NIV

Like newborn babies, crave pure spiritual milk, so that by it you may grow up in your salvation, now that you have tasted that the Lord is good.

January 4, 2013

> *1 Peter 3:10-12, 14, 15 NIV*
>
> *For whoever would love life and see good days must keep their tongue from evil and their lips from deceitful speech. They must turn from evil and do good; they must seek peace and pursue it. For the eyes of the Lord are on the righteous and his ears are attentive to their prayer. Always be prepared to give an answer to everyone who asks you to give the reason for the hope that you have. But do this with gentleness and respect...*

Today was much better than yesterday. I have eaten some and feel some renewed strength. I went to the doctor today, and he has set up a procedure next Tuesday to try to expand the esophagus with an endoscopy. He thinks it will buy me some time. If it works, I may well be eating a good meal next week. Thanks for your prayers. My brother Lyle and wife Lynn are here for a few days... they are always an encouragement.

January 5, 2013

Should I live to be 68, this is one of the most thought-provoking quotes that I have understood for some time:

> *"Perhaps the most valuable result of all education is the ability to make yourself do the thing you have to do, whether you like it or not."*[25]
>
> —*Thomas Henry Huxley.*

In this new year as we all struggle to find that fine line of survival, there are things we just have to make our mind up to do whether we like it or not. That is the difference between failure and success, triumph or defeat; is making ourselves do what is not the easiest, but what is the best or the necessary.

My prayer for you who have every reason to succeed in 2013 is that you get your head out of wasteful periods of time watching computers or television, video games and make a meaningful contribution to family, your community, your job, and the world around you. Excel is more than a Microsoft program... Excel this year should be your goal in every good thing that matters.

James 1:16-18 MSG

So, my very dear friends, don't get thrown off course. Every desirable and beneficial gift comes out of heaven. The gifts are rivers of light cascading down from the Father of Light. There is nothing deceitful in God, nothing two-faced, nothing fickle. He brought us to life using the true Word, showing us off as the crown of all his creatures.

Hit the ground running and Excel!

January 6, 2013

Ever notice that when you write something that seems to make incredible sense to you that no one picks up on it and when you write something that has no depth to it at all everyone understands, and then you wonder what you really meant by what you wrote? I haven't either. It was just a question. I really didn't want to write about my battle with swallowing again, so I won't and didn't want to tell about my extreme weight loss. I have to be the biggest loser. I honestly feel like a loser, not because of weight, but because I have had to miss so many great opportunities to live life to its fullest this past year because of cancer and treatment. Complaining doesn't help, but it sure helps shift the blame from me to something else. I have noticed that it is so much easier to complain than to actually get up and do something about it because you have to include God in the equation...

Philippians 2:12-15 MSG

Now that I'm separated from you, keep it up. Better yet, redouble your efforts. Be energetic in your life of salvation, reverent and sensitive before God. That energy is God's energy, an energy deep within you, God himself willing and working at what will give him the most pleasure. Do everything readily and cheerfully — no bickering, no second-guessing allowed! Go out into the world uncorrupted, a breath of fresh air in this squalid and polluted society. Provide people with a glimpse of good living and of the living God. Carry the light-giving Message into the night...

My precious wife who has been such a great caregiver is tonight the recipient of care. She became very ill on Friday night and still is battling a stomach flu. My brother and his wife are here at the right time helping us both. It is hard to see your loved one suffer. I think she is getting better. It will be home church for us today. I have come to realize God hears the cry of our heart but also the praise of our lips and know that even as we cry for help, our praise can release the healing we need.

Psalm 9:1, 2 NIV

I will give thanks to you, Lord, with all my heart I will tell of all your wonderful deeds. I will be glad and rejoice in you; I will sing the praises of your name, O Most High.

It has been very difficult to think about journaling lately as I have physically felt so depleted. The reason for that is when the body's intake is limited, there is very little natural energy to do what is necessary for daily survival. Then that, in turn, saps the inner energy we all try to hold in reserve. I always taught that reserve was endless, but the Bible teaches it must be renewed: Paul says it like this:

2 Corinthians 4:16 NKJV

Therefore we do not lose heart. Even though our outward man is perishing, yet the inward man is being renewed day by day.

The battle ends up in the mind even though it seems to be the body having the greatest difficulty. Tonight, I drove my brother and his wife to the airport. I came home and felt depressed again because all I could think about was what I was thinking about and what I was thinking about had no good outcome or resolution. I surfed the channels and found nothing I wanted to watch until I came upon a program called *Reflections.* Pretty pictures, nice music, and verses of the Bible. I began to recall verses that spoke to my situations:

Romans 12:1-2 NKJV

I beseech you therefore, brethren, by the mercies of God, that you present your bodies a living sacrifice, holy, acceptable to God, which is your reasonable service. And do not be conformed to this world, but be transformed by the renewing of your mind, that you may prove what is that good and acceptable and perfect will of God.

I realized I needed my mind renewed. It was being attacked by every stronghold of the enemy. I was letting myself get sucked into a black hole of despair and hopelessness. I was letting myself...no one was making it happen... my outward man may be perishing or getting weaker, yet there is no reason my inner man should succumb to that kind of deceit yet it was happening... for over a week I have felt numbness of the soul coming on, yet I didn't even care. It is like, "I have been around this block too many times to care anymore... " But I have found out again that I do care and not just because I care but that I remember He cares.

January 7, 2013

Thomas Huxley coined the word "agnostic" to try to explain his quest for answers. I oppose much of what he wrote on evolution, but there were some gems of brilliance I have discovered in his writings: Example:

> *"We live in a world which is full of misery and ignorance, and the plain duty of each and all of us is to try to make the little corner he can influence somewhat less miserable and somewhat less ignorant than it was before he entered."*[26]
> —*Thomas Henry Huxley*

Wouldn't that be a good goal for today that by what we do and say we can relieve some misery and bring revelation wisdom to someone whose mind is blinded by sin and deceit?

Matthew 5:13, 14 NKJV

Jesus said, "You are the salt of the earth; but if the salt loses its flavor, how shall it be seasoned? It is then good for nothing but to be thrown out and trampled underfoot by men. You are the light of the world. A city that is set on a hill cannot be hidden.

January 8, 2013

As you may remember, I have complained about my great difficulty in swallowing food and liquids. I went outside Hospice to seek some treatment that may help me gain weight and strength. Tomorrow morning, I am going to have the procedure called esophagogastroduodenoscopy which will also be used to enlarge or expand the esophagus (Esophageal Dilation). If it works, I may be able to eat and drink somewhat normally again.

Although I am not concerned about the safety of this procedure, I think my daughter, Suzi, may be a little bit because she drove here from Phoenix to be with us tomorrow. I have four awesome kids who all would do anything for us, but I am really blessed that she was able to be with me at this time. It means a lot to me. We were talking about a number of things that Fran and I have had to endure in our years as pastors, and we know that some think it is really unfair or "How could God let all this happen?" But Fran and I made life choices long ago that we would live by faith and not by obvious circumstances... Jesus said this:

Matthew 5:45 NLT

In that way, you will be acting as true children of your Father in heaven. For He gives His sunlight to both the evil and the good, and He sends rain on the just and the unjust alike.

We just got a lot wetter than we thought we would. Lol...

We believe that God is with us through this, and we find our faith stretched at times, but it always brings us back to peace. A peace that goes beyond human understanding and a peace no one can take from us. So regardless of the outcome tomorrow... we have peace... but I sure would like to eat an In-N-Out hamburger tomorrow... thanks for your prayers...

January 9, 2013

I am convinced people were praying for me today. Prayer is an act of faith by people like you and me that says, "God I believe you are God..." while also admitting we are not God which means we cannot manipulate any answer we want.

People prayed for me and hoped and believed for a good report after my procedure to attempt to enlarge the esophagus. The good report is that I still have a faith in the God whom I have committed my life to and I do have a peace that transcends my understanding.

The procedure, however, was unsuccessful as the problem I have in swallowing is from the tumor at the top of my stomach and couldn't be expanded nor could a feeding tube be inserted into the stomach for the same reasons. I have to admit I couldn't help but tear up as the doctor gave me the news. I realized it just rained again and got wetter than expected. (*Matthew 5:45*). So, no hamburger today.

My next option is a feeding tube surgically inserted into the opening of the small intestine. I have an appointment on Thursday to see if this is possible. I have a friend who survived more than ten years with one, so I am not giving up on hope or my faith in Jesus Christ. He is still my light in the darkness of this situation.

John 8:12 NKJV

Then Jesus spoke to them again, saying, I am the light of the world. He who follows Me shall not walk in darkness, but have the light of life.

January 10, 2013

After being a patient at the hospital on Tuesday and hearing some less than encouraging words from my doctor after a failed attempt to dilate my esophagus so I could swallow better, God knew I needed to get my eyes off my troubles. Jonathan and Rebekah came to visit and for a few hours, my one-year-old grandson, Caiden did everything he could to entertain all of us. It was a wonderful evening watching the little guy exert more energy than all of us had combined. God saw Fran, and I needed a distraction. I was ready for bed when they left. However, Suzi and I stayed up and talked for a long time. She is such a good daughter…laughs at all my jokes…While I was in the recovery room, she was such a blessing as Fran could only cry when she got the bad news about my condition.

After Suzi left for Phoenix this morning, I decided to work on my boat. I felt so good this morning, and as I worked trying to get the boat ready for winter, I got hungry, and I actually ate (very slowly) a taco and some fruit. I think the working helped the food go down.

Fran and I had such a precious time of prayer tonight and sensed a precious anointing of God's presence in our hearts and home. I cannot explain to those who this may seem foreign to, how amazingly strengthening it is to pray in such a way that you are aware you are pleasing to God… This scripture may help explain it:

Hebrews 11:6 MSG

It's impossible to please God apart from faith. And why? Because anyone who wants to approach God must believe both that He exists and that He cares enough to respond to those who seek Him.

We both knew we had approached God in faith and that He responded to us with peace and hope. Max Lucado says,

"Faith is not the belief that God will do what you want. Faith is the belief that God will do what is right."[27]

I have a short bucket list, and one of the things I want to do is write a devotional book journaling my battle with cancer and to write several children's short stories based on all the stories about a girl and her cat that I told my grandkids as they were growing up. Reality is that typing sometimes is hard because my fingers are numb from the chemo treatments I took. I received a speech to text program called Dragon as a gift at Christmas from my family. However, my laptop was so ancient that I really needed a new one. Over the weekend some pastors and my family got together and bought me a wonderful new laptop that will do everything I need except dictate the books. I am so blessed. Now I have to use my time wisely. This scripture from the Message Bible is my testimony tonight:

Ephesians 3:20 MSG

God can do anything, you know — far more than you could ever imagine or guess or request in your wildest dreams! He does it not by pushing us around but by working within us, his Spirit deeply and gently within us.

January 11, 2013

It is cold in Boulder City; in fact, it is supposed to get in the low 20's this weekend. I realized we had four faucets that might be vulnerable to freeze so Fran and I were outside after 10:00 P. M. wrapping insulation around them. I came back into our warm house and fell asleep in my big chair while listening to a preacher (not me), and Fran just left me there and went to bed. I just woke up a little while ago and so decided to do an update on my daily saga with my battle with cancer.

If you read my post from yesterday, you know that I had a procedure attempted that was to expand my esophagus so I could swallow better. That failed and was told that soon my only option for getting nutrition and hydration would be a feeding tube surgically inserted into the opening of my small intestine. I decided this option would be worth it so today I met with the surgeon who had operated on me before. After reviewing all my recent history with cancer treatment, he said that a feeding tube may not be an option because the fluid that had built up in my abdomen may have spread cancer in such a way that any surgery would be life-threatening. He said if he cut through cancer, infected tissue could cause infections that would not be good. He had another option of doing an endoscopy and can possibly insert a tube in the stomach because he is a surgeon. I told him I wanted to at least try. He agreed, and he is willing to explore the possibilities.

If not, then without a miracle, hospice will be my best friend. This has not been a week of good news, but again I grab hold of my faith and am finding peace and hope. I am not afraid to die, but I certainly don't want to if God has a provision that is available that will extend my life even for a season. I would cherish your prayers for wisdom and guidance by the Holy Spirit in the days ahead. It is not by might, not by power, but it is by the Spirit of God that a miracle can even be imagined. This again is a truth I hold on to:

Philippians 4:6-7 NKJV

Be anxious for nothing, but in everything by prayer and supplication, with thanksgiving, let your requests be made known to God; and the peace of God, which surpasses all understanding, will guard your hearts and minds through Christ Jesus.

One of the things on my bucket list is to be on the Oregon coast during the winter. A cousin is letting us stay at their beach house south of Seaside, Oregon this next week. We also are going to a service where the focus is on prayer for healing. This is a special time for Fran and me, so we are not saying a lot about it, but I am confident that God has a plan for this trip. Although I am struggling to eat and drink, I believe it will be worth the effort. Please remember us on Sunday and Monday. My two sons and family will be helping us to get there. It is actually going to be as warm on the Oregon beach as it is forecasted here in the Vegas area.

James 5:13-17 NKJV

Is anyone among you suffering? Let him pray. Is anyone cheerful? Let him sing psalms. Is anyone among you sick? Let him call for the elders of the church, and let them pray over him, anointing him with oil in the name of the Lord. And the prayer of faith will save the sick, and the Lord will raise him up. And if he has committed sins, he will be forgiven. Confess your trespasses to one another, and pray for one another, that you may be healed. The effective, fervent prayer of a righteous man avails much.

Believing for a miracle, resting in His plan...

January 15, 2013

Life is never dull for us, just complicated by cancer and getting older. We flew to Portland on Saturday and met with lots of family. Sunday, we went to church at City Bible Church with more family and enjoyed a great service there. Then met more family for lunch. Our youngest son and family flew in from Las Vegas, and we picked them up at the airport and then drove to Cannon Beach where a cousin has graciously opened their beach house to us.

We had a wonderful night sitting in front of a fire in the fireplace and listening to the surf come in. This morning Jon drove us back to Portland on the Sunset Highway and went through the coastal mountains seeing lots and lots of snow along the highway. Fran and I got on a plane for Medford and drove to Redding, California to a healing service hoping for a divine encounter with God. It happened but not like we supposed.

We pulled into the hotel we were going to stay at (which I had almost hesitated from staying at for various reasons, but chose it anyway) and as I walked in to get my reservation taken care of there were two people walking towards me that had been in the church I pastored in Prineville, Oregon. A minute either way and I would have missed them.

It had been 17 years since I had seen them. We had no idea that Dave and Peggy were on their way home from Tucson and at the last moment decided to stay in Redding at the same hotel we were booked at. It was a wonderful reunion, and as the four of us stood in the parking lot, Dave asked if he could pray for me. Dave, a very large and rugged man, began to weep as he prayed and we all forgot we were not in a church and we prayed with a great freedom. People watching probably thought we were crazy, but it didn't matter, God met us there. I have been able to finally eat some nourishment tonight. I ate more tonight than I have for days. We all went to the healing service. At least a thousand people were there. The service was good, but after three hours we needed to go, and I was never prayed for. I know I heard God tell me that His intended encounter with me had started in the parking lot of our hotel. We are still very amazed. I don't know what will happen in the future, but tonight I fully understand that God still is making me know that He is so aware of me.

Jeremiah 29:11-13 NKJV

For I know the thoughts that I think toward you, says the Lord, thoughts of peace and not of evil, to give you a future and a hope. Then you will call upon Me and go and pray to Me, and I will listen to you. And you will seek Me and find Me, when you search for Me with all your heart.

January 17, 2013

Facebook asked me how I am feeling? I feel so loved and noticed by FB. I have done so much better since my encounter with God through Dave and Peggy and the healing service I attended. Just being around thousands of almost sane appearing people who believe God can heal is faith building. It is imperative to have faith. It is a given gift from God but unless it is used it becomes only a word. But faith acknowledged and exercised is a God-pleasing act.

Hebrews 11:6 NKJV

But without faith it is impossible to please Him, for he who comes to God must believe that He is, and that He is a rewarder of those who diligently seek Him.

By the measure of faith, I have, I am believing for more than a feeding tube to sustain my life. I am believing for healing and a new beginning.

January 18, 2013

Fran and I had an incredible trip back to Cannon Beach from Redding, California. We had flown on Horizon Air from Portland to Medford and rented a car. I was telling my son the night I reserved a car in Medford that I really would like an all-wheel-drive SUV. He told me there was not much hope of that and that the price would be close to $100 a day. So, I went with a standard car. Would you believe we got a new Volvo C60 SUV all-wheel drive with sunroof, leather interior and all the fun stuff I really like in a car? And for the same price as I would have paid for a Ford Fusion.

Then the roads were clear over the Siskiyou Mountains, the sun was shining, Mt. Shasta was spectacular, and I already wrote the rest. On our way home, again the roads were dry, with snow piled high along roadways. Shasta Lake and Mt. Shasta were beautiful.

We got to Phoenix, Oregon and I remembered Elvin Houston, a college friend from Northwest lived in the area. I called him, and since we had several free hours in Medford, he met us at the airport and took us to his home.

Another God ordained appointment. What a joy to meet a friend I haven't seen for over 40 years. We had a good time remembering and then believing for our futures being in God's hands.

Our flight to Portland was so smooth, and son Jonathan picked us up at the airport. Enjoyed a Doritos Taco and a smoothie with no problems. Got up Wednesday morning in Cannon Beach, sun shining, and it got to be nearly 70 degrees (it was in the sunshine). Just a beautiful day.

We ended the day with a fire on the beach and watching my family make S'mores... I did not feel like going, and my bed felt so good, but I knew this would be the last chance to be with Jon, Re, and Caiden in a setting or time like this, so I decided to try to make it. And I did very well.

I decided to make a s'more and managed to get it down... too rich. Then made one with just graham crackers and marshmallows and it was very good. Just watching my 14-month old grandson get his first taste of a marshmallow was worth the effort. When he was finally convinced to taste it, his eyes lit up, and he grabbed it and put it all in his mouth, looking for another.

The fire was wonderful, the surf pounding and the stars so clear and prolific. Just an awesome time. It was a time to talk honestly about my life and possible death. I shared:

Ecclesiastes 3:1-2,11

To everything there is a season, A time for every purpose under heaven: A time to be born, and a time to die. He has made everything beautiful in its time. Also He has put eternity in their hearts, except that no one can find out the work that God does from beginning to end.

...and told my kids that my death will not be a random chance of bad timing, but will be in the divine plan of God and that it will be right, and I will be OK and so will they in time. There were tears and hugs, and I believe heaven was very close to us all at that moment.

Although I am eating more, there are still daily challenges that I have to deal with... but it is *"...not by might, nor by power but by His Spirit,"* says the Lord of Hosts. *(Zechariah 4:6 NKJV)*

My cousins were so gracious to give us the time at their beach house.

We overlook the beach, and it is so beautiful. I can see Haystack Rock from my bedroom window and hear the surf all the time. So soothing at night. From all the front of the house, we have an unobstructed view of the Pacific. No words are enough to explain or say thanks for this awesome gift. God has given me a desire of my heart.

On the way to the airport so Jon and family can get home. Friday night two more of my kids will be here. Something meaningful is going on here. I have noticed that each time I need more strength than I have, God intervenes:

Isaiah 40:29-31 NKJV

He gives power to the weak, and to those who have no might He increases strength. Even the youths shall faint and be weary, And the young men shall utterly fall, but those who wait on the Lord Shall renew their strength; They shall mount up with wings like eagles, they shall run and not be weary, they shall walk and not faint.

January 20, 2013

I am struggling daily to swallow and get hungry very quickly. Yesterday was rough when several times what I ate never reached my stomach. It was discouraging. Today was much the same but at my lowest Dave and Peggy called and prayed with me. It was what I needed most. Again, at the right time, God brought a prayer warrior to intercede for me. This Psalm reminds me that God satisfies us with good things. As I go to sleep, I hear the surf pounding and the sound soothes the mind as God soothes the soul...

Psalm 107:1-3, 6, 8, 9 NIV

Give thanks to the Lord, for he is good; his love endures forever. Let the redeemed of the Lord tell their story—those he redeemed from the hand of the foe, those he gathered from the lands, from east and west, from north and south. Then they cried out to the Lord in their trouble, and he delivered them from their distress. Let them give thanks to the Lord for his unfailing love and his wonderful deeds for mankind, for he satisfies the thirsty and fills the hungry with good things.

January 21, 2013

Tonight, I was on an Alaska Airline's plane flying at 41,000 on my way back home after a week of wonder. Fran and I went to Portland, then to Silverton, then back to Portland, then to Cannon Beach, then to Portland, flew to Medford, Oregon, drove to Redding, California, then back to Medford, then flew to Portland, then back to Cannon Beach. From there to Astoria and Long Beach, Washington, and back to Cannon Beach, then on Friday to Portland to take Jon to the airport, then back to Cannon Beach and then today back to Portland and now on our way home to Las Vegas (Boulder City). Lots of travel for a guy in my condition. Not bragging, just saying this is what we did, and making memories with the three kids who were able to join us in Cannon Beach.

I believe I was on a mission this week, led and ordained by God. I went to find a new touch of God in my life and did through many events that occurred during the week. I know God is well aware of my ongoing battle with cancer. I know God has touched my spirit, but my body is wasting away... I look like a man who has been in a concentration camp for months... but I walk not by sight, but by faith... regardless of the outcome of this week, I know I was where I needed to be...

Psalm 37:23, 24 NKJV

The steps of a good man are ordered by the Lord, And He delights in his way. Though he fall, he shall not be utterly cast down; For the Lord upholds him with His hand.

January 22, 2013

My wife, Fran, has been able to stay with me for the last two months because of her sick leave and the awesome people who work at the City of Henderson who have donated leave to her. We are forever in their debt. Although I am able to move around still, it is getting harder and harder for both of us because I am unable to eat enough to gain strength or weight. Fran wants to take care of me yet the food I need that she can prepare (very well) I cannot swallow. I can guarantee anyone who wants to lose weight, all they have to do is to stop swallowing food, and the weight begins to go away. I know God is so aware of my situation. I am not discouraged, I am not mad at God, and I am not abandoning my faith just because I have not yet experienced healing.

Some have told me that I am healed already and that I need to claim it, lay hold of it, grasp it, or embrace it, but no one has told me how to do that. Many who have told me this are struggling in their own way with their health or eyesight and so I am at a loss to know how to grasp what seems to be like thin air. If there is something you know healed you totally from a terminal disease, please tell me.

I confess that He heals all my diseases, but this one God has not yet done...

I asked the Lord how to press through the crowd and touch the hem of His garment as in Mark 5 and Luke 8, and I believed I was to go to Redding. I did and had an encounter with God, but as of yet, there is no obvious healing although there has been strength given. Thankfully, those praying for me have not given up.

Today, at two different times, the food I ate would not stay down so if nothing changes they will attempt to insert a feeding tube on February 1.

Tonight, as Fran and I prayed we also read Psalm 103 which just makes my faith even stronger... I do Bless the Lord; I do believe He is my healer and the One who renews my strength...

Psalm 103:1-5 NKJV

Bless the Lord, O my soul; And all that is within me, bless His holy name! Bless the Lord, O my soul, and forget not all His benefits: Who forgives all your iniquities, Who heals all your diseases, Who redeems your life from destruction, Who crowns you with lovingkindness and tender mercies, Who satisfies your mouth with good things, so that your youth is renewed like the eagle's.

January 23, 2013

My hospice nurse made her weekly visit today, and I was giving her a condensed version of the things Fran and I did last week in our travels. I told her about my reason for wanting to go to Redding, California, and that I believed that God had prompted me to do what the woman in Mark 5 and Luke 8 had done to be healed. By going, making the effort, for that one night was my way of pressing through the crowd and touching Jesus. I told her about the flights, the car rentals, the things that just kept falling into place, the wonderful weather, the scenery that was a touch of heaven in itself and then the miraculous coincidences in meeting people who I know God wanted me to meet and then more...

I said to the nurse; "All this but I am not healed." She looked at me and kind of sighed as though she was tired, and then laughed as she said, "Do you realize how many miracles God gave you on this trip? I am tired and amazed just listening to all the things you did. He gave you the miracle of strength and so much more." We talked for a while about this, and she reminded me that often it is not till we look back do we see the miracles God has done.

And you know what? She is right. It reminded me of:

Psalms 68:19 KJV

Blessed be the Lord, who daily loadeth us with benefits, even the God of our salvation. He loads us daily with benefits

...forget not His benefits (Psalm 103:2); He gives us this day our daily bread. (Matthew 6:11)

We all have amazing miracles that happen daily that we take for granted. I believe we need to be more aware of those wonderful touches of God on our lives. I may not yet have a miracle of healing, but have had multiple miracles of blessings that I must give thanks for....

1 Corinthians 2: 9-10 NKJV

But as it is written: "Eye has not seen, nor ear heard, nor have entered into the heart of man. The things which God has prepared for those who love Him." But God has revealed them to us through His Spirit...

As He reveals or we become aware of the daily miracles, we should give thanks and live in appreciation of the goodness of God in our lives...

January 24, 2013

Sunday night, Jonathan and Re were coming to pick us up at the Las Vegas airport. We were standing in the passenger pick up area looking for Jon's car when a lovely black lady gave a little scream and ran over to me and hugged my neck and was calling my name. I was so surprised... it was a friend who was just returning from Kenya and was also waiting for her ride. We have known each other for several years but had not seen each other for months, and here we were.

Another chance meeting? We were only able to talk a couple of minutes, as Jon arrived, but Fran and I were so blessed to have that wonderful chance (?) meeting. She is an RN, so she asked that "so how are you really doing?" question. Then she reminded me that she is believing I am being healed.

As we drove away, I asked Jon what the odds were to have that kind of meeting. She had just flown for nearly 20 hours and came from the east coast, and I had flown from Portland... Jon laughed and said, "For anyone else, the odds would be high, but not for you Dad, it happens to you all the time."

I do believe God is so involved in our lives that He orchestrates such events for our good and His glory and to keep life exciting. I love these chance meetings and events. I used these verses a few days ago, but they fit again:

Psalm 37:23-26 KJV

The steps of a good man are ordered by the Lord: and he delighteth in his way. Though he fall, he shall not be utterly cast down: for the Lord upholdeth him with his hand. I have been young, and now am old; yet have I not seen the righteous forsaken, nor his seed begging bread. He is ever merciful, and lendeth; and his seed is blessed.

January 25, 2013

I have read this many times, but just came across it again today and wanted to share it.

What Cancer Cannot Do:

Cancer is so limited...
It cannot cripple love.
It cannot shatter hope.
It cannot corrode faith.
It cannot destroy peace.
It cannot kill friendship.
It cannot suppress memories.
It cannot silence courage.
It cannot invade the soul.
It cannot steal eternal life.
It cannot conquer the spirit.

-Author Unknown

This poem reminds me of a portion of scripture:

Isaiah 54:17 NKJV

No weapon formed against you shall prosper...

Cancer cannot separate us from the love of God... if anything it will drive us closer to Him if we let it. So far in this battle with cancer, I have had choices I can make about my attitude. Will there come a time when I have no choices? Probably not, but if so, I choose before that happens to have an attitude of faith, praise and thanksgiving even when I cannot express it. I will always believe that Jesus is my healer...

Romans 8:31, 34-35, 37-39

What then shall we say to these things? If God is for us, who can be against us? ... It is Christ who died, and furthermore is also risen, who is even at the right hand of God, who also makes intercession for us. Who shall separate us from the love of Christ? Shall tribulation, or distress, or persecution, or famine, or nakedness, or peril, or sword? ... Yet in all these things we are more than conquerors through Him who loved us. For I am persuaded that neither death nor life, nor angels nor principalities nor powers, nor things present nor things to come, nor height nor depth, nor any other created thing, shall be able to separate us from the love of God which is in Christ Jesus our Lord.

January 26, 2013

When I was a kid, and someone asked me why I did something, my pat answer if I did not want to answer the question accurately was, "Because." My Mom would say, "Because why?" And I would answer, "Just because." That usually didn't work well with her, and she would eventually get the answer she wanted.

When people ask me why about something that has to do with cancer, I want to answer, "Because." Why didn't chemo cure me? Why hasn't God healed me? Why haven't I taken every miracle cure that has come down the pike? About all I have to say is. "Because." Because I don't know what the answers are. Life is what it is; because.

However, there are some powerful uses of the "Because" in the Bible. Two that I remember well:

The first one is in Luke 4:18 where Jesus is reading from Isaiah 61 and reads,

"The Spirit of the Lord is upon me because..." and then reads the rest, *"... He has anointed me to preach the good news to the poor, to heal the broken hearted, to set at liberty those who are oppressed and to proclaim the year of God's favor..."*

There is a good reason why the Spirit was upon Jesus, and it was because...

James 4:2 says, *you have not because*... you ask not, or you ask wrongly or for the wrong reasons... There can be good reasons why prayers are not answered... because...we fail to ask or go with the wrong motives...

I could say that I have cancer because... "The Because" may not be known until I look back and see the many things that God opened up to me because of cancer. I have had so many things revealed to me and opportunities opened to me because of cancer... Did God give me the cancer? I certainly don't think so, but I believe He causes all things to work together for good to those who love Him and because they have been called for His purposes...

There have been some recent days that I have struggled more than other days, and I look back, and it was the day I chose not to keep my prayer time because I was discouraged or tired and I did not receive because I did not ask. I let an excuse keep me from my victory for that day... because I didn't feel like praying. But I needed to pray even when I didn't feel like praying so I could have what I needed. You see I have found that God has not yet given me a complete healing, but I have seen Him give me grace for the day I needed it the most when I would pray and believe. I had not because I prayed not...

I believe there is an anointing of the Holy Spirit that can be ours if we are willing to be preachers, healers, deliverers, and proclaimers as in *Luke 4:18*. Because when we make ourselves available to God, He produces in and through us messages, healings, deliverance, and proclamations that would not have happened otherwise.

Tonight, I am walking in a victory because... of an anointing (divinely equipped to do the job) and because I am asking and am asking for the right motives... why would I do this? Because... Just because.

———

Fran and I attended the wedding of a young couple who met in the youth group of Boulder City Assembly. Both dedicated their lives to Jesus Christ, and I believe they will be testimonies of God's grace through their lives. They celebrated their marriage with music and dance, and all seemed to have a great time.

Brings back memories of my two marriages and the awesome joy I had in being married to Mary K. Jordan and Mary F. Jordan. Mary K. is in heaven, and Mary F. is doing all she can do to make my time as good as it can be before I go to heaven.

Tonight, after I had lost two battles of trying to swallow food and it wouldn't stay down, Fran began to weep saying, "It just isn't right!" I understood her frustration, but I reminded her that faith is the belief that God will always do what is right... From talking about her fear of me not being here with her should I die soon got us talking about faith and it led to a time of prayer proclaiming Jesus as my healer but also being reminded of *John 3:16*:

> *"For God so loved the world that He gave His only begotten son that whoever believes in Him should not perish but have everlasting life."*

Notice He did not say temporal or earthly life, but everlasting life... That verse got our attention, and some very strong ideas about heaven began to fill our hearts. I prayed, "Lord I want to be as excited about heaven as I am about my life here." And honestly, something began to stir in me as I got little glimpses of what heaven could be... Paul wrote,

> *"For me to live is Christ, but to die is gain..." Philippians 1:21*

He saw both sides and realized that heaven was not to be dreaded, but to be embraced and excited about. We saw scriptures like *1 Thessalonians 4:13* that says we sorrow not like those who have no hope, and then Paul saying it is a hard thing handling the difference that dying brings great reward compared to leaving loved ones behind that brings them sorrow...I am going through that and Fran, and I tried to talk as truthfully as possible about life and life after death.

We have had a number of miracles, and one is I am alive six months longer than the surgeon told my family. And at this point, I believe it could be more than that. However, like David wrote in Psalm 23:

> *...even if I walk through the valley of the shadow of death I do not fear any evil for You are with me...and surely goodness and mercy has followed me all the days of my life and I have the promise that I will dwell in the house of the Lord forever....*

Again, it is well with my soul....

January 27, 2013

It was good to be in church today and sense the presence of the Lord. What an incredible sense of completeness that comes when the human spirit acknowledges the Holy Spirit as happens in church. It is not any certain song or Bible verse; it is just knowing this is where you need to be. It is like putting the last piece in a puzzle, and you feel a sense of satisfaction as the puzzle is completed and you get to see the finished picture that you have been trying to put together.

Blaise Pascal said long ago, *"What is it, then, that this desire and this inability proclaim to us, but that there was once in man a true happiness of which there now remain to him only the mark and empty trace, which he in vain tries to fill from all his surroundings, seeking from things absent the help he does not obtain in things present? But these are all inadequate, because the infinite abyss can only be filled by an infinite and immutable object, that is to say, only by God Himself."*[28] A paraphrase of this quote has surfaced from an unknown source: *"There is a God-shaped vacuum in the heart of every man which cannot be filled by any created thing, but only by God, the Creator, made known through Jesus."*

That is what I experienced today. It was good to have that very real experience because the very little that I ate today made it to my stomach. I am not sick to my stomach, just the tumor is closing off the opening to the stomach. Medically speaking my options are very limited; there may be some B17 injections that might help but maybe not in time, so I am holding on to the hope I have from the pages of the Bible and from my faith. Here are some verses from the Message Bible that I am holding on to:

Philippians 4:6-7

Don't fret or worry. Instead of worrying, pray. Let petitions and praises shape your worries into prayers, letting God know your concerns. Before you know it, a sense of God's wholeness, everything coming together for good, will come and settle you down.

It's wonderful what happens when Christ displaces worry at the center of your life. I have read and reread this in many translations and in meditating on the words I notice it never says that God will answer my prayers but that He will cause a sense of peace, completeness, and wholeness to surpass my attempts to understand all my unanswered questions about what is going on in my life. I have a peace tonight that God is not at all surprised or shaken that cancer is still fighting my body and that He will do what is right just in time... *as the author and the completer of my faith... (Hebrews 12:2).*

January 29, 2013

Another day without food getting to the stomach... such a shame as food tastes so good when it is chewed... however not so good when it comes back up. Even though I have stomach cancer, I am not sick to my stomach, but the food I eat does not want to get past the tumor at the top of the stomach and gets lodged somewhere before the esophagus enters the stomach, and that causes all kinds of trouble...

However, Fran and I prayed specifically that the esophagus would open and let water and fluids get into the stomach. I have had two people call me and pray for me as well.

After prayer, it seems like that has happened. Where a sip was too much before, now almost a full 16 oz. bottle has been drunk. That was a direct answer to Fran's prayer. Maybe something is happening... it sure needs to happen as my weight is dropping faster than the "Biggest Losers" ... So, I am experimenting by trying to eat a cracker with peanut butter on it. If it stays down, I may be able to eat something more solid. So far it is staying down... thank you, Lord. What a battle.

Friday is the day the surgeon will try to insert a feeding tube. Then perhaps I can chew my food and spit it in the tube (disgusting). It will be a time I can eat without regard to the taste or texture. The cracker stayed down, so there is some hope tonight.

Proverbs 3:1-6 NIV

My son, do not forget my teaching, but keep my commands in your heart, for they will prolong your life many years and bring you peace and prosperity. Let love and faithfulness never leave you; bind them around your neck, write them on the tablet of your heart. Then you will win favor and a good name in the sight of God and man. Trust in the Lord with all your heart and lean not on your own understanding; in all your ways submit to him, and he will make your paths straight.

January 31, 2013

Isaiah 26:3 NKJV

You will keep him in perfect peace, whose mind is stayed on You,
because he trusts in You.

I am still among the living... just have had some struggles with getting any nourishment or hydration into my body. Tomorrow a surgeon will attempt to insert a feeding tube. This may not be possible if the cancer has spread too much. If it works, it will sustain my life and perhaps give me more energy and might stop my weight loss. I am in no pain other than being hungry. I hurt mostly for Fran who tries hard not to cry when she knows nothing seems to stay down that I eat or drink and sees such a skinny husband. But she is a woman of faith, and we both find strength and peace in our faith and when discouragement seems to try to overwhelm us.

—

Still up at almost 1:00 A. M., winding down after a very busy day. Because I am having surgery, I had to sign out of hospice today, but after surgery, I can get back on. My son Jon, went to the airport to get Rob, my son from Oregon tonight and my daughter, Suzi and her two girls drove up from Phoenix. So, all my kids will join Fran and me at the hospital as I go in for surgery in about nine hours. Inserting a feeding tube is still part of believing for a greater miracle.

There is still hope that someday I will again have a steak dinner or some good Chinese food, but for now, I am a non-eater. But as Jesus said, *"Man does not live by bread alone but by every Word that proceeds from God."* *(Matthew 4:4)* I may not have the best cuisine in me, but Jesus said, *"He that believeth on me, as the scripture hath said, from within him shall flow rivers of living water." (John 7:38 ASV)*. He was talking about the Holy Spirit.

Regardless of what happens tomorrow I am confident His Spirit is in me, and God will cause all things to work together for good, because I love Him and have been called for His purposes, and God is forming me by this into the image of His Son. (Romans 8:28, 29) My surgery is at 10:00 A. M. on February 1, thanks for asking for God's favor in this.

——

If you see this, would you for Fran's sake post a word of encouragement for her? By all outward signs, I am dying, she saw the same weight loss in a good friend who died from cancer in December, so she is really struggling with my loss of 65 pounds and at least 10 pounds in the last couple of weeks.

The doctors are not encouraging us much about this surgery thinking the cancer may have progressed too much, so I may not have a feeding tube when I wake up. If the tube doesn't work, I will slowly starve. At least I will not be in a lot of pain if that happens, but I know what it is like to watch a spouse slowly have life ebb away, and Fran and my kids and grandkids will need their family and friends.

It is easier for me than them because I have settled that for me to live is Christ, but to die is gain. They will have to live without me, but I will live in the presence of God in a place Jesus said He was preparing for us. That is our ultimate goal... that is as good as it gets... this is everything for me. I shall dwell in the house of the Lord forever and forever, and forever... no comparison to life here... for those who are left behind it will be years for them before they get to taste what I may experience soon, but for me, it will be like a blink of the eye till I see them again... I feel a little homesick tonight for this part to be done... I hope you and my family will not sorrow and grieve as those who have no hope... live in the Hope of our resurrected Lord and His promise of everlasting life.

I have been so blessed to have loved Fran Jordan... she has been my Treasure in this life. My daughter, Suzi, has been a joy to me all her life; my son Rob brought me so much happiness in his life (though there were the times as he was learning to be a man). I could say the same about my second son Jonathan who was a true gift to me when my love for Fran brought him and his sister Jennifer into my life. I love the man Jon has become. My second daughter Jenny has brought me more joy than she will ever know. She and I never always saw life the same, but I loved her as my daughter all the years she has been in my life. I love the girl she was and the woman she became.

Each of my kids brought me the gift of Grandchildren, and I love them so much. Matthew, Erika, Mary, Amy, Kalani, Kaia, Abbey, and Caiden. They are all my favorites. I could never love one more than the other. If I live to be 80, on that birthday, I will tell them who my favorite one was.

Each of my children brought their spouse into my life, and I have loved them as my own kids. Ed, Jenny Jordan, Mike, and Rebekah. Mike has a daughter named Janae who calls me grandpa, and I gladly add her to my grandkids. I had 10 sisters and brothers who I loved so much.

My brother, Lyle, has truly been my best friend for all our lives. My living sisters, Clara, Lewanna, Carol, and Patricia are some of the most precious women in the world. Their spouses and children are my beloved family.

My first wife's sister's family, the Newells are as close as any family could be, and I love each of them and their families with all my heart.

Fran's brothers and sisters and their families are so loved by me that it is like God gave me more than I ever deserved.

If I die today, it can be said of me I was a wealthy man because of such an awesome family that I loved, and they sure acted like they loved me as we loved our God who so loved us. This was important for me to write. If you read this far, you might think this was a goodbye. It may be, but it may just be a reminder of how blessed Martin Duane Jordan is.

Jon's Facebook Post
February 1, 2013

> As most of you already know my father had surgery for a feeding tube today. Things didn't go completely according to plan, but they were able to put one in his intestine instead of his stomach, but this means he has to stay in the hospital for up to five days. Prayers are much needed since the surgeon said he will be slow to heal since he is malnourished due to him not being able to eat for days at a time.

February 2, 2013

I have now been in the hospital in Henderson, Nevada for 24 hours. The plan was to have a feeding tube inserted into my stomach which would have been a short and simpler procedure, but cancer caused the lining of the stomach to harden and made this option unavailable. So, the surgeon decided to open the abdomen and insert an "F" tube in the top of the small intestine. So now I will be in the hospital for a few days healing. On

Sunday, my Super Bowl party will be watching the "Tube" and enjoying food through a tube... This is not a cure, but gives me a chance to gain my strength and have more time to see Romans 8:28 played out in my life. Thanks for all your prayers for me. I am confident my life is in God's hands.

February 5, 2013

Philippians 1:6 KJV

Being confident of this very thing, that he which hath begun a good work in you will perform it until the day of Jesus Christ.

This is my fourth day in the hospital. It has been a most challenging time, to say the least. To tell you all that has happened would be TMI. There has been the good with the bad...I will forget the bad and focus on the good.

The good is having most of my family with me, as well as Pastors Gary Moorfield, and Bill Kilwakski. Secretary-Treasurer Jay Herndon, and Superintendent Jim Braddy of the Northern California/Nevada District Council of the Assembly of God came to pray for me. Each visit was a blessing.

Today, an instructor nurse and a student came to change the dressings on my incisions. As they finished, they asked if there was something else they could do. We had mentioned how prayer was powerful and a positive thing in our lives so I told them they could pray for me. They said they would, and soon we were holding hands around the bed. Rob, the instructor, me, and the student nurse. The student prayed, and she knew how... quoting scriptures and putting those scriptures with faith-releasing-words I felt the presence of the Lord there in a real way. Tears were flowing, and I knew God heard this prayer meeting. There were hugs and love there.

Tonight, after throwing up many times, IVs failing and more pain than I want to talk about. I am still believing.

Suzi's Facebook Posts
February 6, 2013

A brief update on my dad's status. Dad is still in the hospital. He's had some tough days. I won't go into details, but things aren't working YET as they should. (Feeding tube issues, blood clot, feeling pretty miserable and more...). Please keep him in your prayers for miracles of healing, strength, and a huge dose of encouragement. He usually closes his amazing posts with an applicable verse so I will try it too. This is an encouraging verse when going through things you just can't understand.

Isaiah 41:10 ESV

Fear not, for I am with you; be not dismayed, for I am your God; I will strengthen you, I will help you, I will uphold you with my righteous right hand.

February 7, 2013

I don't have a lot of details, but I was told yesterday Dad had a much better day. Things were working better; he felt better... I believe it was from all the prayers of everyone standing in the gap for him. Thank you! I trust he'll be updating himself soon. His brother, Lyle Jordan, posted these verses yesterday...

2 Corinthians 1:8-11 MSG

We don't want you in the dark, friends, about how hard it was when all this came down on us in Asia province. It was so bad we didn't think we were going to make it. We felt like we'd been sent to death row, that it was all over for us. As it turned out, it was the best thing that could have happened. Instead of trusting in our own strength or wits to get out of it, we were forced to trust God totally—not a bad idea since he's the God who raises the dead! And he did it, rescued us from certain doom. And he'll do it again, rescuing us as many times as we need rescuing. You and your prayers are part of the rescue operation—I don't want you in the dark about that either. I can see your faces even now, lifted in praise for God's deliverance of us, a rescue in which your prayers played such a crucial part.

———

So... lots of ups and downs. Sounds like it's been a very rough day. Please continue to keep my dad, Fran, and the rest of us in your prayers.

Psalms 9:10 ESV

And those who know Your name put their trust in You, for You, O Lord , have not forsaken those who seek You.

February 8, 2013

Psalm 73:26, 28 NKJV

My flesh and my heart fail; But God is the strength of my heart and my portion forever. But it is good for me to draw near to God; I have put my trust in the Lord God, that I may declare all your works.

This has been such a hard seven days. I had surgery last Friday to insert a feeding tube in my abdomen. I have a row of 15 staples going from just below my navel towards the middle of my chest. The incision circles my navel like a question mark. The whole goal was to give me the chance to have a way to feed myself.

It has been over two weeks since I've had any food in my body. The hospital stay has been a daily challenge. My personal dignity has been tested daily. Ladies, I know how you must feel when under the care of a male doctor. I had to have two women install a catheter, give me suppositories, give me shots in my buttocks, and many more things than I care to remember. LOL.

The hardest times have been the waves of despair and spiritual warfare. So many hard and painful things happening every day. My latest problem has been that my body cannot accept food because my bowels are not working then I begin vomiting bile. That is so hard to deal with, it hurts and tastes so terrible, and I am getting weaker daily.

I have had a lot of godly men and women who have prayed with me and have spoken faith to me. The problem is my spirit has resisted because I see the obvious and have had so many bad things happen.

Tonight, however, brought a change again. Talking with Fran and Rob about the possibility of my death and how I did not want my family being angry or discouraged with God. I read out of Philippians and 2 Timothy and then Psalms 73 where the writer was complaining about the bad things happening to him and non-believers having good things happening. It appears that he went to church and realized what a great mistake he would have made if he were to have continued spewing words that would devastate the faith of a younger generation. He repented and began to talk about the goodness of God.

As I have mentioned before, a spirit of repentance, a change in direction, or voicing something in faith changes everything. I know in whom I have believed and am persuaded that He is able to keep all His promises...

February 12, 2013

12 days in the hospital. I think I have gotten to meet most of the nursing staff on this floor. What a wonderful bunch of people. Still not able to take nourishment, not looking too hopeful at this moment. May go on IV feeding tomorrow. My visitors always talk about food and then realize I can't eat and get embarrassed but it doesn't bother me... I enjoy hearing about good food. I can imagine a good breakfast or mashed potatoes and gravy with turkey... lol. Many have prayed for a miracle of healing, and that would be awesome, but the greatest prayer any could pray would be a surrender of your lives to Jesus Christ. When you get to a place like I am there is nothing left to trust except truths like John 3:16. For 50 some years I have had an unshakeable faith in the truths of the Bible and lying on this bed today I know I have nothing to be ashamed of. For I know whom I have believed... Not sure how many more times I will find the strength to type... but to you who have bothered to respond to my daily posts, thank you and know I love you all.

February 15, 2013

Today is the Day that The Lord has made, we will rejoice and be glad in it.

I have had so many tests, shots, medical procedures, and trials that I am not sure which way is up.

Last time I wrote, there was no hope offered, and I could see little time left down the road, but another feeding function has been put back on the table ... and I am on my first nourishment in weeks. I am running on adrenaline right now but wanted to be among the living again. This TPN that Barbara suggested I take was finally OK'd over the objections of the surgeon, and I sense a little more energy so I could take a walk and sit up for a little while. I had to quote this as I stood up to try to walk:

Isaiah 40:29-31 NKJV

He gives power to the weak, and to those who have no might He increases strength. Even the youths shall faint and be weary, And the young men shall utterly fall, but those who wait on the Lord shall renew their strength; They shall mount up with wings like eagles, they shall run and not be weary, they shall walk and not faint.

Today my hope is built on Jesus Christ and His righteousness!

Discouragement is the greatest battle I am facing right now because no one really has an answer. It was a life-preserving act coming into the hospital, but now there are more questions than answers. However, we know that God does not forsake us or abandon us even in the middle of our questions.

Isaiah 57:18, 19 NKJV

"I have seen his ways, and will heal him; I will also lead him, and restore comforts to him and to his mourners. I create the fruit of the lips: Peace, peace to him who is far off and to him who is near," says the Lord, "And I will heal him."

February 19, 2013

Facebook wanted to know how I was feeling. That is a question I get a lot as people visit me in the hospital. No good answer, except where there is breath there is hope. Going on 19 days in this "Last Resort..." there have been many discouraging words, but still, there is Hope.

The feeding tube will not work but has saved my life as a drain from fluid buildup in my intestines and lower stomach. Had I not had the surgery I would not be here today. As it is, I am still alive and holding on to the God of Hope. Will I be healed? No sign of it yet, but I sure haven't rolled over and given up. Heaven may be my healing and if so that is cool. If my healing comes before my death, I know I will be finding some good food to eat... lol. I may go home at the end of the week coordinated with home health care and others... everything has to be in place for me to come home.

Glad there are people who love to do this kind of thing. We have had lots of company the last two days: Albert and Nancy Johnson, niece Pam and Wayne and Dawson, Gordon and Shirley, all my kids and grandkids; Pastors Blayne, Dean Sanner, Kurt and Suzi Hedlund, Ned and Valerie, and many others I cannot remember. Each brought a wonderful blessing to my day.

Hebrews 13:1, 2 NKJV

Let brotherly love continue. Do not forget to entertain strangers, for by so doing some have unwittingly entertained angels.

Been a bunch of angels.

February 21, 2013

I would imagine that all who read my journals...know that I have a faith in Jesus Christ that goes beyond a church service or traditions. I believe you have figured out that my life depends upon my faith and the relationship I have with God. I have known and watched men and women with far greater problems and suffering than I have and yet never wavered in their faith. People like that are an inspiration to me not to give up.

Right now, here at St. Rose Hospital, starting day 21 I am inspired to listen to Kari Jobe sing the song, *"Healer"* over and over while I confess Jesus as my Healer and read these scriptures from Hebrews 12, Message Bible:

Hebrews 12:1-3

Do you see what this means—all these pioneers who blazed the way, all these veterans cheering us on? It means we'd better get on with it. Strip down, start running—and never quit! No extra spiritual fat, no parasitic sins. Keep your eyes on Jesus, who both began and finished this race we're in. Study how he did it. Because he never lost sight of where he was headed—that exhilarating finish in and with God—he could put up with anything along the way: Cross, shame, whatever. And now he's there, in the place of honor, right alongside God. When you find yourselves flagging in your faith, go over that story again, item by item, that long litany of hostility he plowed through. That will shoot adrenaline into your souls!

Today required Dilaudid painkiller because of new pain, and symptoms show that the tumor has completely shut off my stomach from the esophagus which causes lots of ramifications. But the plans are still being put in place that I will be going home in a few days. Someone said when needing a miracle and no sign of it happening, "You don't need the ticket until you get on the plane..." I am not sure exactly when I really need the miracle of healing, but it must not be tonight...

February 23, 2013

Today was one of those days that I rejoiced in the Lord, enjoying feeling better than I have for several days. I asked Jonathan to walk with me. I had not walked for a couple of days because they are experimenting with pain patches for when I get to go home on the first of the week (we hope).

Lots of things to coordinate by the time they let me go. Wow... But I needed to walk, and so we did. This hospital, St. Rose, Siena campus is so grandeur in its five-story-lobby entrance. I sat in a chair on the third floor looking out on the lobby and felt like a pope, so I started waving my arms in blessings on those coming and going... Jon said he was going to get me a papal hat so I could practice for the role as he heard there was an opening... lol.

I told Jon I wanted to go outside and he asked if I felt like it, and of course, I didn't but wanted to anyway. We headed down the elevator, through the lobby, and out the door. A lady told me I was going to freeze, but I told her that would feel good after three weeks of not being outside. I was rolling my IV tower, and they have Valet Parking here, so I rolled over to the check-in counter and asked to check in my tower... caught the guys by surprise, and all they could do was laugh. Then more pictures in the sunshine and back to the fourth floor for pictures with Mickey Mouse (after we saw the pictures we posted on Facebook we were surprised by what was on the TV behind us). Then back to the third floor and back to bed.

What a wonderful time. No scriptural lesson other than

Proverbs 17:22 KJV

A merry heart doeth good like a medicine:
but a broken spirit drieth the bones.

Suzi's Facebook Post
February 27, 2013

Quick update regarding Dad. (I'm not there but am getting updates from family.) He was released from the hospital Monday night. Lots of stuff to set up with his IV food (TPN) and pain management... Sounds like there were some challenges. Then last night chills, fever, and infection set in and was taken to ER. It looks like a kidney infection, and he'll be admitted to hospital again. Please keep everyone in your prayers. This is a tough journey.

Isaiah 26:3, 4 ESV

You keep him in perfect peace whose mind is stayed on you, because he trusts in you. Trust in the Lord forever, for the Lord God is an everlasting rock.

Quick report: Dad is doing better and resting well. Will probably be in the hospital for a few more days.

March 1, 2013

Hi to our good Facebook friends. This is Fran attempting to give you an update on what is happening with Duane.

As some of you may know Duane went into the Hospital on February 1, 2013, to see if they could put a feeding tube in either his stomach or in the small intestine. He was having such difficulty swallowing that he was literally starving to death.

So, we checked out of Hospice to get this procedure done. Duane went in as an outpatient, but before the surgery was completed, it turned into an inpatient at the hospital. Duane had complications with the feeding tube, too numerous to write them all. One thing led to another: A blood clot in his left arm; feeding tube wouldn't work as a feeding tube so they are pumping out bile from his stomach and small intestine with it (which in essence is saving his life) his body would not receive the food they gave him in the feeding tube and would just pump into his body cavity distending his stomach. We found out later that whenever you do surgery on your intestines they automatically shut down and Duane's have not woken up yet, and other complications... They let him go for 10 days without any food at all thinking his intestines would wake up. He was very weak, and we weren't sure he would make it, so they started him on TPN (intravenous food).

He seemed to be doing better. They put a pic line in his blood vein, and that was how he would receive his food. Since he had been in the hospital since February 1st, they decided he was good enough to be sent home on the 25th.

He was home on the evening of the 25th but kept throwing up and felt miserable. This continued for the whole next day and evening of the 26th. We were giving him the required dosages of pain and nausea meds. We couldn't figure out why he was doing so poorly. If the kids, especially Rob, had not been there I wouldn't have been able to keep going with all the problems we were having.

So... the morning of the 27th at about 6:00 A. M. Duane began shaking saying he was cold, so I put more blankets on him. He continued shaking, and it turned into violent shakes as to where the whole bed was moving! I ran and woke Rob up, and we ended up calling 911. Apparently, he had a fever of 104 and had gone into septic shock! (I am a really bad nurse because I thought I had overdosed him on Morphine!)

We found out later in the hospital that he had an infection in his blood. The culture has not come back yet as to trace where it started but the samples of lungs, kidneys, and blood all came up with bacteria. Poor fellow! Can't seem to get better and get out of here! He has been sooooo sick! He is doing a little bit better now. Lots of fluids and antibiotics have really helped.

We want to thank all of you for your prayers! I don't think Duane or our family would have made it without so much support! You can actually feel God holding you up to do what you have no strength to do on your own! An old, old song comes to mind:

> *"God answers prayer in the morning, God answers prayer at noon,*
> *God answers prayer in the evening, so keep your heart in tune."*[29]

It is as though we had lost faith (heart) in God that He is going to answer our requests for Duane's healing. But we must not lose heart (faith) if we keep our heart in tune with God, then God's perfect will WILL be done in Duane's life. We must surrender to God's will, all the while making our requests known to Him and He will do what is best for Duane's life. We only have to believe that God sees further down the road than we do and that He knows what is best for Duane.

So we are diligently trying to keep in tune with our Heavenly Father for we know it is because of love we even exist!

Love you guys and thanks so much for your faith and prayers at this time! One never knows when God will do a miracle!

March 6, 2013

Hi everyone. This is Fran again giving a short update on what's happening with Duane. He has been in the hospital this second time for seven days. He came in because of a UTI that he brought home from the hospital. It was let go so long that they determined it caused his septic shock which resulted in their diagnosis of a blood infection. He has since developed a cold sore/fever blisters virus that has his bottom lip looking pretty rough.

The doctor said his body has been in and still is under stress. That's why all the blisters are around his mouth. Yesterday morning, he began shaking again around 4:00 A.M. I was asleep on the little bed by the window, and I heard someone calling my name. It was Duane saying, "I'm shaking again"! I called the nurse, and there were about four of them trying to take blood pressure, temp, oxygen level, heart rate, etc. He was shaking for about 45 minutes. It wasn't as bad as the first time. The doctor said he had developed yet another infection! He has five bags of antibiotics going plus his TPN Food. He is very weak and has a weak voice.

He told us about a dream he had the morning he started shaking. It sounded like he had been with old friends and he said he just couldn't describe the feeling of relationships that he was having with these old friends. We have been wondering if Jesus didn't give him in his spirit a vision of Heaven, at least the "feelings" part of it! He said he was having a hard time trying to get back here from the other place he was at. I was reading Psalm 30 the other day and crying out to the Lord for my desires. You'll have to read it. I have to go take care of Duane. He's hurting now. Love you all. Fran for Duane.

The Dream
(excerpt from Fran's journal)

Life is made up of the most important things, like laughter, crying, the love for your children and marriage to a wonderful lifelong friend! When tough things happen in life, how do you find the willpower to go on without your best friend? That is what I questioned and felt when I stood by the bed of my dear husband, Martin Duane Jordan when it had become apparent that he was going to pass from this life into Jesus' arms of healing, wholeness and complete joy in Heaven forever!

Very early one morning, the last week Duane was in the hospital, I was asleep on the little window seat bed where I could be close to him. He woke up and whispered my name. Of course, I was immediately awake, and he asked me to get a chair and come over and sit by him. I got a chair, and as I sat down, he took my hand and began to tell me of a dream he had just woke up from.

He said his body was hurting and he didn't know if he was awake or asleep, but he was being drawn towards a room. He opened the door, and he saw many people that he hadn't seen in years all visiting with each other! He said it was great to see them but that he couldn't forget the reason he had been drawn to that room. It was the awesome feeling of love, friendship, fellowship, closeness, contentment and pure joy that he felt when he opened the door! Duane said it was so wonderful that he just couldn't even begin to tell me the deepness of the feelings! He was so overcome while sharing this with me he could hardly speak! We were both crying! He said it was all so wonderful that he wanted to stay forever but he also wanted to come back and get me so I could feel what he was feeling! Somehow, he said, he didn't quite know how he was back in the hospital room and woke up and wanted to share his "dream" with me.

We were both weeping! I told him I thought the Lord had let him see a glimpse of Heaven! He said "Yes. That was it." I think that was the moment Duane knew that he was going to leave this earth and be forever in Heaven.

March 10, 2013

I am still alive; have been in the hospital since February 1, except for two days. These have been the most difficult days of my life, and I broke down and cried last night just wanting to go home. I have suffered from so many maladies that it is hard to keep track.

Imagine not being able to ever swallow food or drink again, having bile suctioned out of your body because your body can't process it... suction of bile and suction of water that gets into your mouth.

Thousands of prayers offered in faith, but no answer yet, the way I want it to happen, and maybe it won't. Kutless has a great song called "*Even If*" ...It talks about God being good even if He doesn't heal.

That's where I am right now. Holding on to my faith but ready to go home which will mean hospice again, but I fulfilled some goals that couldn't have happened without being in the hospital. Love you all... this may be the last I can be on here, but will try. My faith is based on Jesus Christ and his righteousness...

March 12, 2013

Laying here in the hospital for 38 days, I've been so weak (in fact my daughter Suzi is typing this for me) (*and I was weeping while I typed-Suzi*) that I couldn't answer all the personal messages my friends have sent me, but I want you to know each one of them is appreciated, and if I could, I would personally answer each one of them.

It appears going home is going to be sooner than later. That means more than just going to my house... Psalm 23 is still impactful that going through the valley of the shadow of death, I will fear no evil because God is with me. Also, I know that I have had goodness and mercy following me all the days of my life and I will dwell in the house of the Lord forever. In John 14, Jesus said, *"In my Father's House are many mansions, if it were not so, I would have told you. I go to prepare a place for you that where I am, there you may be also."*

So, going home is not a bad thing. For all my friends and family, I pray that eventually, they'll all join me in that place Jesus has prepared for us. I'm still trying to get my mind wrapped around what Paul said: *"For me to live is Christ, but to die is gain."* But I'm sure I have fought the good fight, I've kept the faith, and there is laid up for me a crown of righteousness which is not just for me, but for all those who love His appearing. Remember the old song,

> *"Oh, I want to see Him, look upon His face.*
> *There to sing forever, of His saving grace...* "[30]

As I can, I will read the posts that you put here. Keep Fran and my family in your prayers. Love you all.

Suzi's Facebook Post
March 15, 2013

Quick update for those concerned about dad, Duane Jordan. I'm not in Nevada anymore so someone else may update his status. But he is home now. My brothers both say he's doing well and getting settled. Keep the prayers coming and stay tuned as they might post more details.

An Entry from Fran's Journal

My husband Duane had just been told by the hospital specialists that there was nothing else medically they could do for him. They asked him to decide if he wanted to go to an acute care center or to go home. Whatever his decision; his life was coming to an end. We knew his desire was to go home.

We had to get things set up with hospice before we could transport him to our house. This took some fast doing because he wanted to leave the hospital as soon as possible. One request that Duane made was that the hospital bed from hospice be put in the living room "where all the action was"! He didn't want to miss one thing!

We arrived home in the early afternoon. The hospice nurse was there to help do everything that medically needed to be done before leaving. That left our son Rob, Duane and I the only ones in the house. I asked Duane if he needed anything and he said, "Yes!" "Get me out of this bed!" "I want to go outside!" I thought he would be too tired after the trip home and all, but he was determined! So Rob and I helped him into the wheelchair and out on our front porch. He just sat there for a minute in his housecoat, and with a big smile said: "Oh that sun feels so good!"

About that time the house phone rang, and I went to answer it. After a short conversation, I came back out to the front porch, and Duane and Rob were nowhere to be seen! I thought maybe they went into the garage. Not there either! Calling their names, I checked in the backyard. They weren't there either! I was really puzzled! I knew they just couldn't disappear! I walked to the front of the house and looked up the street. There they were! Rob was running, pushing his Dad in the wheelchair. They had gone quite a ways up the street and then turned around on their way back. Both were laughing! Duane had the biggest smile on his face, hair blowing in the wind, and giggling like a little boy, holding up his catheter! What a sight they made! Just looking at them made me laugh! It was hilarious! Literally his last fling!

Just about that time the Ice Cream Truck came into our neighborhood. You cannot believe how much Duane liked Ice Cream! Our neighbors came out of their house with their two little children and bought us all a treat! Duane in his housecoat, holding his catheter, eating Ice Cream! We both knew it wouldn't stay down for long but for now, one last time he was enjoying his favorite dessert! Just the thing close to his heart! Talking with little kids and eating Ice Cream!

We brought Duane into the house and laid him in bed. Two days later he said, "Please call the kids. I am going to die in two days." In tears, I called the children. Everyone arrived as soon as they could get here. With loving care, we all sat by his bed. He left this world to meet Jesus in Heaven; two days later, March 20, 2013, which was exactly one year from his first exploratory surgery.

Looking Upon His Face
March 20, 2013

Dear Friends and Family, just wanted to let you all know that our dad and husband, went home to be with Jesus this morning about 7:30 A. M. One of his favorite scriptures,

Isaiah 40:28-31 NLT

The Lord is the everlasting God, the Creator of all the earth. He never grows weary. No one can measure the depths of his understanding. He gives power to the weak and strength to the powerless. Even youths will become weak and tired, and young men will fall in exhaustion. But those who trust in The Lord will find new strength. They will soar high on wings like eagles, they will run and not be weary, they will walk and not faint.

He has found new strength this morning and is rejoicing in heaven with our Savior. Thank you all so much for your support, prayers, and friendship. It has meant so much to each one of us. We love you all, and we will let you know of service times for the celebration of his life ~ Fran and kids.

Thank you, everyone, for your kind words, thoughts, prayers, and support! We feel so loved and are so thankful for you.

EPILOGUE

On March 30, 2014, The Boulder City Minister's Association gathered at Boulder City Assembly to plant a tree in memory of Duane. The tree chosen was an African Sumac because it stays green year-round. At the gathering, a local pastor, Kurt Hedlund, shared this story:

> "...I heard him (Duane) share different stories that showed me he was an observer of life, and I was looking for spiritual applications. One that stuck with me most was about his family. He talked about one of his daughters.
>
> Fran and Duane had moved to Boulder City, and one of their daughters was living in California. If I remember the story correctly, she had never been to Boulder City; had never been to the house here. But on one occasion had called home and talked to Dad and said, "Dad, can I come home?" Duane's point was: She'd never been to Boulder City; never been to the house they were located at, but because her father was here, she knew this was home. I think of that in relationship to Duane knowing that he had never been to heaven, but he knew his Father. So, we as Christians and as family can be confident that he (Duane) is truly home. As Christians, we all individually look forward to the time that we too will all go home someday."

> *"...the instant my spirit leaves my body, I will be forever in the presence of the Lord enjoying the beginning of everlasting life. Cancer and disease will have no power at that second... sin will be powerless, death will be defeated, and I will dwell in the house of the Lord forever and ever and ever..."*

—*Duane*

This is not the end…

On December 14, 2013, Rob and Fran were getting out the Christmas decorations and found this note. This was quite a shock and tears were shed, but what a special thing to find. (See Duane's post December 29, 2012.)

Christmas 2012

It was a good time going to the mountain with all my family (except Kalani)- As I have packed all the Christmas things, I realize I probably won't be here for Christmas 2013. That makes me sad but it is what it is-I will not know what it is to miss my family, but I know they will miss me-I believe I will be in heaven with the Lord waiting for my family- I pray everyone makes a choice for Jesus Christ. Please take care of my "Franny" whom I love so much-Thanks kids for being such wonderful children to me-Suzi, Rob, Jon & Jen-Thanks Grandkids for loving me – Thanks Ed, Jenny, Re, and Mike for loving your father-in-law-See you in heaven. – Dad

The Floyd & Laura Jordan Family 1949
Back row left to right: Laurance, Theda, Clara, Laura holding
Patricia, Floyd, Norma in front of him, Vera.
Front row left to right: Lyle, Pearl with Duane in front of her,
Carol, Lewanna.

*The Siblings at their mother Laura's wedding
to William (Bill) Burley June 1978.
Back: Patricia, Lyle, Duane, Lewanna, Carol, Pearl, Norma
Front: Laurance, Theda, Vera, Laura, Bill, Clara*

Duane & Fran at their 25th Anniversary Celebration, 2012

*The Jordan's at Duane & Fran's 25th Anniversary Party, June 2012
Duane, Fran, their four children and spouses and grandchildren*

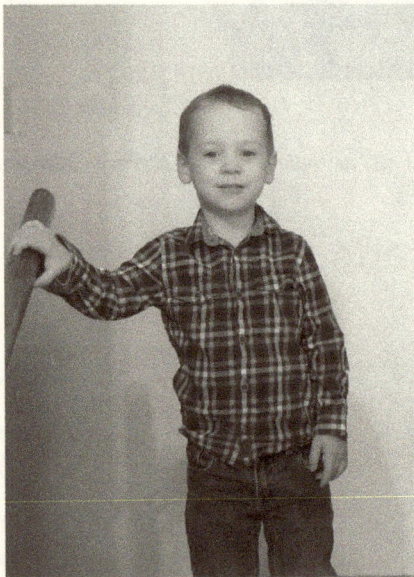

The newest member of the Jordan family arrived in 2015.

NOTES

March 2012

1. *Solid Rock,* WORDS: Edward Mote, ca.1834. MUSIC: "Solid Rock"; William B. Bradbury, 1863. Public Domain

April 2012

2. *It Is Well,* WORDS: Horatio G. Spafford, 1873. MUSIC: "Ville Du Havre"; Phillip P. Bliss, 1876. Public Domain

3. *Solid Rock,* WORDS: Edward Mote, ca.1834. MUSIC: "Solid Rock"; William B. Bradbury, 1863. Public Domain

May 2012

4. *In The Garden,* WORDS and MUSIC: Charles A. Miles, 1913. Public Domain

5. *Great Is Thy Faithfulness*
Words: Thomas O. Chisholm
Music: William M. Runyan
©1923, Ren: 1951 Hope Publishing Company, Carol Stream, IL 60188,
www.hopepublishing.com. All rights reserved. Used by permission

6. I Know Whom I've Believed, WORDS: Daniel W. Whittle, pub. 1883. MUSIC: "El Nathan"; James McGranahan, pub. 1883. Public Domain.

June 2012

7. *Wonderful Peace*, WORDS: Warren D. Cornell and William G.
    Cooper, 1889. MUSIC: W.G.C., 1889. Public Domain

July 2012

8. *I Know Who Holds Tomorrow*
    Writer: Ira F. Stanphill
    Label Copy:
    Copyright ©1950 New Spring Publishing Inc. (ASCAP) (adm.
    At CapitolCMGPublishing.com) All rights reserved.
    Used by permission.

9. *Jim Elliot, The Journals of Jim Elliot (Michigan: Revell, 1978) 174*

10. *Blessed Assurance*, WORDS: Frances J. Crosby, 1873. MUSIC
    "Assurance"; Phoebe P. Knapp, 1873. Public Domain.

11. *It Is Well*, WORDS: Horatio G. Spafford, 1873. MUSIC: "Ville
    Du Havre"; Phillip P. Bliss, 1876. Public Domain

12. *Wonderful Peace*, WORDS: Warren D. Cornell and William G.
    Cooper, 1889. MUSIC: W.G.C., 1889. Public Domain

13. *Great Is Thy Faithfulness*
    Words: Thomas O. Chisholm
    Music: William M. Runyan
    ©1923, Ren: 1951 Hope Publishing Company, Carol Stream,
    IL 60188,
    www.hopepublishing.com. All rights reserved. Used by
    permission

14. *Grace Greater Than All Our Sin,* WORDS: Julia H. Johnston,
    pub. 1910. MUSIC: "Moody"; Daniel B. Towner, 1910. Public
    Domain.

September 2012

15. *"Fransis of Assisi, Prayer of Peace"*, La Clochette, 1912;
     anonymous; L'Osservatore Romano 1916; translated into
     English by 1927 source: *http://www.franciscan-archive.org/
     franciscana/peace.html*

16. *"HE LIVES"*
     Words and Music by Alfred Ackley
     ©1933 Word Music LLC (ASCAP)
     All rights administered by WB Music Corp.
     WB Music Corp. 100%
     On behalf of Word Music LLC

October 2012

17. *Sonia Todd Obituary*, Published in Idaho Statesman on Oct. 19,
     2012. Used with permission from Brian Todd.

November 2012

18. Song Title: *I Will Rise*
     Writer(s): Chris Tomlin, Jesse Reeves, Louie Giglio, Matt Maher
     Label Copy:
     Copyright ©2008 Thank You Music (PRS) (adm. worldwide at
     CapitolCMGPublishing.com excluding Europe which is adm.
     by Integrity Music, part of the David C Cook family. **Songs@
     integritymusic.com)/worshiptogether.com** Songs (ASCAP)
     sixsteps Music (ASCAP) Spiritandsong.Com Pub (BMI) Vamos
     Publishing (ASCAPE) (adm. At CapitolCMGPublishing.com)
     All rights reserved. Used by permission

19. *What a Friend We Have in Jesus*, WORDS: Joseph M. Scriven,
     1855. MUSIC. "Erie"; Charles C. Converse, 1868. Public
     Domain.

20. *Your Grace Is Enough*
     © 2003, (2008,) Thankyou Music (PRS) (administered

worldwide at CapitolCMGPublishing.com excluding Europe which is administered by Kingswaysongs) and Matt Maher. Published by Spirit & Song®, a division of OCP. All rights reserved.

Song Title: *Your Grace Is Enough*
Writer(s): Matt Maher
Label Copy:
Copyright ©2004 Thankyou Music (PRS) (adm. worldwide at CapitolCMGPublishing.com excluding Europe which is adm. by Integrity Music, part of the David C Cook family. **Songs@ integritymusic.com**) /Spiritandsong.com Pub (BMI) All rights reserved. Used by permission.

21.   Song Title: *I Know Who Holds Tomorrow*
Writer: Ira F. Stanphill
Label Copy:
Copyright ©1950 New Spring Publishing Inc. (ASCAP) (adm. At CapitolCMGPublishing.com) All rights reserved. Used by permission.

December 2012

22.   *Live Like That*
Song Title: Live Like That
Writer(s) Ben Glover, Ben McDonald, David Fey
Label Copy:
Copyright ©2012 9t One Songs (ASCAP) Ariose Music (ASCAP) (adm. at CapitolCMGPublishing.com)/Warner Chappell Music (ASCAP) All rights reserved. Used by permission.
Capitol CMG Percent Control: 33.34%
"Live Like That"
Words and Music by David Frey, Ben McDonald and Ben Glover
©2012 Dayspring Music LLC (BMI)
All rights on behalf of Dayspring Music LLC administered by Warner-Tamerlane Publishing Corp.
Warner-Tamerlane Publishing Corp. 66.666%

On behalf of Dayspring Music LLC
(Frey and McDonald)

23. Song Title: *A Quiet Place*
Writer(s): Ralph Carmichael
Label Copy:
Copyright ©1967 Bud John Songs (ASCAP) (adm. at
CapitolCMGPublishing.com) All rights reserved. Used by
permission

24. Song Title: *Everlasting God*
Writers(s): Brenton Brown, Ken Riley
Label Copy:
Copyright ©2005 Thank You Music (PRS) (adm. Worldwide at
CapitolCMGPublishing.com excluding Europe which is adm.
by Integrity Music, part of the David C Cook family. **Songs@
integritymusic.com**) All rights reserved. Used by permission.

January 2013

25. Thomas Huxley, *Science and Education: Essays* (New York: D.
Appleton and Company, 1897) 414

26. Thomas Huxley, *On The Physical Basis of Life* (Yale College, New
Haven, Conn "The College Courant", 1869) 23

27. Max Lucado, *He Still Moves Stones* (Tennessee: Thomas Nelson,
1993,1999) 53

28. Blaise Pascal, *Pensees VII(425)* (New York: E.P. Dutton & Co.,
Inc., 1958) 97

March 2013

29. *Whisper A Prayer*, Composer: Unknown. Public Domain.

30. *Oh I Want To See Him. WORDS and MUSIC: Rufus H.
Cornelius, 1916. Public Domain.*

www.ingramcontent.com/pod-product-compliance
Lightning Source LLC
Chambersburg PA
CBHW021826090426

42811CB00032B/2037/J

* 9 7 8 1 7 3 2 7 5 5 7 0 3 *